The Conscience of a Libertarian

The Conscience of a Libertarian

Empowering the Citizen Revolution with God, Guns, Gambling, and Tax Cuts

Wayne Allyn Root

WILEY

John Wiley & Sons, Inc.

Published by John Wiley & Sons, Inc., Hoboken, New Jersey.
Published simultaneously in Canada.

Statue of Liberty image: Corbis Digital Stock

For general information on our other products and services or for technical support, please
contact our Customer Care Department within the United States at (800) 762–2974,
outside the United States at (317) 572–3993 or fax (317) 572–4002.

Wiley also publishes its books in a variety of electronic formats. Some content that appears
in print may not be available in electronic books. For more information about Wiley
products, visit our web site at www.wiley.com.

Library of Congress Cataloging-in-Publication Data:

Root, Wayne Allyn.
     The conscience of a libertarian : empowering the citizen revolution with god, guns,
  gambling & tax cuts / Wayne Allyn Root.
        p. cm.
     Includes index.
     ISBN 978-0-470-45265-3 (cloth)
        1. Libertarianism—United States.   2. Political participation—United
  States.   3. United States—Politics and government—1989—   I. Title.
     JC599.U5R67 2009
     320.51'2—dc22
                                                                    2009013316

Printed in the United States of America
10 9 8 7 6 5 4 3 2 1

A12005 655354

Dedicated to

My parents in heaven David and Stella Root—who gave me my foundation in life.

My grandmother Meta Reis—who taught me the meaning of courage and chutzpah.

My grandfather Simon Reis—who taught me the value of entrepreneurship and salesmanship.

My wife Debra and four wonderful children Dakota, Hudson, Remington Reagan, and Contessa—who teach me the meaning of love every second of every day.

My political heroes and role models—Barry Goldwater, Ronald Reagan, and Thomas Jefferson.

And most importantly, to God—who inspired my words and ideas, and to whom I dedicate my life.

Contents

Acknowledgments

L et me start with God. God is my foundation, my motivation, my source of inspiration. I pray to God to start every day. I prayed to God for the creativity and wisdom to write this book. I now pray that this book will empower, improve, and enrich the lives of readers (and voters) all over this great country. I hope (and pray) that this book encourages a whole generation of Americans to fight for smaller government, reduced spending, reduced entitlements and handouts, dramatically lower taxes, more economic and personal freedom, more rights for the individual, and more respect for the Constitution.

Next I must acknowledge my family. Let me start with my wife Debra Parks Root. Talk about blessings! She is a stunningly beautiful and brilliant wife, mother, and partner. She is college educated, with a master's and PhD in Homeopathy (the science of healthy living and holistic healing). She speaks five languages. She's a former Miss Oklahoma, and a former lead singer for music legends like Ginger Baker and Emerson, Lake & Palmer. Too good to be true? I'm just getting warmed up. She's a gourmet cook and a spiritual dynamo (she comes from a family of devoted, selfless Christian ministers and missionaries). Many men say that their wives are the perfect wives and mothers. *Debra really is.* She gave up all the beauty contests, stadiums full of music fans, and a television-acting career, to be Mrs. Wayne Root; to be my rock, and to be the mother of Dakota, Hudson, Remington, and Contessa; and to serve as CEO of the Root household. That frees me to follow my passions: write books, host TV and radio shows, create and run businesses, and spread my message of economic and personal freedom across this country. Debra makes it easy to be me—because she does *everything else*! All I have to do is show up and be me. God has blessed me—and Debra is the ultimate blessing.

Then there are the wonderful children that Debra has created, raised, and educated. My daughter Dakota has been a source of joy to me from the first day of her birth. I am proud of her talents—she can out-talk and out-debate her father (a pretty fair debater); she's beautiful like her mother; and she is a world-class scholar and athlete. She earned her black belt at age 15, and has qualified for multiple fencing junior Olympics, nationals and international World Cup events (representing the United States). But the proudest moment of my life was when Dakota gave the Libertarian presidential nominating speech for her father on C-Span. In front of a live audience at the Libertarian convention and a national television viewing audience, my 16-year-old daughter showed poise, class, and communication skills that would shame any veteran, polished, political leader. She hit a home run out of the ballpark. Don't take my word for it—Google "Dakota Root" and watch her speech. Remember the name Dakota Root. In about 20 years (or sooner) she will be a star on the U.S. political scene.

But Dakota is not the only special Root. Nine-year-old Hudson and five-year-old Remington Reagan (named after my hero President Ronald Reagan) are both smart-as-a-whip, strong-as-a-bull, macho daddy's boys, who love to start their days by roughhousing with yours truly.

We start our days with football, car racing, tackling on the living room floor, and morning walks together. When you put Daddy, Hudson, and Remington together it spells *testosterone*.

And then there's the new baby of the family—Contessa Churchill Antoinette Root. She is one year old (as I write this book) and she is the apple of daddy's eye. I bound out of bed every morning to see Contessa playing in her crib. She makes daddy melt with one look of her dazzling smile! Dakota, Hudson, Remington Reagan, and Contessa are the lights of my life.

Speaking of best friends and family, there are a few close friends that must be acknowledged here. Doug Miller is at the top of any list. Best friend, mentor, and my loyal business partner for many years (he is now retired). He was the first adult who ever believed in me, and my talents. Without his counsel, advice, and wisdom, I could not and would not be where I am today. Roger Harrison is the best friend any man could have. He is the finest, fairest, and most honest individual I've ever met. Our discussions about politics have been a great source of joy, education, and entertainment for me for many years. But most importantly, he is "Uncle Roger" to my children. Hollis "Harvard" Barnhart has been by my side as friend, advisor, executive of my many entrepreneurial ventures, and, of course, "poker-player-extraordinaire." Last but certainly not least is my attorney and trusted advisor Lee Sacks. Lee is that rarest of the rare—a true spiritual warrior. Lee is another business associate who has grown into a beloved member of my family. Every significant deal of my life has been done with Lee Sacks at my side. These friends are the heart and soul of Team Root. I love you all like brothers.

Other family members who must be acknowledged: my in-laws Ralph and Martha Parks, who after the death of my parents literally just took over as my mom and dad. Married more than 50 years, they are the reason Debra is a world-class wife and mother. They moved two blocks away from us to be in their grandchildren's lives on a daily basis. If my life sounds like a fairy tale—*it is*! The Parks family is the reason why. Many people talk about God and spirituality. The Parks family *lives* it. Thanks also to my sister Lori Brown and her husband Doug, and my siblings-in-law Minister Charlie and Darla Finnochiaro, and to my parents David and Stella Root, and grandparents Simon and Meta Reis. They are all up in heaven, but I feel their wisdom, motivation, and presence in my life every day. They were the original foundation in my life. I think of them often.

Now, to a few business acknowledgments: First, my publisher and editor at John Wiley & Sons: Debra Englander and Kelly O'Connor. I am forever grateful for your faith, professionalism, work ethic, and teamwork. Wiley is the finest publisher I have had the honor of working with. I am forever grateful to my literary agent, Nancy Ellis—I call her my bulldog. She is the most tenacious and relentless person I've ever met—other than me, of course! She was responsible for getting me book deals on both *Millionaire Republican* (Tarcher/Penguin, 2005) and (after my political conversion) *The Conscience of a Libertarian*. Thank you, Nancy, for helping turn a Las Vegas odds maker and small businessman into a nationally recognized political author. And special thanks must go to my trusted publicist Sandy Frazier, who has landed me nonstop national media appearances for many years now. Sandy has taken my raw talent and molded me into a national television political pundit. Sandy is also relentless; she never gives up until she achieves her goal (which just happens to be my goal, too). I seem to attract relentless dynamos into my life!

Now to the talented team that has encouraged, empowered, and energized me as I wrote this book. Very few politicians write their own books. I'm proud to report that I wrote every word of this book—with no co-author or ghostwriter. But I had help from some very special people who read, reread, suggested, added, subtracted, and analyzed every word in this book. I could not have written this book without the heroic efforts of Aaron Starr, my Libertarian political guru, advisor, wordsmith, and trusted counselor. Thank you, Aaron, for all your efforts from the day I declared my intensions to run for the Libertarian presidential nomination, through my vice presidential campaign, and through the long days of writing this book. Your efforts were invaluable and greatly appreciated. Others who contributed so greatly to this book were Doug Miller, Roger Harrison, Hollis "Harvard" Barnhart, Doug Bandow (the policy advisor to the Barr/Root campaign), Kip Herraige (of Wealth Masters), John Lester,, and Tim Claiborne. Each of them added invaluable words, themes, and ideas to this book. Then there's my wife Debra and daughter Dakota who each spent far too many hours reading the raw manuscript for this book and made countless suggestions. What a "Dream Team."

Other key players at Team Root who must be acknowledged: Doug Fleming, my high school principal back in New Rochelle, New York, 25 years ago. Doug and I have a truly unique relationship. How many students count their high school principal as a close friend a quarter century later? People often talk about a favorite educator who changed their life and inspired their success. In my lifetime that one favorite educator who made such a difference in my life was Doug Fleming (along with Annemarie and all my wonderful friends at Thornton Donovan School). I must also recognize Joe Sugarman, a man I consider a trusted friend and mentor. Joe is one of smartest, savviest, most creative and successful marketing experts in the history of U.S. business. I've learned so much from the endless reservoir of knowledge that Joe possesses. I am blessed to count him as a friend. I hope to learn from him for many years to come.

Special thanks are owed to two professionals who have been with me forever. First to my trusted webmaster and web guru for so many years—Will Habdas. When you look up loyal, brilliant, creative and tech savvy in the dictionary—Will's picture is there. He has designed and run all of my web sites for many years. Allyn Moskowitz deserves special mention here too as my loyal and dedicated accountant and friend for over 20 years.

I am forever indebted to a few very special Libertarian political gurus whose support and counsel led to the birth of many ideas in this book: First and foremost is Congressman Bob Barr, my Presidential running mate. It was a great honor learning how to run a national political campaign, at the side of a true patriot. I hope this country appreciates Bob Barr and all he has done for us. I must also thank Aaron Starr (again), Manny Klausner, M. Carling, Bruce Cohen, Martha DeForest, Mark Schreiber, Jeff Dimit, and Scott Lieberman. Without their help, I would never have become a vice presidential nominee. Also, I am forever indebted for the political support of many Libertarian leaders. Let me mention a few that mean so much to me: Kevin Knedler, Lou Jasikoff, Travis Nicks, Kevin Takenaga, Steve Kubby, Stewart Flood, Bill Redpath (Chairman of the Libertarian Party), Richard Burke, Peter Beary, and Sam Goldstein. Outside of the Libertarian party, I owe a debt of gratitude for the political friendship, counsel, and support of Rick Williams, Chuck Muth, Matt Brooks, Kieran Mahoney, Larry Greenfield, Jake Witmer and Eric Dondero (whose original blog that recommended me for the Libertarian presidential nomination got me started on this long journey).

I owe a debt of gratitude to business supporters like George Abraham, Wil Rondini, Richard Spring, Monte Weiner, Steve and Charlene Richman, Fred Zeidman, Tim Connolly, Tim Keating, Petar Lasic, Steve Carlston, Jeff and Erica Combs, Jeff Peterman, Danny Goldberg, Rudy Ruettiger, Bruce Merrin, Kevin Hogan, Bobby Consentino. Robert Ringer (the author who inspired my writing career), and my great friends from Wealth Masters International Kip Herraige and Karl Bessey.

I thank all of you for your support, friendship, hard work, and generosity. These remarkable people have always been there when I needed them. And I will always be there for you.

Some media personalities who must be mentioned and thanked for their support and generosity include Neil Cavuto (host of *Your World* and *Cavuto*), who has featured my opinions so often at FOX News Channel and FOX Business; nationally syndicated radio hosts Michael Savage (host of *Savage Nation*), Mancow Muller (host of *The Mancow Show*), and Jerry Doyle (host of the *Jerry Doyle Show*) who have made me a regular part of their shows; KABC Los Angeles radio host Al Rantel, who was the first major radio personality in the country to feature me regularly on his show; Rita Cosby who has been such a big supporter; and Chris Ruddy, publisher of *Newsmax*, who has featured me on the pages of his popular conservative magazine and Newsmax. com web site so often. Extra special thanks are necessary for Mancow Muller, whose early support and nomination speech on my behalf at the Libertarian National Convention was instrumental in boosting my vice presidential nomination. Mancow Muller defines "class act."

Finally, I must give thanks and acknowledgment to the critics. No statue has ever been built to honor a critic. You are the people who sit back and achieve, accomplish, and create absolutely *nothing*. You have the easiest job in the world—you just criticize and insult the creativity and work of others. But you do serve a purpose—you have inspired my success every step of the way. To all of you who didn't see the spark, didn't recognize my potential, never acknowledged my talents, criticized me or attempted to humiliate me—you have been a valuable resource toward my success! Thank you. It is you who produced my energy, enthusiasm, passion, commitment, tenacity, fire, drive, and determination. It was your inspiration that led to the publication and success of this book. It is your ignorant and mean-spirited words that make me *relentless*!

Publisher's Note

The views expressed in this book are those of the author and do not necessarily represent the views of the publisher or any organization with which the author is or may have been associated. The publisher and the author make no representations or warranties with respect to the accuracy or completeness of the contents of this work and specifically disclaim all warranties, including without limitation warranties of fitness for a particular purpose. No warranty may be created or extended by sales or promotional materials. Neither the publisher nor the author shall be liable for damages arising herefrom. The fact that an organization or web site is referred to in this work as a citation and/or a potential source of further information does not mean that the author or the publisher endorses the information the organization or web site may provide or recommendations it may make. Further, readers should be aware that Internet web sites listed in this work may have changed or disappeared between when this work was written and when it is read.

Introduction

Citizen Politician—
Citizen Revolution

Open your wallets and purses.
Look inside.
Vote for me.
And I promise to stay the hell out of there!

—WAYNE ALLYN ROOT

M y name is Wayne Allyn Root. I'm not your typical politician.
As a matter of fact, some might call me the *anti-politician.*
Politically, I'm a combination of Barry Goldwater, Ronald
Reagan, and Ron Paul—a Libertarian conservative, supercharged, and
on steroids!

Who am I? I was the 2008 Libertarian Party vice presidential nominee. Today I am a leading contender for the 2012 Libertarian presidential

nomination. But those are just titles. Who I am? I am an S.O.B.—a blue-collar *son of a butcher*—just what the United States so desperately needs right now.

I'm not some fancy Ivy League lawyer, with the perfect resume, running for president. Actually, my resume defines the phrase "breaking the status quo."

I'm a small businessman, a second-generation U.S. citizen, a home-school father of four young children, the quintessential citizen politician, just what the Founding Fathers envisioned back in 1776. I'm also the first-ever Nevadan on a presidential ticket—my adopted home-town is Las Vegas, Nevada. And I'm a big-mouthed New Yorker (born and raised) with a chip on my shoulder and a strong, loud, colorful, passionate opinion on most every issue. I will forever be my father's son—a rebel with a pitchfork, or in my case, a meat cleaver.

I'm also a college classmate of our new President Barack Obama. We both graduated Columbia University on the same day in 1983, from the same class, both political science majors, both pre-Law. That's where our paths diverged. Obama's world revolved from that day forward around Chicago, Illinois. My life revolves around Las Vegas, Nevada. Never have there been two such contrasting polar opposites. Nevada represents smaller government, among the lowest taxes in the United States, entrepreneurship, personal and economic freedom, and personal responsibility. Conversely, Chicago represents big government, big unions, corrupt politicians, high taxes, high murder rates, and strict gun control—a "Nanny State."

No, Nevada is not a place that big-government-loving Beltway Insiders like Barack Obama understand. I'm about as far from a Beltway Insider as you get. I'm not a lobbyist. I'm not a lawyer. I'm not a career politician or bureaucrat. I'm not an establishment insider. As a matter of fact, in my entire life, I've only stepped foot in Washington, DC, three times and that was as a citizen parent proudly showing and teaching my children the history of this country I love so much. I've never worked for local, state, or federal government. I've never done business with government. I've never taken a check from government, other than an IRS refund of my own money, or a student loan (which I paid back in full, with interest).

What I am is the same as all of you—a taxpaying citizen of these United States of America. I'm a proud member of that small group of entrepreneurs and businesspeople who actually creates most of the jobs and pays most of the taxes in this country. Small business is the economic engine of the United States. We have created the majority of all nongovernment jobs in the United States, and 75 percent of all new jobs. We're the group that pays for others to live the American Dream. We work the long hours and pay the taxes that allow government to hire all the unnecessary government employees, pay for their bloated pensions, and keep expanding government programs. We may dislike government, but ironically, we pay for it all!

The fact is that almost *everyone* lives off the small group of us who daily put our money, energy, and talents on the line to create and expand our businesses. While liberal politicians pollute the air by talking nonstop about the problems of health insurance, we actually pay the health insurance for tens of millions of U.S. workers. When you hear experts talk about the wasteful spending and outrageous earmarks in Congress, we're the group that pays for it all.

We're also the group that pays for the legal bribery called "corporate welfare." When government gives away more than $100 billion per year in corporate welfare to special interest groups, it's our tax money being wasted. We're the group that pays the tab for the special interest cabal in DC—all the lobbyists, lawyers, and defense contractors who legally bribe the politicians by the millions, so their clients can fleece the system by the billions. We're the group that paid for the trillion dollar wars in Iraq and Afghanistan. We're the group that paid for the trillion dollar Wall Street banking bailout of 2008—the greatest taxpayer rip-off in history. We're the group that paid for Obama's first big act as president—his trillion dollar economic stimulus plan. You know, the one who gave tax cuts to people who don't pay taxes in the first place. We not only paid for it with our blood, sweat, tears, and taxes, but most of us won't even share in it. You see, small business owners make too much money according to politicians like Obama, so we don't get a stimulus check. We pay for it, but the checks don't go to us. We create most of the jobs, but the politicians think that we must be punished for our hard work and success.

Government tends to forget (or purposely ignore) our contributions—without our tax dollars, there are no "pet projects" or earmarks or wars or entitlements. Taxpayers are the heroes who make it all possible. And small business owners form the solid foundation of the taxpayers union. I know what you're thinking—there is no taxpayers union. Well there should be. We're the group that is "too big to fail." We're the group that needs a union to fight taxation without representation. Government tends to forget that it's our money in the first place. Politicians tend to forget that without taxpayers there could be no government. Without businesspeople there would be no taxpayers. So, how does government choose to treat those of us who risk all we have to create the wealth that pays the freight for everyone else? They tax us more! They punish us for our efforts.

As a child I understood the meaning of the nursery rhyme, "Jack and the Bean Stalk." Only a fool would kill the golden goose. But, that is exactly what government is doing. Inch by inch, or more properly, a percent here, a percent there, and the golden goose is being strangled. And, once the goose is dead there are no more golden eggs. As one of my heroes Ronald Reagan once said, "Government is not the solution, government is the problem."

■ ■ ■

Speaking of government often being the problem, I immediately think of the IRS. A few years back I was a guest on ABC's *Politically Incorrect with Bill Maher*. When asked about the IRS, I said that I preferred the Mafia to the IRS. The crowd and host Bill Maher were shocked. Then I explained, "The Mafia comes to a small businessman like me. They ask for 10 percent of my profits and they say that in return they'll protect me. The IRS demands 50 percent (or more) and they don't even protect me. *I choose organized crime!* It's a much better deal." The crowd exploded into a roaring ovation. Fellow guest actor and rapper Ice Cube responded, "I thought the IRS was organized crime." "They are," I responded. Ice Cube and I shook hands to the laughter, cheers, and deafening ovation of the ABC TV audience.

It would be funny if it weren't the truth. Think about it. Government wants half of your money when you succeed—even though they never helped you one bit. They never risked a dime. They never worked late. They never helped you with your payroll or health insurance. And where is the government when you fail? When you're close to going out of business, is that same 50/50 partner there to help you? When you need a loan to stay in business, does the government agree to personally guarantee half of it? (I guess if your company employed enough union workers they might.) When you go bankrupt, are they there to hand you back half your losses? What exactly do they do for you to deserve that 50 percent cut of your profits? When the Mafia asks for 10 percent in return for providing "protection," that's called *extortion*. They go to jail for that crime for many years. But when the government asks for 50 percent and provides nothing in return, that's called legal taxation. It's all a matter of how you word it.

But the best example of the incompetence of government and the folly of depending on big government to improve your life, to save your life, to come up with solutions to save the economy, to best decide what to do with your money, is again found in my home state of Nevada. In Nevada, prostitution is legal in certain rural counties—the only place in the United States with legalized prostitution. The most famous brothel ever was the Mustang Ranch run by Joe Conforte. Mr. Conforte made more than $100 million, and paid taxes on very little of his fortune. He was indicted for income tax evasion and escaped to Brazil as a fugitive from the U.S. government. The IRS seized the Mustang Ranch and rather than selling it, decided to keep running it. In less than a year, under government management, the same brothel that produced profits of more than $100 million went broke! Bankrupt. Out of business. Can you imagine? *The federal government can't even run a brothel!!!*

Yet we allow the same corrupt, incompetent government to run our economy and our schools. Is it any wonder that our children and educational standards are rapidly falling far behind the rest of the world? And now, this same incompetent government appears to have convinced the public to let the government run our health care system as well. How can we possibly even be considering it? How can you want government to keep even more of *your* money? Do you think they'll make better decisions with your money than you would? Do you think they'll choose the best doctors for your family? Do you think they'll make the right medical decisions to save your life? Do you want them to control your life—to decide what you do in your bedroom, what choices you make on your computer, what shows you're allowed to watch on TV?

Do you want government to solve the banking crisis? These are the people who *caused* the crisis in the first place. Then these same people claimed they had the solution to that banking crisis. They gave away several trillion dollars in bailouts, and things got worse. Credit tightened further. Housing continued to spiral downward. Businesses closed by the tens of thousands. Jobs are lost by the hundreds of thousands per month. So did government have the solution? Do you want the people who brainstormed the bailout to bring us more solutions? With friends like that, who needs enemies? These are the people who hand billions of dollars of taxpayer money to banks—with no oversight, and no stipulations. Then those banks turn around and deny us (the citizens and taxpayers) credit, or home loans, because they claim our credit is shaky. Really? Well, what was the credit rating of the banks when they stood at the brink of bankruptcy, on their knees, begging Uncle Sam to rescue them? How could they deny us credit, or reduce our credit, when they only survived based on a loan from our tax money?

Do you want to put the people who ran the post-Iraq war planning . . . Hurricane Katrina . . . the Great Society war on poverty . . . the Walter Reed hospital crisis, in control of your life? Do you want Eliot Spitzer, the same guy who prosecuted Wall Street executives for minor crimes while he was frequenting illegal prostitutes, to define morality for you? Do you want Mark Foley deciding whether your moral behavior is legal or not—while he sends suggestive messages to male pages on Capitol Hill? Do you want Congressman Barney Frank overseeing Fannie Mae and Freddie Mac while he points fingers at everyone—everyone, that is, except his lover who ran the programs at Fannie Mae that helped to bankrupt the housing and banking industry? If the Republicans had taken control of Congress, Frank would undoubtedly have been investigated and quite possibly forced to resign. Instead he has become one of the most powerful politicians in Congress—a man with the power to control our economic future—amazing. *Absolutely amazing!* Is this the change you were looking for?

If your answer to these questions is *no*, then you'd better stand up now and start doing something about it today—tomorrow may be too late. And, unfortunately, "doing something about it" no longer means you can vote for the other, out-of-power political party. The fact is, the two major political parties, the Democrats and the Republicans, have morphed into what can best be called "The Big Brother Bureaucracy." Sadly, a vote for either Republicans or Democrats is a vote for more of the same: bigger government, more power for government, more government spending, and far less power for the people.

The government doesn't have the solution. *They are the problem.*

■ ■ ■

Here's the good news. I'm not on a power trip. I don't want to control your lives. I'm one of you—the people. I'm part of that unrepresented group—the taxpayers. I don't have any fancy connections in Washington, DC (or anywhere else for that matter). The only connection I ever had growing up, was if I wanted a nice piece of bologna. Let me tell you about my family. I'm a second-generation American whose father David Root owned a tiny two-man butcher store (hence the bologna connection). Every morning before sunrise he went to work where he donned his white, bloodstained apron. My maternal grandfather arrived at Ellis Island from Germany. He and two of my uncles also owned small butcher stores.

My paternal grandfather Louis Root arrived at Ellis Island from Russia and died a sad, unnecessary death in the poor ward of a Brooklyn hospital. He left behind seven children (including my father) and a wife with no assets or income. But my grandmother, Anna Root, never took a penny in welfare or entitlements in her entire life. Those seven young children all went to work (my dad shined shoes on the streets of Brooklyn). Later in life, those seven loving and grateful children each chipped in to pay for my grandmother's retirement. Through sheer determination, tenacity, and personal responsibility, that young, immigrant family survived and thrived, without asking government for help.

They did it for their own survival, but more than that they did it for their children and their children's children—it's called pursuing the American Dream. And, today here I am, the beneficiary of their hard work and sacrifice living the American Dream. What a great country the United States is. Today, virtually every grandchild of my paternal grandparents, Louis and Anna Root, and my maternal grandparents, Simon and Meta Reis, is an educated contributing member of society. Today, in three generations' time, as the grandchild of penniless immigrants, as the son of a blue-collar butcher, I have achieved business and personal success—and most remarkably earned the Libertarian Party's nomination for Vice President of the United States. *Only in America.*

As an experienced small businessman and citizen-politician, my vision of how to achieve the American Dream is different from that of most politicians. You see, I don't think Beltway Insiders, politicians, or government bureaucrats have anything to do with achieving that dream—at least nothing positive. The American Dream isn't about entitlements or handouts. It isn't about lawyers or lawsuits. It isn't about affirmative action or quotas. It is about one thing—*freedom*. It is about the freedom to pursue your dreams without government interference or persecution; the freedom to let talent, smarts, and hard work determine your level of success in a free market capitalist society; the freedom to keep more of your own money, without the government choosing to punish your success and redistribute it to others. It is up to the individual U.S. citizen, as it has always been, to achieve the American Dream. *If it is to be, it is up to me.* Government has no positive part in this dream—the only role of government should be to get out of the way.

I guess this background of mine—with the butcher father and grandfather, with my ownership of small businesses—fuels this burning passion of mine to change government, to limit its size and scope and power, to give power back to the people, just as the Founding Fathers intended. It fuels my Don Quixote–like journey to win the White House someday, so that someone represents the people, instead of the lawyers, lobbyists, big unions, and big corporations. It's a long shot, but hey what were the odds that a B-movie actor who played second fiddle to a chimp named Bonzo would become president? My hero Ronald Reagan tilted at windmills, too. My goal may be crazy, it may be a long shot, it may be laughable to liberals like Obama, but I'm a street fighter from the mean streets of New York. And I've never backed down from a fight in my life. This is the fight of my life. This is the fight I was born to lead. I won't rest until I win the battle to get respect and representation for the taxpayers. I won't rest until I get government out of the way and give the power and control back to the people.

Because of my background, I look at things from a completely different perspective than our new president. Even though we graduated in the same class at Columbia University, and got there in similar ways (both of our young lives were saved and shaped by our grandparents), I'm fighting a completely different battle than Obama. I'm representing a completely different group. As a small businessman, I have seen (and experienced) up close and personal the damage lawyers due to business. I call them "job killers." I have seen the damage that government bureaucrats have done to business. I have seen the damage that taxes do to small business owners. I see the daily struggle for small business owners to survive in spite of government, not because of it. I consciously chose not to go to law school when I graduated Columbia. I chose to start businesses, to risk my own money on my ideas and passions. I chose to live in a low-tax state like Nevada, so I could keep more of my own money and make my own decisions about what to do with it. My choices and decisions could not have been more polar opposite than Obama's. But I discuss those choices in detail in a later chapter.

I guess by the standards of Obama, and the ultraliberal media, and the big-government-loving Beltway politicians, lobbyists, and bureaucrats, I'm completely unqualified to lead this great nation. But those big government snobs will be surprised to find out that I agree with them. I *am* unqualified to run the U.S. government. At least by the standards of the bums who have been running it into the ground for decades. They are the very people who have bankrupted our economy and crippled our country with debt for generations to come.

Thank goodness I'm not qualified to run this bloated, wasteful, arrogant Nanny State government. Who wants someone "qualified" in charge who has done all this damage to the average U.S. citizen, voter, and taxpayer?

There is no better example of the damage done by politicians to taxpayers and the U.S. economy than the amazing story of the Congressional Effect Fund. This Wall Street mutual fund is run by a friend of mine, Eric Singer. Eric has studied the effects of Congress on the U.S. economy over the last half century. Since 1964, every time Congress is in session, the stock market goes up an average of 1.7 percent. During that same period, when Congress is *not* in session, the stock market is up an average of 17.7 percent. *Amazing!* Concrete proof of the damage that politicians do to the U.S. economy. The Congressional Effect Fund provides the answer to the question, "How do you know when a politician is doing damage to the economy?" The answer, "When he's sitting in his seat in Congress."

It's time for a change. "Business as usual" has led us to the point where 90 percent of Americans are dissatisfied with government; where

90 percent of Americans believe our country is on the "wrong track."*
Who could possibly want more of the same? I'm proud to be nothing like the bums who now occupy all levels of government. The only
thing they are qualified for is to continue to lead us straight down the
path of debt, deficit, bankruptcy, and loss of freedom and individual
rights.

I neither need, nor want, to be "qualified" by standards of the liberal
media or Beltway Insiders to accomplish my goals. You see, my goals are
very different from the current leaders of our government. I don't want
to run government. I don't want to expand government. I don't want to
grow government. I don't want to manage government.

I only want to dismantle it—bring it down to a size where it is
responsive to the people and is capable of being efficiently and effectively managed.

I want to dramatically cut the power, size, and scope of all levels
of government. I may be the only politician in history who actually
wants to make my office less important, less powerful, and less visible—
certainly one of the only politicians since our Founding Fathers. The
Founding Fathers—Jefferson, Washington, Madison, Adams—were small
businessmen. They were home-school fathers. They were citizen politicians, not career politicians. They were schooled in what happens when
government gets too big and too powerful and too controlling; they saw
it all up close and personal at the foot and muzzle of the British King
and his army of ruthless tyrants.

■ ■ ■

As a student of the American Revolution, I understand only too well
the lessons our Founding Fathers learned about big government. I
have not forgotten their sacrifices. I have not forgotten or forsaken the
Constitution they were willing to fight and die for. I understand that
the "taxation without representation" for which they fought a revolution to overturn is alive and well today. Their principles and ideals fuel
my fire, my passion, my burning desire to revolt against the tyrants who

---

*Thee, Megan. "Poll: Record High for Wrong-Track Rating." October 14, 2008,
New York Times. The Caucus.

run our government today. It fuels my desire to make government so small you could fit it into one line in the phone directory. I want to make government so unimportant, that you won't even notice it's missing. All I want to do is give the power back to the people.

For all that, I have the *perfect* qualifications. I'll forever be the butcher's son, a rebel with a meat cleaver, a maverick with a pitchfork, a Las Vegas small businessman with a chip on his shoulder. There's never been a more qualified American to dramatically cut government down to size, to protect and uphold the constitution, and to restore our nation to the vision of our Founding Fathers. For all of those goals, I am uniquely qualified.

I can hear the snide comments coming all the way from Washington, DC—the "experts" and the media snobs and the lifelong government bureaucrats howling with laughter and smirking and slapping each other on the back. They're saying, "A small businessman from Nevada thinks he can change Washington, DC?" They are falling over with laughter.

But the Beltway Insiders won't be laughing for long. Maybe a Las Vegas odds maker is *exactly* what this country needs. In Vegas, you may lose your money, but at least you have a chance. No one cheated you. The game was fair. And even if you lose, you get free drinks and a nice room. You get entertained for your money. You walk away feeling good about your trip.

In Washington, DC, the game is rigged. The system is fixed—and it is fixed against *you*, the taxpayer. You don't have a chance. You are screwed before you ever step foot in Washington, DC, and you don't even get a free drink or a comped room. There is no entertainment. They fleece you, pick your pockets, kick you in the butt, and send you back home—with the laughter of lawyers, lobbyists, bureaucrats, unions and politicians ringing in your ears. I'll take Vegas anytime. Nevada may allow legal prostitution, but the real pimps and whores wear nice suits and reside in Washington, DC.

No, I'm not your typical politician looking to win and retain power. I want no power over your life. I actually *respect* you—I think you're smart enough to run your own life. I think you're smart enough to keep your own money, and make your own decisions about what to do with it. I think you're smart enough to figure out how to educate your own children. They're your kids—you should decide how to best educate them. You should have the power to determine their futures. I'm actually willing to give you school choice and parental control. *Can you imagine?* I know this must baffle the media elite and Beltway Insiders.

I can hear the comments from the career bureaucrats right now: "You can't let the people think for themselves? You cannot possibly let the common man or woman in the streets have control over their own lives? What this Root guy is proposing is *dangerous* to the people." What they really mean is that this kind of thinking is dangerous to their power as government officials. Actually, this kind of thinking from our political leaders is nothing new. Thinking like this used to be prevalent and it is this kind of thinking from which our great democracy was born. Americans fought and died in a revolution to free ourselves from the grasp of political tyrants *much less* oppressive than our current government. The Boston Tea Party was an act of rebellion against a tax on tea, which was much less than most sales taxes today. Remember, there was no income tax. Working people kept their entire earnings in those days. What would the colonists' reaction have been if the king had attempted to impose an income tax? They fought a revolution over a small sales tax on *one* product (tea)!

It is time for a new revolution—a citizen revolution led by a citizen politician. My goal may be considered "revolutionary" by today's big government Nanny State standards. But, my philosophy is strictly based on the Constitution—you know, that silly bunch of words written by our Founding Fathers, the same words upon which our entire nation was founded. Just as our brilliant Founding Fathers intended, my goal on the day that I take office is to give the power back to *you*—the citizens and taxpayers. For that job, an S.O.B. (son of a butcher), small businessman, home-school dad—a citizen politician—who just happens to be an odds maker from Las Vegas, Nevada, is ideal.

Remember, my home state of Nevada is a place where the Constitution, including the Second Amendment, is respected; where personal and economic freedom is honored; where personal responsibility is encouraged; where state income tax, business income tax, and inheritance tax is *zero*; where income taxes are actually banned by our state constitution. It's a place where property taxes are limited by law. It's a place where big government is considered a foreign idea.

So here at this intersection of big government, big taxes, government bailouts of Wall Street, economic stimulus packages, government intrusion into every aspect of our lives, warrantless wiretaps of U.S. citizens, IRS undercover stings on U.S. taxpayers, redistribution of wealth, and, of course, the election of President Barack Obama, the biggest proponent of big government in U.S. political history stands the loyal opposition—W.A.R. (Wayne Allyn Root) and the Libertarian Party, "America's Third Party."

We are the party of rebels with pitchforks and meat cleavers; decent, hardworking U.S. taxpayers who despise government, lobbyists, lawyers, power brokers, corrupt union leaders, career politicians, and overpaid government bureaucrats. And I hope you'll agree that we now have the ideal candidate—the anti-politician, anti-establishment, home-schooling, small businessman, proud gun owner, citizen politician. Some might call me the Anti-Obama. Yes, I am the loyal opposition to President Obama and his big-government, tax-and-spend ideology. But I'm also the anti-Bush, anti-Republican, anti-Democrat, anti-lobbyist, anti-lawyer, anti-corporate fat cats. I'm the equal opportunity anti-politician. Both parties have got one heck of a problem on their hands. It's called a *Citizen Revolution. And we have only just begun.*

The Constitution is an instrument, above all,
for limiting the functions of government . . .
Throughout history, government has proved to be
the chief instrument for thwarting man's liberty.
Government represents power in the hands of some
men to control and regulate the lives of other men.

Barry Goldwater

Part One

A REVOLUTION IS BREWING

Chapter 1

It's All Familiar

The Journey Begins with Barry Goldwater

"The government must begin to withdraw from a whole series of programs that are outside its constitutional mandate . . . By reducing taxes and spending we will not only return to the individual the means with which he can assert his freedom and dignity, but also guarantee to the nation the economic strength that will always be its ultimate defense against foreign foes."

—BARRY GOLDWATER, THE CONSCIENCE OF A
CONSERVATIVE, 60-61

My journey for the White House actually began in 1964, at the age of 3, in my father's arms, when we handed out political literature for Barry Goldwater in front of a supermarket in Mt. Vernon, New York. I remember it like it was yesterday—it is one of the strongest memories from my childhood. I can still feel my father's strong arms wrapped around my body. I can still see his big smile as we greeted shoppers and handed them each a Goldwater pamphlet, button, or bumper sticker. My dad loved Barry Goldwater, and, of course, I did, too. As far as I was concerned, my father always knew best. By the time I was in sixth grade, I was reading Barry Goldwater's best-selling book *The Conscience of a Conservative*. By the time I graduated high school, I had read that book probably a dozen times. Today I still carry it in my briefcase. When I have a question about a controversial issue in the news, I always refer back to it. The answer is always there. That book has political wisdom and common sense for the ages. It has never gone, and will never go, out of style.

Barry Goldwater's signature book *The Conscience of a Conservative**
was published in 1960 (a year before I was born). This best-selling conservative book of all time was authored by Goldwater in 1959. At the moment this book, *The Conscience of a Libertarian*, hits bookstores, it will be the 50th anniversary of when Goldwater put pen to paper. Coincidence . . . I think not. After all, Goldwater dealt with many of the same political, economic, and social issues and criticisms that I discuss in this book 50 years later. What's more, Goldwater often offered similar solutions to those that I propose today. When you compare these two books, you'll realize that nothing in politics ever really changes. Not the issues, not the problems, not the obvious solutions, not the debates. They are all virtually the same 50 years later! A half century has vanished and the more things change, *the more they stay the same*.

Not only have the same problems never changed, in most cases they've gotten far worse. In the next few pages, I discuss a few specific examples:

- The growth of government and rampant government spending
- The increase in taxation
- Bloated and irresponsible education spending and the poor results
- Spending-gone-wild on specific government departments, wars, foreign aid, and foreign military spending

In this chapter, I quote liberally (excuse the pun) from Barry Goldwater to give you a sense of the man's political ideology and brilliant thinking. As you read his words, you start to get a sense of the familiarity between his words and the severity of the same situation (only worsened) today. After all, if you leave an injury (even a minor one) untreated for many years, it gets worse. Eventually you need to

---

*I quoted from the 30th Anniversary Edition, published by Regnery Gateway, 1990.

be hospitalized. At that point, you often need to take dramatic steps to save the patient's life. We are at this point in the United States today. Without those drastic steps, the patient will die.

Let's hope the battle doesn't go on for another half century before anyone bothers to listen (or take action). I fear we are coming to the end of the road. We don't have 50 more years of unabated government expansion and spending. The time to make changes (and dramatic cuts) is now. That is why I wrote this book. We didn't listen to Barry Goldwater. But Barry was probably too nice of a guy. He had manners and class. He came from a wealthy family. I don't. I'm a big-mouthed, bold, passionate, self-made New Yorker who isn't afraid of anyone or anything. I will scream from the highest mountains, and I will never stop screaming. I am *relentless*. Perhaps I can get your attention, whereas Barry was too nice to hit you over the head with a 2 by 4, or to tell voters that they are voting for idiots. I'm not too nice. It's time to throw niceties overboard. It's time to suspend manners. We don't have time for nice. Being nice hasn't gotten us anywhere. While we've been nice, the problem has reached the critical stage. It's time for action. This book is the opening shot across the bow of the *Titanic*. The United States is the *Titanic* nearing the end of a long journey. The iceberg is ahead. Someone has got to get the taxpayers' attention before we all perish. Now is not the time for nice. But before I get rough and raw and loud (with the rest of my book), let's first examine the remarkable record of Barry Goldwater.

■ ■ ■

In 1959 Barry Goldwater predicted the descent of our nation. His main issues were always government over-spending, over-reaching, and interference in the lives of individuals, which often goes hand in hand. He said,

> It is in the area of spending that the Republican Party's perform-ance, in its 7 years of power, has been most disappointing. (57)

Sound familiar? I could not have said it any better when referring to the first seven years (or any year) under President George W. Bush (in 2007). In Eisenhower and Bush, we have two Republican presidents, with virtually identical disappointing results, a half century apart. The biggest problem, of course, was unrestrained government spending and growth. In Bush's case, the sins included the doubling of spending during his reign, the dramatic increases in corporate welfare, dramatic increases in military spending to fight wars on multiple fronts, and the passage of a prescription-drug entitlement added to Medicare. All of these actions dramatically expanded the size and scope of government.

Another timeless issue that Goldwater discussed nearly a half century ago was the president's unending promise to lower taxes. Goldwater said,

> Where is the politician who has not promised to fight to the death for lower taxes—and who has not proceeded to vote for the very spending projects that make tax cuts impossible? (52)

Sound familiar? Goldwater was, of course, referring to Eisenhower and other big-government Republicans of the 1950s. Yet, those identical words could be spoken in 2009 when looking back at George W. Bush and the GOP Congress. The size of government expanded under Bush by historical levels, yet Bush didn't veto a single spending bill in his first term. The first veto of his entire presidency came in his second term—against stem cell research. Embarrassing.

As always, the issue of increased taxes always leads me back to the issue of government spending. Goldwater also said,

> I believe that as a practical matter spending cuts must come before tax cuts. If we reduce taxes before firm, principled decisions are made about expenditures, we will court deficit spending. . . . (56)

Sound familiar? We experienced the same exact problem in 1959 as in 2008—Bush dramatically cut taxes, but let spending grow unchecked. The result? Gigantic budget deficits that will result in President Obama taking away those same tax cuts (and then some). Tax cuts that could have been permanent, if spending was reduced to make up the difference, instead became temporary, just as Goldwater predicted. Same mistake, same result, a half century apart. But, of course, this isn't a Republican problem. President Obama has promised gigantic middle-class tax cuts, and even tax cuts for people who never paid taxes in the first place, at the same time he expands government spending dramatically. Both major parties spend irresponsibly—it is only what they choose to spend the money on that changes. What's the difference? Either way, we're spending money we don't have, with a blank check paid by taxpayers, and our children and grandchildren. Either way, we are headed for bankruptcy, insolvency, and crisis. In Obama's case, he seems to believe that we can solve the problems of overspending, deficit, and debt with more spending, higher deficits, and far more debt. And you wonder why we are in economic crisis? President Obama's first-year deficit is four times higher than the *worst* year under Bush. Obama's own budget projections predict a tripling of our national debt. The long-term budget Obama laid out in his first year is bigger than all the budgets in U.S. history *combined*—from George Washington to George W. Bush. Amazing. This is not how you solve a crisis. This is how you bankrupt a country.

Although Goldwater specifically supported his thesis by exposing the actions of Republican President Eisenhower, he understood that the blame (and irresponsibility) was assigned to both parties. In fact, he often said that although Republicans are irresponsible, Democrats are even worse. Goldwater said,

> Every year the Democratic national leadership demands that the federal government spend more than it is spending, and that Republicans propose to spend . . . and (this year) the Democratic National Advisory Council issued a manifesto calling for profligate spending increases in nearly every department of the federal government; the demands for increases in domestic spending alone could hardly cost less than $20 billion a year. (59)

Sound familiar? If I didn't know better, I'd think Goldwater was talking about the Democratic Congress of 2006–2009. Wait until we all experience the pain of President Obama's spending plans. Obama's economic proposals and promises during the 2008 campaign alone suggested the biggest spending increases of any president in history. That was before Obama supported the trillion dollar government bailouts. That was before Obama proposed an almost trillion dollar stimulus package. But the reality of his actual spending plans once in office is far more than even I could have imagined. Obama isn't just bankrupting this generation—he is bankrupting America for generations to come.

But how do we cut spending? Goldwater had the suggestions a half century ago. He said,

> The Constitution is an instrument, above all, for limiting the functions of government. (10)

In other words, our brilliant Founding Fathers never intended for the federal government to be involved in all areas of our life. They created a Constitution specifically to spell out the limits on government. All these years later, Congress and our political leaders have abandoned even the pretense of following the Constitution. A 2008 poll by the Intercollegiate Studies Institute explains how this has happened—the poll proves that most U.S. citizens cannot even pick the key points of the Constitution or Bill of Rights out of a lineup. But here's the real shocker: Elected officials fared even worse than ordinary citizens. (If you don't believe me, log onto to www.americancivicliteracy.org/ for the civic liberty report.) Even when given multiple-choice answers, leading politicians and government officials did not recognize the Constitution. How can you follow it, if you've never read it?

What specific cuts did Barry Goldwater have in mind? He said,

> The only way to curtail spending substantially, is to eliminate the programs on which excess spending is consumed . . . government must begin to withdraw from a whole series of programs that are outside its constitutional mandate—from social welfare programs, education, public power, agriculture, public housing, urban renewal and all the other activities that can be better performed by lower levels of government or by private institutions or by individuals. (60)

Sound familiar? Since Goldwater wrote his book, the federal government has created multiple new cabinet departments, including Homeland Security, Energy, Education, Transportation, Veterans' Affairs, and HUD (Housing and Urban Development). The federal government is involved in more areas than ever before—with more bureaucrats, more power, more rules and regulations, and dramatically increased spending (correlating with our dramatically increased deficit). And, of course, what goes with bigger government, more spending, and more power is automatically more government employees, more powerful government employee unions, bigger salaries, bigger pensions, and lifetime health care for this "privileged class." Unfunded liabilities for government employees today threaten to bankrupt local, state, and federal government. Barry Goldwater saw it all coming in 1959. Nothing has changed in half a century—it has only gotten worse. Far worse.

Want some specific examples? Goldwater said,

> The federal government has moved into every field in which it believes its services are needed . . . the result is a Leviathan, a vast national authority out of touch with people, and out of their control. This monopoly of power is bounded only by the will of those who sit in high places." (13 and 14)

Sound familiar? Goldwater used as his example of government growth and waste going unchecked during the Eisenhower presidency, the creation of the Department of Health, Education and Welfare. Goldwater raged about its budget of $15 billion per year back in 1959. But that same agency is today called the Department of Health and Human Services *and* its budget is now more than $737 billion. Yes, I said $737 billion versus $15 billion in "the good old Goldwater days." Thus, proof that once a government agency or program is created, it never goes away. It simply grows out of control.

Goldwater saw this main issue of government spending and over-involvement coming a half century ago. One Goldwater quote sums it all up:

> The root evil is that the government is engaged in activities in which it has no legitimate business. As long as the federal government acknowledges responsibility in a given social or economic field, its spending in that field cannot be substantially reduced . . . the only way to curtail spending substantially, is to eliminate the programs on which excess spending is consumed. (59–60)

Amen. Nothing about government has changed in a half century. Yet, just like a wound or injury that goes untreated, it has only gotten more infected and more expensive to maintain.

■ ■ ■

Goldwater outlined numerous areas in which the growth of government was rampant and consequently spending too much money. One such area was education, which is certainly on the top of my list as well. Goldwater said back in 1959,

> ... education is one of the great problems of our day ... (lobbyists) tend to see the problem in quantitative terms—not enough schools, not enough teachers, not enough equipment. I think it has to do with quality: How good are the schools we have? Their solution is to spend more money. Mine is to raise standards. Their resource is the federal government. Mine is to the local school board, the private school, the individual citizen—as far away from the federal government as one can possibly go. And I suspect that if we knew which of these two views on education will eventually prevail, we would know also whether Western civilization is due to survive, or will pass away. (70)

Sound familiar? When George W. Bush took over the presidency, the federal budget for education was less than $33 billion. That's $33 billion more than in Goldwater's day, when there was no such agency on the federal level. Today the budget approaches $70 billion and touches every school and student in the United States. But the Department of Education budget does not include the extra $130 billion or so that Obama will spend on education through his economic stimulus plan. So actually $33 billion in the year 2000 has turned into $200 billion in 2009.

Since our education spending has doubled during the Bush years, does anyone believe our schools have doubled in performance? Does anyone believe our students are twice as smart as they were when Bush took office in 2000? Does anyone believe that doubling the spending has improved the education system at all? Does anyone think that we got our money's worth?

The federal government now spends almost $70 billion annually on education (or more honestly $200 billion—see above), despite the fact that the Constitution doesn't mention the word education. Our educational spending is at the top of the industrialized world, yet our results are at the bottom. A 2006 study of education in industrialized nations reported that U.S. 15-year-olds score significantly below average compared to our chief economic rivals. Out of 30 industrialized countries, U.S. students ranked 25th in math and 21st in science. Polls also show that Americans believe that good academic performance leads to financial success later in life. If that is true, we are facing a dismal future.*

Goldwater said it best a half century ago: We need quality, not quantity. In other words, the more involved the federal government has gotten in our education system, the more dismal the results. And yet with those dismal, disappointing, and devastating results come ever increasing spending on education. Are we getting our money's worth? Shouldn't we demand accountability for education? Why is education the only business I know of where the worse the results, the more money that education bureaucrats demand? Why should we reward failure with more money? Based on Goldwater's amazing track record, and his gut instincts about education leading to the success or failure of Western civilization, we are in grave danger.

■ ■ ■

Another area in which Goldwater also saw the over-involvement of government was "corporate welfare." In 1959 Goldwater was aghast at the money lavished on big corporate farms by the Department of Agriculture. He said,

> No power over agriculture was given to any branch of the national government . . . disregard of the Constitution in this field has brought about the inevitable loss of personal freedom; and it has created economic chaos . . . I doubt if the folly of ignoring the principle of limited government has ever been more convincingly demonstrated . . . Doing something about it means—and there can be no equivocation here—prompt and final termination of the farm subsidy program. (33)

Sound familiar? Nothing ever changes—the same government programs just grow bigger (and more entrenched). In 2002, President Bush dramatically increased corporate welfare spending for farmers at a time of record farm profits. Why? Politics is the answer. Senators

---

*Snyder, Elizabeth. "Leading Economists Warn That Education Gap Between the U.S. and Industrialized Countries. . . . " Reuters. June 27, 2008.

and Congresspersons from farm states pushed hard to bring home the bacon (excuse the pun) for their constituents. Lobbyists pushed hard to increase the lard (excuse the pun) on behalf of billion dollar farm conglomerates. And so spending went up, even while profits reached record highs. Does this make any sense for taxpayers? Spending on the farm welfare program back in 1959 pales when compared to the almost $100 billion per year now lavished by our federal government on corporate welfare. Goldwater saw it coming, but he'd be shocked and embarrassed by the 2002 farm bill signed by President Bush.

■ ■ ■

Yet, Goldwater did not only focus on domestic issues, he also discussed the overarching growth and spending by government in international affairs. Foreign military aid, foreign aid in the form of bribes, and the financial burden imposed by the United Nations are three areas where Goldwater suggested dramatic spending cuts. He said,

> For many years now, our allies in Western Europe have devoted smaller portions of their national budgets to military forces than we have. The result is that the American people, in the name of military aid, have been giving an economic handout to these nations; we have permitted them to transfer to their domestic economy funds which, in justice, should have been used in the common defense effort. (90)

Sound familiar? It is almost unfathomable that a half century later U.S. taxpayers are still paying for the national defense of wealthy countries like Germany, Japan, and South Korea. In a time of economic crisis, why on earth are we paying billions of dollars annually to defend them? The Cold War is over. Let them pay for their own defense. That was Barry Goldwater's gut instinct a half century ago. We still haven't listened.

Perhaps, more than listening, we haven't been told that we are paying for the national defense of wealthy nations. This is welfare for our allies. Do the taxpayers understand that this is money our "friends" can use to prop up their economies and major industries to compete against us? Does this make sense decades after World War II and the Cold War ended? Nothing ever changes—not when government is involved.

And then there's foreign aid in the form of bribes to other governments. Goldwater said,

> . . . the Constitution does not empower our government to undertake that job in foreign countries, no matter how worthwhile it might be. Therefore, except as it can be shown to promote America's national interests, the Foreign Aid program is unconstitutional. (89)

More common sense from my hero Barry Goldwater,

> Increasingly, our foreign aid goes not to our friends, but to professed neutrals—and even to professed enemies . . . our present Foreign Aid program, in sum, is not only ill-administered, but ill-conceived. It has not, in the majority of cases, made the free world stronger; it has made America weaker . . . . (93)

Sound familiar? Has anything changed in half a century? We waste billions of dollars today on countries led by tin-pot dictators, who steal it all and give nothing to the people. What do we gain from it? Do any of these nations actually do anything for us? For the U.S. taxpayer? Do they even vote our way at the United Nations? I say it is time to drastically cut foreign aid. It comes 50 years too late, but better late than never. Can you even imagine the savings for the U.S. taxpayer if we had heeded Barry Goldwater's advice a half century ago?

Finally there is Goldwater's wisdom about the United Nations. He said,

> The UN places an unwarranted financial burden on the American taxpayer . . . the United States is currently defraying roughly a third of all UN expenses. That assessment should be drastically reduced . . . we should not be surprised that many of the policies that emerge from the deliberations of the United Nations are not the policies that are in the best interests of the United States . . . it becomes clear that our present commitment to the UN deserves re-examination. (108)

Sound familiar? Nothing ever really changes, does it? How many billions of dollars could we have saved from 1959 to 2009 by demanding proportional payments from each member nation of the United Nations?

■ ■ ■

Goldwater not only criticized the government, he also posed solutions to end government spending and slow the formation of a welfare and entitlement state. Using different terms, he suggested obvious solutions that would reduce the federal budget. Goldwater's goal was to stop the government bailout madness (for both individuals and corporations) before it got out of control. Goldwater predicted it all a half century ago. Sadly, we didn't listen. He said,

> . . . the Welfare State can be erected by the simple expedient of buying votes with promises of "free" federal benefits—"free" housing, "free" school aid, "free" hospitalization, "free" retirement pay and so on . . . the effect of Welfarism on freedom will be felt later on—after its beneficiaries have become its victims, after dependence on government has turned into bondage and it is too late to unlock the jail. (64)

Sound familiar? Think of the lost souls in the streets of New Orleans after Hurricane Katrina. They waited desperately and helplessly for government assistance. Think of where this "something for free" mentality has led—to Bear Stearns, AIG, Citibank, the Big 3 automakers, Bank of America, and our biggest banks begging the federal government to bail them out of financial Armageddon in the fall of 2008 (and beyond). The desire for "something for free" from government now permeates all areas of our society from the welfare mother to the CEO suite. Think of LBJ's Great Society promises. Has a half-century of welfare solved the problem of poverty? Hardly. Have poverty-stricken inner cities been improved by spending trillions of dollars on welfare, entitlements, handouts, free school breakfast and lunch programs, free housing, or free medical? To the contrary, a half-century later we have created a welfare mentality: the expectation and desperate need for handouts from government. Worse, it has extended from individuals to corporations to entire industries. We have "enabled" an entire generation of addicts. No, I'm not referring to drug addicts. I'm referring to entitlement addicts. But just like drug or alcohol addicts, you cannot help them by providing them with a crutch. You cannot help drug addicts by giving them money. It just makes them worse. Only discipline and personal responsibility (and a strong faith in

God) can save an addict. "If it is to be, it is up to me." Goldwater saw it a half century ago. If only we had listened.

But the problem is that government entitlement and welfare programs have never been about helping the poor. They've always been about giving more power and control to politicians and government. Once again Goldwater understood this problem 50 years ago. He said of the welfare state,

> The long range consequences of Welfarism are plain enough: as we have seen, the State that is able to deal its citizens as wards and dependents has gathered unto itself unlimited political and economic power and is thus able to rule as absolutely as any . . . despot. Consider the consequences to the recipient of welfarism . . . he concedes to the government the ultimate in political power—the power to grant or withhold from him the necessities of life as the government sees fit. (66–67)

Sound familiar? What is so frightening is what is happening before our very eyes here in the United States in 2009. This economic crisis, which may yet be called a depression (as I predicted back in early 2008), has caused more people than ever to run into the arms of big government. It has caused voters to elect the ultimate Big Brother politician Barack Obama, who, in turn, sees big government as the answer to every problem; who spends *more* to solve the problem of looming bankruptcy; who adds millions of new government employees in response to growing unemployment; who gives over $100 billion to state and local governments so that their government union employees do not have to be laid off (worse, so that they can get their annual pay increases); who bails out banks so that government can have authority and apply pressure to bankers to dole out bank loans and mortgages to the "right kind of people" (those who support Obama—unions, union projects, environmentally conscious "green" projects, politically correct projects). Overnight, virtually all of America has become dependent on the welfare state. Corporate CEOs are now bigger welfare queens than welfare mothers and fathers. Unions, big corporations, cities, states, banks—they all beg the federal government on hands and knees to save them.

The welfare state now is on the verge of being the official state of affairs. Crisis and fear has driven Americans into the arms of socialism, without even realizing we have cut a deal with the devil. We are going quietly to our deaths—at least the death of capitalism—willingly and quietly. We are jumping off a cliff like lemmings following a Pied Piper. Barry Goldwater must be rolling over in his grave. The welfare state he predicted has come to pass, except worse than even he ever imagined.

■ ■ ■

How did this all happen? Goldwater said it best a half century ago,

> . . . we were swindled. There are occasions when we have elevated men and political parties to power that promised to restore limited government and then proceeded, after their election, to expand the activities of government. (15)

Sound familiar? We have only ourselves to blame. We—the citizens, voters, taxpayers—let it happen. We voted for two major parties that outdid each other to bribe the voters. Getting elected, gaining and retaining power, making government bigger (thereby increasing their power)—those were their only goals.

But Goldwater doesn't stop there. He uses his crystal ball to predict the reasons for Obama's election as well. He said,

> But let us be honest with ourselves. Broken promises are not the major causes of our trouble. Kept promises are. All too often we have put men in office who have suggested spending a little more on this, a little more on that, who have proposed a new welfare program . . . We can be conquered by bombs or by subversion; but we can also be conquered by neglect—by ignoring the Constitution and disregarding the principles of limited government . . . Like so many nations before us, we may succumb through internal weakness rather than fall before a foreign foe. (15–16)

Sound familiar? If Obama keeps his promises to expand government, increase government spending, increase stimulus packages from the billions to the trillions, increase entitlements, create government-run health care, and provide tax cuts to people who don't pay taxes in the first place, he will most certainly bankrupt the United States. We will be conquered from within. I am left to only imagine what historians will be saying about Barack Obama and his effect on the United States 50 years from now (the 100th anniversary of Barry Goldwater's book).

The only way for Obama to keep his promises without bankrupting the United States is to dramatically increase taxes on successful U.S. citizens to levels that will destroy motivation and productivity. Obama thinks it's "fair" to spread the wealth around. Goldwater had the answer to that scheme as well. He said,

> . . . a man's earnings are his property as much as his land and the house in which he lives. It has been the fashion in recent years to disparage property rights—to associate them with greed and materialism. This attack on property rights is actually an attack on freedom . . . How can (a citizen) be free if the fruits of his labor are not his to dispose of, but are treated, instead, as part of a common pool of public wealth? Property and freedom are inseparable: to the extent government takes the one in the form of taxes, it intrudes on the other . . . The very imposition of heavy taxes is a limit on a man's freedom. (53–54)

Sound familiar? Obama, and his running mate Joe Biden, explained why higher taxes on successful citizens are fair by using this same attack on "greed and materialism" as liberal politicians used in the 1950s. There is no doubt that President Obama will use this identical argument to dramatically grab the property (income) of business owners, taxpayers, and job creators, so he can spread the wealth around to those who have not earned it (his voters).

Does Goldwater think we therefore have no obligation to pay taxes to our country? Of course not. Goldwater said of taxes,

> Having said that each man has an inalienable right to his property, it also must be said that every citizen has an obligation to contribute his fair share to the legitimate functions of government. (54)

But the key word is *legitimate*. As Goldwater pointed out back in 1959, the Constitution is the proper arbiter of what is legitimate. If we simply limit the spending of the federal government to programs authorized by the Constitution, spending and taxes would drop dramatically. As Goldwater points out,

... when the federal government enacts programs that are not authorized by its delegated powers, the taxes needed to pay for such programs exceed the government's rightful claim on our wealth. (55)

If only we had listened to Barry Goldwater back in 1959—spending, taxes, and the national debt would be far lower in 2009.

Goldwater foresaw Obama's argument on what is a fair level of taxation. He said,

... the graduated tax is a confiscatory tax. Its effect, and to a large extent its aim, is to bring down all men to a common level. Many of the leading proponents of the graduated tax frankly admit that their purpose is to redistribute the nation's wealth. Their aim ... does violence both to the charter of the Republic and the laws of Nature. (56)

Sound familiar? The tax battle rages on unabated a half century later.

■ ■ ■

Although I have been discussing Goldwater's commentary on political and economic issues, his brilliance and foresight also expanded to social issues. Think of the biggest social and personal freedom issues of our day: abortion, gay marriage, stem cell research, online gaming, the right to die (assisted suicide), and medical marijuana. Goldwater had the solution a half century ago,

The Tenth Amendment is not a "general assumption," but a prohibitory rule of law ... States' Rights mean that the States have a right to act or not to act, as they see fit, in the areas reserved to them ... today neither of our two parties maintains a meaningful commitment to the principle of States' Rights. (18, 22)

Sound familiar? Quite simply, these issues are none of the federal government's darn business. One size does not fit all. Half a century later we can solve all of these issues on the state and local level—where it is closer to the people—without federal interference.

Later in life, it was revealed that Barry Goldwater, the man who literally *invented* the conservative movement was quite centrist and libertarian on the topics of personal and social issues. Goldwater felt that abortion was a personal choice, not intended for government intervention. He was also supportive of gays in the military. Goldwater said,

> You don't have to be straight to be in the military; you just have to shoot straight . . . Everyone knows that gays have served honorably in the military since at least the time of Julius Caesar.

After his retirement from the U.S. Senate, Goldwater endorsed an Arizona voter initiative for legalization of medical marijuana. All of these were consistent with his views to get government out of our lives. But more importantly, they were part and parcel of his belief in States' Rights. Whether Goldwater personally supported abortion, gay rights, or medical marijuana would be of no matter, if in fact the citizens of each state make their own decisions on personal freedom issues like these.

Goldwater even foresaw the issue of warrantless wiretaps by the Bush administration. Goldwater often argued that faithfulness to the Constitution was more important than any reform that might come of restricting the freedoms the Constitution guaranteed.

Sound familiar? If we heeded the wisdom of Barry Goldwater, the federal government would not have the right to listen into your phone calls or read your e-mail messages (without a warrant). Goldwater often opined that the Constitution was not just a piece of paper to be ignored if you disagreed with a certain issue. The Constitution is the law of the land—to be obeyed no matter the circumstances at the moment. The authority of the Constitution is more important than the government's immediate needs during a war on terror. If one presidential administration overrides the Constitution over warrantless wiretaps, what will the next administration decide to override in the name of a "national emergency?" Like my hero Barry Goldwater, I am today uncomfortable with any administration overriding or ignoring the Constitution for any reason. Or as Benjamin Franklin once said, "They that give up essential liberty to obtain a little temporary safety, deserve neither liberty nor safety."

■ ■ ■

It's one thing to read all of the quotes listed above. It's quite another to realize that all of these brilliant observations, conclusions, and solutions were uttered by Barry Goldwater a half-century ago. I am not the soothsayer that Barry Goldwater was back in 1959. I've had the luxury of a half-century to figure out that Goldwater was right (excuse the pun). But my role is that of the town crier. I believe that I was put here at this moment in time to translate Goldwater's wisdom to a new generation, and to make sure that this generation *listens. My job is to wake up the citizenry.*

The old political saying goes, "A billion here, a billion there, and pretty soon you're talking about *real* money." Well, just think for a moment what the result would be if we'd saved billions per year on each of Goldwater's recommendations since 1959? Add up cuts in waste, cuts of entire federal cabinets, cuts of welfare and entitlements, cuts of corporate welfare, cuts in foreign aid, cuts in foreign military spending, and cuts in United Nations contributions. A billion here, a billion there, saved for a half century and we'd have some *real* savings— perhaps enough to eliminate the entire national debt, with enough left over to easily fund the entire $9.7 trillion bailout. Of course, with Goldwater (or myself) in charge, there never would have been a bailout in the first place. Barry Goldwater is my hero. His wisdom applies now, more than ever.

Chapter 2

The Libertarian Model

Meet the Original Rebels with Pitchforks

Libertarianism is the very heart and soul of conservatism.
—RONALD REAGAN

Before we discuss the need for libertarian thinking and a dramatic change in government, let me first tell you a bit about myself and the evolution of the Libertarian political model.

■ ■ ■

When people ask me who I am, I always define myself as an S.O.B.— son of a butcher. Yes, my dad was a butcher, the owner of a tiny two-man local butcher shop. Every morning, before sunrise, he went to work where he donned his white, bloodstained apron. But he wasn't just *any* butcher—David Root was a Jewish Republican–conservative butcher from Brownsville, Brooklyn. Now that's *unique*!

But, what people may find even more unique was that my father was also one of the original founders of the New York State Conservative Party. In 1962, David Root responded to an advertisement in a New York newspaper to start a new party to defeat the liberal, arrogant, out-of-touch, big-government GOP as represented by Republican U.S. Senator Jacob Javits and Republican Governor Nelson Rockefeller. My dad and mom attended that first meeting of the founders of the Conservative Party, led by J. Daniel Mahoney (a future New York Supreme Court Justice). It was a meeting of peasants and rebels looking to start a revolution and take down the King and his court (the powerful New York State GOP led by Javits and Rockefeller). I don't think that you could find longer odds than my parents and their Conservative Party friends faced back then. This was the ultimate long-shot third party. They had no money, no name recognition, no high-profile candidates, and of course, no shot-in-heck of victory. They were laughed at, taunted, and, perhaps worst of all, ignored by prominent Republicans and the New York media. Today's mainstream media would have said that my father and his ragtag bunch of third-party rebels were involved in a hopeless cause. But they would have been wrong then, just as they are now about the Libertarian Party.

After a few years of torture, humiliation, and nonstop defeat, my father and his friends elected James L. Buckley in 1971, the first *ever* Conservative Party U.S. Senator. They became the first third party in New York State history to send a U.S. Senator to Washington. The GOP wasn't laughing anymore. They accomplished this miracle victory in ultraliberal New York State, in the ultraliberal 1960s and 1970s. The only revolution in the air in those days was a peace-loving, anti-war, ultraliberal flower child revolution. The fact that my parents' third-party long-shot victory was achieved in the midst of *that* political environment makes it even more remarkable.

The New York State Conservative Party went on to help elect other "hopeless underdogs," like Senator Al D'Amato (who defeated the legendary and supposedly unbeatable Jacob Javits in a GOP primary) and Ronald Reagan (who was derided as a B-movie actor co-starring with a chimpanzee). President Reagan said of the Conservative Party, "The Conservative Party has established itself as a preeminent force in New York politics and an important part of our political history." My parents' proudest moment in life was receiving their invitation to President Reagan's inauguration in 1980. Can you imagine a blue-collar butcher invited to the swearing-in ceremony of the President of the United States? "Only in America" my dad used to say (long before Don King coined the phrase).

Conservative Party (CP) candidates twice received a remarkable one million votes in statewide elections. They also helped to elect countless conservative-endorsed state assemblypeople, senators, mayors, councilpeople, congresspeople, and judges—the list was long. Twice they provided the margin of victory for New York Governor George Pataki. Eventually J. Daniel Mahoney (the CP founder) became a New York State Supreme Court Justice. Each of these powerful politicians owed their victories to this ragtag long-shot third party.

I'm very proud of what my parents David and Stella Root helped to accomplish. My father, the butcher with a high school degree, has his DNA forever on New York State political history and will forever be my hero. He raised his children to do better, to become educated, and to literally change the world. That blue-collar butcher from Brooklyn sent both his children to Ivy League universities (and my sister to Columbia Law School as well). David and Stella Root were remarkable parents. They taught me that in this great country *nothing* is impossible.

And anyone who doubts the chances of a long-shot presidential candidate in this great country needs a quick history lesson.

■ ■ ■

While studying at Columbia University, I learned that history repeats itself again and again. Yet, it wasn't until a few years ago that I saw the clear connection between my father's history in helping to build the Conservative Party and my own in bringing the Libertarian Party's ideas to the forefront of political discourse.

You see, my dad helped found the Conservative Party in the 1960s because he felt that the GOP had lost its way. He felt they were ignoring, the principles and ideals of Barry Goldwater. All these decades later, *I feel the exact same way*.

Yes, history repeats—especially political history. On the fiscal side, I want to reintroduce this country to the commonsense, rugged individualism, personal responsibility, fiscal conservatism, limited government, anti-tax, pro-freedom, pro-constitution principles of Barry Goldwater.

As indicated in the previous chapter, on the social side, Goldwater was against government interference in the lives (and bedrooms) of individuals. He believed in personal freedoms and individual rights. Today we call that socially *tolerant*. But Goldwater called it "conservative" to not want government in your bedroom. He must be rolling over in his grave at the Big Brother mentality and Nanny State antics of today's GOP. The definition of conservative has been highjacked and twisted out of context. How can it be conservative to want big government (in the name of morality) to limit our personal freedoms and interfere in our private lives? Who in their right mind thinks it's conservative to ban a free American's right to play poker on his or her own computer? Who thinks it's conservative to tell a severely ill cancer or MS patient that they have no right to smoke medical marijuana, even if it's prescribed by an M.D., and the only known medicine that can alleviate their pain.

As a Libertarian, I believe that social and personal freedom issues are quite simply States' Rights' issues. As intended by our forefathers' words in the Constitution, these issues are none of the federal government's darn business. Voters should decide these issues on the state and local level. I simply want the federal government out of the way, and out of my life. Government has no right in my bedroom, in my home, telling me what to do on my computer, what to watch on television, how to spend my own money, where to send my children to school, or deciding what vaccines my children must have forced upon them. *None of it is any of their darn business.*

Last I checked, personal freedom issues are why we fought the American Revolution in the first place—to shorten the long reach of the British government. Eventually our Founding Fathers created a constitution meant to limit the long reach of *any* government. They wanted to return the power back to its rightful place—the citizens. That same long-shot victory in the American Revolution is yet another reminder for the critics, cynics, and two-party apologists of the fact that in the United States a hopeless long shot can win a Citizen Revolution. Remember that the American Revolution was fought over taxes that look miniscule compared to those we willingly pay today, without so much as a whimper. Yet it is valuable to note that many of us have that spark of rebellion coursing through our blood.

The odds may be long, but this S.O.B. is a chip off his old butcher father's block. The battle has just begun. The government bureaucrats, political power players, and two-party apologists may not be frightened yet. But they better get ready. The peasants and rebels and sons of butchers with the pitchforks and muskets and meat cleavers are knocking at the door of the castle. The seeds of the revolution have been planted. The discontent is fermenting. Obama promised "change." He may learn to be careful what he wishes for. The next four to eight years of the Obama socialist agenda, economic crisis, bailouts, bank failures, bigger government, dramatically increasing welfare state, draconian tax increases, trillion dollar economic stimulus packages, deficit, debt, and the eventual chaos, protests, and riots that will result, have the potential to spur another Boston Tea Party. This odds maker's crystal ball senses a turning point (and boiling point) in U.S. political history. Revolution is once again in the air. But before we discuss this political revolution, we must first understand the principles behind it.

Chapter 3

My Libertarian
Awakening

*. . . It cannot be repeated too often that the Constitution is a limita-
tion on the government, not on private individuals—that it does not
prescribe the conduct of private individuals, only the conduct of the
government—that it is not a charter for government power, but a
charter of the citizens' protection against the government.*

—AYN RAND

P eople often ask me why I left the GOP. After all, it's not easy to
change your identification. I'm the guy who wrote the Amazon
best-selling book *Millionaire Republican*. Since birth my political
identification has always been Republican. Just like my father, I had
always been a Republican. My father loved politics and loved his
Republican party. He instilled that love in me at about the same time
that I learned to walk.

"Son," he would say, "when the Democrats try to knock the Republicans for being the party of the rich, they have it all wrong. The GOP is not the party of the rich. The GOP is the party of anyone who *wants* to be rich . . . and desires the *freedom* to make it happen." It worked for my dad. He went from working as a butcher . . . to owning his own butcher store. It wasn't much, it wasn't big, but it was *his*. He was the boss. He was in control of his own destiny. To him, ownership (of a small business) was the American Dream.

That creed guided my lifelong support of the Republican Party. And then something began to change. Republican leaders were no longer practicing conservative politics. Oh, they certainly talked conservative principles, but once in office, they governed much like big-government Democrats. Even now with Obama in office, Republicans *act* like the loyal opposition. They talk conservative. But talking the talk is not the same as walking the walk. When it comes to politicians, don't listen to what they say, watch what they do. We all understand that if Republicans had won the presidency, very little would have changed. Now that they are no longer in power, they protest Obama's bailouts, stimulus packages, reckless spending, and expansion of government. But whenever Republicans take office, they support the same things. Perhaps slightly smaller versions of the same spending programs. But nonetheless, the same expansion of government. It's all a big game. And the object of the game is to make themselves (the politicians) more powerful, more benevolent, more omnipotent, and to make the people more dependent on the "generosity" of politicians.

It was within this sad environment that I chose to leave my formerly beloved GOP. I left because the GOP had abandoned freedom-loving, limited government, anti-tax, fiscal conservatives like me. I left because the expansion of government under President George W. Bush was larger than any Big Brother/Nanny State proponent could have dreamed about under a Democratic president. I left the GOP because of my Republican president's willingness to violate the civil liberties of law-abiding U.S. citizens with warrantless wiretaps. I left because of the willingness of a then Republican-controlled Congress (in 2006) to ban online poker, the popular form of entertainment that millions of U.S. citizens had experienced in the privacy of their own home, on their own computer, with their own money. I left because the

GOP had become so manipulative, hypocritical, and controlling that it tried to force the power of the federal government upon a brain-dead woman, Terri Schiavo, in a coma during the last days of her life. I left because the neoconservative-dominated GOP defended unconscionable overspending (and cost overruns) at the Pentagon (to Republicans anything related to national defense is immune to oversight, transparency, and any kind of budget cut). In truth, I didn't leave the GOP at all—*it was the GOP that left me!*

■ ■ ■

But, nothing made my decision clearer than the morning of October 19, 2008, when I heard the remarkable announcement that General Colin Powell was endorsing Barack Obama for President of the United States. I sat in stunned silence for a few minutes. Then a smile broke across my face. I was finally completely at peace with my decision to leave the Republican Party a few years ago.

Can you even imagine?

The endorsement of Obama by Republican hero Colin Powell made my case that Republican and Democratic Party lines have become blurred. Supporting McCain and his ideas for bigger government would have been bad enough. Enough to make my heroes Thomas Jefferson, Barry Goldwater, and Ronald Reagan roll over in their graves. But Powell didn't choose McCain's vision of big government. Powell chose Obama's vision of far bigger and more intrusive government. Powell chose Obama's vision of redistribution of wealth. Powell chose the most draconian tax increases in modern U.S. history. Powell chose a man who supports the punishment of the successful citizens in our society, in order to reward the rest (Obama's core voters) with handouts, entitlements, and outright bribes. Powell chose a man named by the *National Journal* as the most partisan leftist extremist in the entire U.S. Senate. Powell chose a man who supports the abolition of secret ballots in union voting—thereby enabling virtually the entire country to imitate the success of Detroit and the "Big 3" automakers.

Powell chose a man that is against school choice and vouchers—even when they've been proven to help poor black students in the failing public schools of Washington, DC. Powell chose a man who supports a government takeover of health care. Powell supports a man who has opposed offshore oil drilling his entire career, and supports draco-nian new "Cap and Trade" taxes that will double or triple our electric and gas bills (instead of simply drilling for oil we already know is there). Powell supports a man who, on virtually every issue, is to the extreme left of everything mainstream voters in the United States believe in, let alone what conservatives and Republicans in Powell's own party sup-posedly believe in. Republican icon Colin Powell chose socialism, or at best, Europe's version of big government "social capitalism." Just what the United States needs—a famous and powerful ex-General leading us down the road to become . . . *France!*

If Colin Powell could make that choice, as have several other GOP power players like former U.S. Senator Lincoln Chafee, former Congressman Jim Leach, and former Massachusetts Governor William Weld, then the difference between the two major parties has clearly blurred to the point of indistinguishable. Powell's endorsement of Obama proved that there is no longer a GOP. The party of Goldwater and Reagan is dead. The party of fiscally conservative, limited government principles is long gone. If a Republican like Powell can leave his party to support a radical, left-wing, tax-raising, punish-success, redistribute-the-wealth socialist who supports a government takeover of health care (not to mention a government hijacking of Wall Street and the U.S. banking system), the proof is undeniable—there are no longer any principles left in politics.

Powell sealed the deal for me. When a Republican hero like Colin Powell can choose to support Obama without blinking, the charade is up. Politics is no longer about fighting for what is right. It's now a real-ity show. Welcome to *American Idol.*

■ ■ ■

My decision was solidly reinforced in the fall of 2008 when GOP Presidential candidate John McCain joined Barack Obama in sup-porting the greatest federal power grab, and rip-off of taxpayers in the history of the United States—the trillion dollar bailout of banks, hous-ing, AIG, Citigroup, the Big 3 automakers, and Wall Street. A bailout filled with waste and bribery, yet supported by McCain—the man who claimed to be the hero who had fought against earmarks and waste with his every breath. "Mr. Anti-Earmark" supported a bailout filled with handouts to firms that manufacture wooden arrows, wool, rum in Puerto Rico, and products in American Samoa. He supported a bailout that provided tax breaks for bicycle commuters, clearly an action vital to rescuing the U.S. economy. He supported a bailout that for all intents and purposes nationalized the banking and financial system of the United States. And perhaps worst of all, McCain supported a bailout that gave the IRS expanded powers to fund undercover sting operations against U.S. citizens, featuring IRS agents posing as accountants to entrap and arrest taxpayers choosing questionable tax deductions. Can anyone possibly explain to me what giving expanded powers to the IRS has to do with an emergency rescue of the U.S. economy?

As I write this chapter, the bailout is turning into more of a disaster every day. The insurance giant, AIG, has come back to the federal government for an additional $40 billion (what a surprise). Fannie Mae and Freddie Mac have disclosed that they may need *hundreds* of billions more. The Big 3 U.S. automakers received billions more in "loans" (as if any of this money poured into these failed business models will ever be repaid). The governors of virtually every state in these United States came to Obama, hat in hand, to ask for billions in handouts. The city council of Detroit disclosed that they would ask the government for $10 billion (with a "B"). *A city needs $10 billion?* Could that be because the auto unions have strangled and bankrupted the Big 3 automakers, thereby destroying Detroit and the state of Michigan in the bargain? Yet we gave billions to the automakers so they could keep paying $160,000 (in salary, pension, and benefits) to union members drilling rivets into fenders? Could I be the only one that sees the absurdity, hypocrisy, and bankruptcy that this represents?

Perhaps worst of all, hundreds of billions of dollars had been loaned out to anonymous companies and banks whose names our own Treasury Secretary refuses to disclose. Of course, the treasury secretary had no reason to disclose those names—Congress gave him unprecedented authority and the draconian powers of a dictator in that same bailout. *As with most government programs this has worked out well, don't you think?*

But just when you think it can't get worse, it always does. Although I was actually happy to see Paulsen go, it turns out he was the good guy in comparison to the people chosen by Obama to run the economy. It has been reported that Treasury Secretary Tim Geithner forgot to pay

Social Security taxes (for years). Yet he will oversee taxes in this country. The man Obama picked to lead the health care battle, former Senator Tom Daschle forgot to report more than $100,000 in taxable income on his car and chauffeur. That could happen to anyone right? At least anyone who has a limousine and chauffeur. And Nancy Killefer, the woman picked to be Chief Performance Officer for the U.S. government, forgot to pay her nanny taxes. Keep in mind these are supposed to be the smartest, most powerful people in the country. Personally, I now understand why liberal Democrats are such big proponents of higher taxes—*they themselves don't pay them.*

But let's move from the flawed characters of those who serve in government, back to their flawed decisions—namely the never-ending bailouts of millionaire CEOs and billion dollar corporate giants. Keep in mind where all this bailout money comes from. *It comes from you the taxpayer.* Yet our own government takes the money from the treasury without asking permission of those who pay the taxes, without discussion with the people, without saying "please" or "thank you"; and then refuses to disclose to whom the money is going. Isn't this the very definition of taxation without representation (the very reason our forefathers fought the American Revolution)? I'm speechless. Where will it end? We are already trillions in debt. If you're already broke and in heavy debt, is it possible to go *more* broke? Could our entire nation default on the debt? Our children's children are trillions in debt, and they're not even born yet. No wonder the first thing a baby does at the moment of birth is *scream!*

It's obvious that the people running our government are flawed hypocrites. So what gives them the right to determine who gets the bailout money? Think of the ethical issues and conflicts of interest. I talked about Tom Daschle's tax problems above. But I didn't mention that he made a reported $5 million working for a lobbying firm—much of it from health care companies. So if he had been confirmed as Secretary of Health and Human Services, would you have trusted his decisions on where the trillions of dollars in government funding would be assigned?

Here are some other questions that come instantly to mind about the bailout funds and conflicts of interest: What right has the federal government to determine which private companies should be saved, and which should be allowed to fail? How would we ever protect these decisions from being corrupted by conflicts of interest (from lobbyists and campaign contributions)? With so much money at stake, why on earth would any major U.S. corporation *not* beg the federal government for billions in order to "save jobs?" Of course, corporations then turn around and pay out billions of dollars in bonuses to fat-cat executives. Where will it ever end? Will any of this money ever be repaid to U.S. taxpayers? Does anyone realize there is actually no money in the treasury to pay for this bailout—there's only debt and more debt. Therefore this money just comes from printing presses. They are working day and night at the Federal Reserve to print money that doesn't really exist, to pay bills that *do* exist, and that every action of the federal government makes the debt larger and larger.

Does anyone realize that when this is all over we will undoubtedly face the highest inflation in a generation (simply because obscene levels of printing of money always leads to runaway inflation)? The politicians may simply close their eyes and say "keep printing." All they care about is today—avoiding a deep recession while they are still in office. But that mind-set can, in fact, cause a great and long-lasting depression. Let me tell you all, this is one son of a butcher who says enough is enough: *Stop running the printing presses!* And, I can assure you that I am joined by tens of millions of other hardworking, overtaxed U.S. small business owners and taxpayers who have reached the point where they are beginning to scream that famous line from the movie *Network*—"I'm Mad As Hell And I'm Not Going To Take It Any More."

Here's an interesting question: Who exactly is bailing out small businesspeople like me when we get in trouble? The answer, of course, is *no one*. While banks receive billions of dollars in sweetheart loans from the feds to save themselves, they are saying "no" to virtually every small businessperson who requests a loan or credit line to save their business. While American Express demands billions of dollars from the federal government to save themselves, they lower the credit lines of their customers who have paid every bill honorably and on time. It's a disgrace. Twenty years from now will today's dollar be worth even a nickel for our kids and grandkids? Will capitalism still be alive? Perhaps the real question is, "Is capitalism still alive today?"

If John McCain had chosen to take a stand against the bailout, there is no doubt in my mind that the presidential election would have been his. Yet even in this moment that so clearly defined big government versus limited government, Big Brother and big corporate interests versus U.S. citizens and taxpayers, socialism versus capitalism and personal responsibility, John McCain and the GOP establishment joined hands with Barack Obama and sang *Kum-Ba-Yah*. They proved once and for all that there are no longer any major differences between the two dominant parties. The support of the bailout cost McCain the election and his place in history. It cost the GOP millions of votes and additional losses in the House and Senate. It validated my decision of a few years ago to leave the GOP. But more importantly, it blurred the lines between Democrats and Republicans. All I could think was: *Big and bigger, dumb and dumber.*

■ ■ ■

But lest you think I'm being too harsh on my Republican friends, wait until you hear what I think of my old college classmate Barack Obama. After everything I just said about McCain and the gang-who-couldn't-shoot-straight GOP, they are a breath of fresh air compared to the Obama–Harry Reid–Nancy Pelosi cabal. Obama is a far-left socialist who will expand government far beyond anything ever imagined by big government liberal icons like McGovern, Johnson, Humphrey, Muskie, Dukakis, Gore, or Kerry. He will choose to tax successful citizens to death (literally by bringing back the death tax and raising the rates of taxation on money we all have left on the day we die *after* a lifetime of paying taxes).

He will choose to hire millions of U.S. citizens to work for government, thereby creating an entire "privileged class" dependent on government paychecks and therefore willing to vote reliably for big-government liberal politicians. Just to give you a small taste of the looming disaster for the U.S. economy (and your kids and grandkids), the federal government employee retirement system has an unfunded liability of $5.3 trillion, including $1.2 trillion for medical benefits.* And President Obama ignores the crisis and continues to dramatically expand the roles of government employee unions. I'll discuss the growing problem of government employee unions later in this book. But suffice to say that auto unions have bankrupted the Big 3 automakers, the city of Detroit, and the state of Michigan. Teachers unions have destroyed our public school

USA Today article "A Part of Americana Seeks to Weather the Storm" Feb. 3, 2009.

system, taking it from the envy of the world, to the bottom of the industrialized world. Government employee unions threaten to do the same to our entire country. The more government employees who are hired, the worse things get for U.S. taxpayers. For every government employee hired, there is now a new responsibility for taxpayers to pay his or her salary, pension, and health care for at least a half century into the future.

Perhaps the most frightening aspect of an Obama presidency is that history proves that liberal tax and spenders usually lie by at least *claiming* to support smaller government (see Bill Clinton). Obama never even bothered to lie. He stated in public that he supports "spreading the wealth around." It's true that some people listened and didn't understand. It's true that some people paid no attention. It's true that some people were so sick of George W. Bush, they didn't care—they'd have pulled the lever for Mickey Mouse or Donald Duck. After the big government George Bush and the Republicans gave us during these past eight years, I can sympathize with many of these voters.

But it is not the voters who voted *against* Bush and the Republicans who should give every taxpayer cause for concern. It is the voters who heard Obama loud and clear and cheered his goal to "spread the wealth around." You see, 40 percent of Americans already pay no federal taxes. After Obama's new "tax cut" program is put into effect—rewarding those who pay no taxes with a welfare check disguised as a tax cut— the number will grow higher. After four years of President Obama we'll surely be at or above the "tipping point" where a majority of U.S. citizens pay no taxes and expect some sort of bribe from government (i.e., handout, entitlement, tax credit even though they paid no taxes).

Once the clear-cut majority of people either work for government, or collect a paycheck from government, the majority will vote for higher and higher taxes on the minority (those who earn their own keep, create jobs, risk their money to build businesses). Why not? Taxes aren't painful, as long as someone else has to pay them. The majority will vote for politicians who require them to take less and less personal responsibility, and promise them more and more handouts from government. For a few short years they may even be better off. But sadly, soon the free market system, the "Goose That Lays the Golden Eggs," will lie dead and the United States will be plunged into a downward spiral of an ever-lower quality of life for all.

When the government allows you to keep more of your own money, politicians call it a "giveaway." But, handing a government welfare or stimulus check to someone who doesn't pay taxes in the first place is called a tax cut. How perverse. The American Dream is becoming a . . . *nightmare*. The United States is becoming . . . *Europe*.

Obama might bankrupt the United States even sooner than Bush or McCain by handing the government checkbook to his friends: lawyers, lobbyists, radical environmentalists, obstructionist teachers unions, greedy government employee unions, and government entitlement addicts. These are the people who think government solves problems by creating jobs and money out of the blue. It's easy to think that when you're not the one being asked to contribute. It's easy to solve problems by voting to tax *others*.

No matter who won the 2008 election, government was destined to grow. Neither of the two major parties ran on a platform of drastically cutting the size of government, nor, given their sorry past performance, could anyone have reasonably expected them to, even if they had. No matter who was elected, U.S. taxpayers faced a bleak future. But Obama's election, along with the power gained by some members of Congress—Nancy Pelosi, Harry Reid, Barney Frank, Chris Dodd, and Charles Rangel—will undoubtedly accelerate the pace. *It's big and bigger, dumb and dumber—on steroids.*

■ ■ ■

There is a bright side to all this. I've had my Libertarian Awakening. In the coming years, under big-government proponent Barack Obama, I believe millions of people will come to the same conclusion. Let me once again repeat myself—there is no longer much difference between the Republican and Democratic parties. Whether big government is used to impose the government's will on economic issues or personal freedom/social issues, it really doesn't matter. Big government used for *any* purpose is not in the best interest of the citizens. Any government granted special powers will most certainly someday use those same powers against you. It's only a matter of time. After all, to paraphrase Thomas Jefferson, a government big enough to give you all you want, is also big enough to take it all away.

The good news is that I've experienced this wonderful "awakening." I've awakened to a whole new world of political possibilities.

When the light bulb finally went off for me, I came to the realization that voting for the "lesser of two evils" only leads to the "wrong direction" our country is headed on. I believe if Barry Goldwater or Ronald Reagan were alive today, and witnessed today's government involvement, neither would call himself a Republican. Like me, they'd both label themselves as Libertarians.

Yes, I still believe that when it comes to fiscal issues, the GOP is a slightly better alternative than bleeding-heart, do-gooder, socialist-leaning, spread-the-wealth liberal Democrats—*if that's our only choice.* But I no longer believe that the labels "Republican" and "Democrat" are the only viable choices for U.S. voters. They can't be. Because history proves, although Republicans sound much like Libertarians while on the campaign trail, they govern much like Democrats, expanding government, raising taxes (although by lower amounts), hiring more bureaucrats, violating our civil liberties, and taking away our freedoms. The choice of "the lesser of two evils" has failed our country miserably. The only way to force the change that Obama constantly talks about is to stop voting for either Republicans or Democrats.

■ ■ ■

When I talk about my own political awakening, I am shocked, amazed, and pleased at how many of my fiscal conservative/socially moderate Republican (and even a few Democratic) friends now openly admit to me that they now consider themselves Libertarians. I sense something big happening in the heartland. It's also happening in Hollywood, where celebrities like Drew Carey, Dennis Miller, Bill Maher, Jon Stewart, Kurt Russell, and Penn and Teller openly call themselves Libertarians. Or on FOX News, where Glenn Beck, Neil Cavuto and Judge Andrew Napolitano are openly Libertarian.

Lord knows it hasn't reached the tone-deaf ears of the DC establishment or liberal national media. But the train has left the station and it's barreling down upon the traditional two-party system and the infamous Beltway Insiders. Ross Perot, Jesse "The Body" Ventura, and even Kinky Friedman (the third-party gubernatorial candidate in Texas) have all paved the way for a serious third-party candidate on a national level. As Bob Dylan would say, "The times, they are a-changin." The window of opportunity has opened for the Libertarian Party to become a competitive mainstream party. As a wise man once said, "Timing is not important—it's *everything!*" I'm confident that when voters know there is a viable, credible alternative—a winnable alternative—many people will experience their very own Libertarian awakening. I've made my decision—I've always been a leader, not a follower. I will continue to vote for, support, and contribute to any candidate from any party with Libertarian ideals and principles. But I've moved to the party of principle.

I hope that like my hero Barry Goldwater's book *The Conscience of a Conservative*, this book will have the power to inspire and energize a national movement. And spur the "inner Libertarian" to come out in millions of U.S. voters who are tired and disgusted with the two-party system. I believe the great Silent Majority of fiscally conservative/socially tolerant U.S. taxpayers and voters are exactly where I was a few years ago, and simply do not realize that there is a third choice. I hope to change all that. *It really is this easy.* All you need to do is support, contribute and vote for a third-party candidate who truly reflects your own views. A candidate with commonsense principles, not just campaign slogans. A candidate who isn't bought and paid for by corporate and special interests. Together we can bring genuine change to the world. I'm not talking about the "change" that Obama promised. That is simply rearranging the deck chairs on the Titanic. I'm talking real change—away from bigger government, bigger spending, bigger deficits and national debt, bigger bailouts, and bigger taxes to pay for it all.

Chapter 4

Republicans and Democrats

Big and Bigger, Dumb and Dumber

The Democrats are the party that says government will make you smarter, taller, richer, and remove the crabgrass on your lawn. The Republicans are the party that says government doesn't work and then get elected and prove it.

—P.J. O'Rourke

O ver the past few decades, the difference between the two major parties has all but disappeared. Democrats win. Republicans win. No matter. *Government grows.* And not just by small steps, but by leaps and bounds. After my hero, Barry Goldwater, was defeated for the Presidency in 1964, federal spending in inflation-adjusted dollars has gone from $600 billion to almost $4 trillion today. Through an almost 50-year journey of Republican presidents, Democratic presidents, Republican-controlled Congress, and Democratic-controlled Congress, the line of government growth just grows unabated straight to the heavens (or more accurately, straight down toward *hell*).

The presidential election of 2008 offered the clearest demonstration of the lack of difference between the two major parties. It featured a moderate Democrat versus a socialist. Unfortunately it was John McCain playing the moderate *Democrat*. I'll give you three guesses who was the socialist? Back in 1964, the year of Barry Goldwater's presidential campaign, few voters would have believed that less than 50 years later Americans would be listening to a candidate supporting a trillion dollar taxpayer bailout of Wall Street and (for all intents and purposes) nationalization of banks, demanding government guarantees of bad mortgages entered into freely by consumers and homeowners, and railing against Wall Street greed. *The shocking part was that the candidate was the Republican John McCain!*

And absolutely no one would have believed that his opponent would openly support "spreading the wealth around" and win the election on a platform of punishing the successful, hardworking job creators with draconian new tax hikes while giving welfare payments to millions of people who pay no taxes in the first place by calling them "tax cuts."

No, this wasn't a horror movie, or a sci-fi novel, about the improbable evils of the future. These were our two major party choices in the fall of 2008. The most amazing part of all—the United States chose the *socialist!* Barry Goldwater and Ronald Reagan are rolling over in their graves. The two-party system is a dramatic failure. And the two parties are now a comedy team—*Big and Bigger, Dumb and Dumber.*

■ ■ ■

Are there differences between the GOP and the Democrats? Of course, there are. After all, as I pointed out above, John McCain in 2008 was what Goldwater would have defined as a moderate Democrat back in 1959. And Obama is certainly an extreme left-wing ideologue that Goldwater would have considered a socialist on fiscal issues. But overall the differences are bigger in talk than they are in action. Yes, Republicans talk about smaller government, lower taxes, and more freedom. But once in office, they govern almost exactly like Democrats—expanding government, raising spending, limiting our freedoms. It is still true that the GOP is more supportive of economic freedom than the big-government Democrats (but only a little bit more); and it may still be true that the GOP is more supportive of small businesspeople like me (but only a little bit more); and it may still be true that the GOP is more supportive of lower tax rates, so that the taxpayers who take the risks and create the jobs get to keep more of their own money (but only a little bit more); and it may still be true that on issues like corporate bailouts and economic stimulus packages, Republicans are better than Democrats (but only a little bit more). So yes, there is still a little bit of difference between Republicans and Democrats on fiscal issues, but it's getting smaller all the time. When it comes to talk and rhetoric, Republicans are much better. When it comes to actually governing, not so much so. Big and bigger, dumb and dumber is the best way to describe the differences between Republicans and Democrats.

After all, it was George W. Bush who opened the door for the election of President Barack Obama with obscene government spending and the greatest expansion of government in modern political history. President Bush violated the first rule of Barry Goldwater—that tax cuts, by themselves, are useless and temporary if first you don't cut spending (so that the cuts can be affordable and permanent). Worse, it was Republican President Bush who opened the door to socialism in the fall of 2008 with his support of bailouts, economic stimulus packages, and loans to failed auto companies. But no matter how bad Republicans are in the area of spending, Democrats can one-up them. President Obama will no doubt make Bush's obscene spending seem small by the time it's all over. I fear after we've experienced four years of Obama's spending plans, we'll all be wishing we could travel back to the "good old days of Bush."

But even that slight difference in favor of Republicans is only on the economic side. Of concern to my Libertarian limited-government roots and sensibilities is the fact that on a number of personal freedom, bedroom, and social issues, I find Republicans to be even *more* supportive of Big Brother than Democrats. The fact is, today's Republicans leaders have moved away from the limited government ideals of my heroes Thomas Jefferson, Barry Goldwater, and Ronald Reagan. When it comes to issues like abortion, gay rights, stem cell funding, right to die (think Terri Schiavo), online poker, medical marijuana, and censorship of television, the GOP is actually in *favor* of Big Brother moving into our bedrooms, taking over our televisions and computers, and taking control of our lives.

Democrats, of course, aren't much better with their Nanny State views on issues such as seat belt laws, environmental restrictions, animal rights, and gun control. Just one small example: Liberal animal rights crusaders in California just passed a law that tells egg producers how close they must place their chickens in the coop. The result: Many, if not most, California chicken farms and ranches will pack up and move to other states before the law takes effect. Just another extreme law that never took economics into account, and thereby stands to wipe out an entire industry and cost the state of California millions of dollars in taxes, all in the name of the civil rights of chickens. Please remember that (as I write this chapter) California is more than $43 billion in debt (at least before federal government stimulus handouts) and begging the federal government to save them from bankruptcy. Does it ever occur to liberal Democratic do-gooders in California that there is a correlation between the laws they pass and their massive, record-setting deficit, debt, and bankruptcy? More on that issue in Chapter 10, "California Nightmare."

The truth is, despite the fact that voters have said again and again that they want smaller, less intrusive government, and more individual freedom, it's difficult to find a politician who is a true believer in freedom and in the rights of the individual. Unfortunately both parties now embrace Big Brother at its worst—looking out first for their own vested interests, at the expense of what I value most—*my individual freedom.* Both parties talk the talk of freedom, but neither walks the walk. In politics today, freedom (economic or personal) is merely something to talk about at election time, but the reality is that it is thrown to the wayside in order to expand the scope, size, and power of government.

The Democratic version of big government is all about limiting our economic freedom. Democrats want to tell us what to do with our own money. They are continually pilfering our bank accounts in the name of "fairness." But fairness has nothing to do with it. In reality, the Democrats attempt to steal from the rich in order to bribe the poor (to vote Democratic) by keeping them dependent on Democratic politicians and big-government handouts. Unfortunately they have been very successful at it. Democrats love to play Robin Hood. But there's a problem with that philosophy. When you steal from the rich to give to the poor, it's still *stealing!* At least Barack Obama was honest when describing his philosophy to "Joe the Plumber." Obama said he wanted to "spread the wealth around." Polite political analysts call that income redistribution. But let's call it by its proper name: *socialism.* It's simply Big Brother forcing social engineering upon the taxpayers to create their definition of "fairness." But that definition has nothing to do with fairness, and everything to do with politics. Fleecing the top 20 percent of taxpayers often wins the support, sympathy, and votes of the majority of the other 80 percent of voters. The fact that it is fair, or right or wrong, is immaterial. It is just politics.

Republicans, on the other hand support Big Brother when it comes to our bedrooms. They want to step all over the Constitution, imposing their moral views by controlling what we can and cannot do in our *personal* lives. I'll talk in depth about my views about God, religion, and prayer later in this book. You may be surprised to find out that I'm a deeply religious man who makes God the foundation of my life. My days revolve around a foundation of prayer and family. But that doesn't mean that I want to use government to impose my views on others and trample the rights of U.S. citizens who might not think the same way that I do. A core value, as strong as my religious beliefs, is my belief in freedom, choice, and free will.

Republicans and Democrats believe in Big Brother and the Nanny State. Both parties believe in using government to impose their views on us—it's merely where and how they choose to impose government upon us that is slightly different. Some choice that leaves us on Election Day—a cynic might question if either party actually believes in any of this? It's more likely in my opinion that they are simply willing to violate our rights and destroy our freedoms in order to amass enough special interest votes to win elections. Belief never enters the equation. The only belief or conviction politicians possess is a belief in their own power (and achieving more of it).

I can't stand big government, or government bureaucrats. Their true function is not to help me. Their true function is only to protect their own vested interest. While I'm on my rant of the things that I cannot stand, let me include overreaching laws and governmental intrusion into areas of individual rights and personal freedoms. No, this doesn't mean I'm a fan of abortion or gay marriage or assisted suicide or online gambling. It just means that I believe in the Constitution. In their infinite wisdom, our Founding Fathers created a document that formed a foundation for the greatest country in world history. That document spells it out very clearly—any issue not specifically authorized by the Constitution as the province of the federal government, belongs to the states. When it comes to personal and social issues like those mentioned above, I believe it is up to the voters of each state to decide for themselves.

As one of my heroes, Thomas Jefferson, once said, "The true theory of our Constitution is that States are independent as to *everything* within themselves and united as to everything respecting foreign affairs." Jefferson recognized the right of a state to nullify a federal law within its own borders, even describing federal government intrusion in state matters as "interference by a foreign government." In other words, let the voters decide these issues on the state and local level where government is closer to the voters and keep the federal government out of it. When it comes to personal issues and private choices, I believe the only answer, no matter what the question (unless it is specifically authorized by the Constitution) is: *It's none of the federal government's darn business!*

■ ■ ■

One asterisk here. I am not naïve enough to assume that state governments are always fair, open-minded, and wonderful to the people. State governments can and often are just as intolerable, onerous, close-minded, and mean-spirited as the federal government. But the reality is that state governments are closer to the people and deal with far smaller populations than the federal government. That gives enlightened reformers a chance to get things done on the local level that could never happen on the federal level. For these reasons, state governments are often the place where reform begins.

States are willing to try out solutions that the federal government would never consider. The states are "the riverboat gamblers" of the government. They are often willing to experiment (roll the dice) with ideas. As an example, California legalized medical marijuana, while Nevada has both legalized gambling and prostitution. In both cases, states were willing to go out on a limb to give their residents (as long as they are consenting adults) more personal freedom (usually motivated by higher tax revenues). These experiments on the state level can serve as models for the entire nation and eventually lead to federal breakthroughs and reform. That is why I strongly support States' Rights. I'd prefer that no government (local, state, or federal) limited the personal freedoms of consenting adults, but I am a realist. Incremental success on the state level, which can lead to full-fledged success on the national level, is preferable to no success at all. And even if the freedoms achieved on the state level are never implemented on the national level, it gives citizens a chance to choose to live in the states that allow the most personal freedom that fits their lifestyle.

I'd like to take a moment here to expose the myth that the federal government ever bans freedoms "for the good of the people." The good of the people rarely, if ever, has anything to do with it. The best example may be online gaming and poker. For those of you who for religious or moral reasons want to ban gambling, and think it's your business to tell U.S. citizens what entertainment they have a right to choose in the privacy of their own homes, I'd like to point out that the wonderful new law UIEGA (that for all intensive purposes bans online gaming) has little or *nothing* to do with morality. This new law is riddled with special interest holes. It just happens to carve out exemptions for online horserace gambling, online lotteries (which produce hundreds of millions in tax revenues for state governments, always aimed directly at the poorest and most vulnerable citizens), tribal gaming (on Indian reservations), and Fantasy Football (because the lobbyists from the NFL spent a million dollars protecting their favorite form of online gaming). So once again we have more proof that government isn't out to help the citizens. It is only out to protect interests and profits of the government itself. And if banning online gaming just happens to add a few million votes from the religious right (who want online gaming banned for morality reasons), well then that's one heck of a bonus.

The only thing this law has accomplished is putting credible, legal, licensed gaming web sites out of business, and literally overnight handing control of online gaming to fly-by-night frauds, criminals, and organized crime. This bill is the greatest thing to ever happen to the Gambino Crime Family. This new version of Prohibition should be renamed "The Sopranos Support Bill." Since a vote for UIEGA clearly has nothing to do with morality, the only possible explanation as to why a politician would vote for it is that they are receiving bribes (excuse me, large legal "contributions") from the Mafia. So it's possible (I'd say likely) that many of our leading politicians are privately accepting bribes from the Mafia, while publicly claiming to be champions of morality. Doesn't it make you sleep well at night knowing your government is out to protect you? I talk in more detail on this issue of online gaming in a later chapter in this book.

My point in all of this is that you shouldn't be fooled into thinking that giving power to Big Brother is fine and dandy if the government is on your side on this issue or that. Giving government power is always a dangerous idea. Today government may use that power on your behalf. You may applaud government's decision. But tomorrow government may change sides and decide to use the power you have given them ... *against you.* The best solution is to never give the government that authority, power, or control in the first place—simply because (drum roll please) *it's none of the government's darn business.*

Chapter 5

The Battered Voter Syndrome

No man's life, liberty, or property is safe while the legislature is in session.

—MARK TWAIN (1866)

I f you have ever had the misfortune to know someone who was being abused or mistreated, I am sure the following statements sound frighteningly familiar:

He lies to me all the time. He takes my money and tells me that I can't spend it as well as he can. I've watched him spend us into financial ruin, giving money to his friends, wasting money on irresponsible schemes. We're so far in debt, we'll never get out.

I work extra long hours to support him. I bring home all the money, yet he tells me what to do all day long. He winds up controlling almost every aspect of my life. He even tells me that I don't know how to properly raise my own children.

When he needs me, he's nice to me. He tells me how he wants the same things I do. After he gets what he wants, he goes back to his *real* personality. The truth is that he couldn't care less about me. He couldn't care less about anyone or anything. He only cares about himself. He uses the rest of us to get what he wants.

He keeps hurting me and I don't know what to do. I'm really scared. But he has me convinced that anyone else would treat me worse. He's probably right. So I stay.

It's probably all my fault. I just need to show him that I support him 100 percent. Maybe then he'll treat me better.

Although you may have never known someone who experienced this kind of abuse, everyone has heard of "battered spouse syndrome." Battered spouses lack self-esteem and confidence. They actually *choose* to stay in disastrous, depressing, dangerous, and even deadly relationships. In many cases, the more loyalty they show to their abusive spouse, the worse they are treated and the more abuse they absorb. Most of us cannot understand how someone can choose to stay in a relationship with someone who torments them, hurts them, physically or psychologically, or threatens to kill them or their children.

But the tale of woe you just read above is *not* from a battered spouse. This person is suffering from "battered voter syndrome."

Both Republican and Democratic voters fall victim election after election to such abuse.

Let's start with battered Republicans.

■ ■ ■

How many times can conservative voters be lied to without waking up to the deception? Year after year, at election time, Republicans trot out candidates who portray themselves as libertarian conservatives standing for free markets, smaller government, lower spending, lower taxes, and more freedom. But after they are elected, they govern very differently than they promised. The reality is that Republicans talk about smaller government, but once elected, they expand government just like Democrats, they support spending on programs that will eventually lead to higher taxes, they violate your freedoms in the name of security, they pry into your bedroom in the name of morality. They may support smaller government, but they sure have a funny way of showing it. As a matter of fact, if you didn't know better, you might swear that the politicians doing this to you were big-government Democrats.

Even one of my Republican heroes was guilty of voter abuse. Remember when Ronald Reagan said during his presidential campaign, "The nine worst words in the English language are 'I'm from the government and I'm here to help.'" Yet, when he was elected, he oversaw a dramatic expansion of government. Although he promised voters that he'd eliminate the Department of Education, he obviously didn't. In fact, it is still standing almost three decades later—not only standing, but *growing* at an alarming rate, with a budget of almost $70 billion. *Seventy billion dollars.* Now Obama has included $130 billion in education spending to his stimulus package. That's $130 billion in *extra* spending. Reagan was one of my heroes. He was about as good as a president gets in modern political history. But certainly this story proves that he was far from perfect. Even the Gipper battered his voters. But he was one of the good guys compared to the rest.

Let me give you another example of a Republican candidate battering his voters. Remember when George H.W. Bush, daddy of W, said, "Read my lips, no new taxes." Then after his election, he promptly *raised* taxes. Of course, Bush 41 increased spending and expanded government, too. That's the typical Republican "Triple Crown"—increase taxes, increase spending, and expand government—while campaigning as a tax cutter who stands for limited government. Now that's abusive. That's a cold slap in the face to Republican voters.

And I guess the old saying, "the apple doesn't fall far from the tree" is as good as any when I ask you to remember George W. Bush's promises to cut government and reduce spending. Like father, like son—or should I say like Republican, like Republican. When he was elected, W went on a spending rampage that would embarrass a drunken sailor. The first veto of his presidency was against stem cell research. But earmarks, pork, waste, and bloated budgets never seemed to bother W. Those issues never caused him to lift his hand to sign a veto. W called himself a compassionate conservative. But he sure didn't show much compassion to the taxpayers. The federal government literally exploded in size under Bush 43.

The 2008 election featured John McCain, yet another Republican presidential candidate promising to be a conservative free market libertarian. But in his prior political life McCain voted against tax cuts, supported amnesty for illegal aliens whose demands for government spending and entitlements threaten to bankrupt our nation, supported more government regulation, more bureaucrats, and dramatically higher taxes in the name of global warming, supported violations of our civil liberties like warrantless wiretaps, and created a campaign finance bill (McCain-Feingold) that eroded our free speech.

And that was all *before* McCain joined with Barack Obama to support the trillion dollar government bailout in the fall of 2008.

Yet the GOP once again relied on "the fear factor" to get their battered voters back in line—a fear of Big Brother himself: Barack Obama. But here's the thing. While Barack is a big government proponent, it was Republicans like Bush and McCain who brought us bigger government, runaway spending, and the nationalization of the U.S. banking system. With friends like that, who needs enemies?

Fear is a powerful motivator. Every four years the Republicans trot out the same sad, pathetic words, "well the Republican candidate is the lesser of two evils." But is that good enough? Republicans threaten us with the specter of bigger government. Then they get elected and give us *bigger government*. Would anyone have been surprised if John McCain had been elected and then chose to govern in much the same way as prior Republican presidents? Any fiscally conservative, small-government advocate that chose to vote for McCain was certainly suffering from battered voter syndrome.

■ ■ ■

But Republicans don't own the franchise on battered voter syndrome. Democrats have spent their fair share of time being abused by their own heroes, too. Democratic politicians promise responsible government that will help "the little guy," and then give us Congressman Barney Frank to oversee Fannie Mae and Freddie Mac.

Then there is President Obama—the man of reform and "change." Well he did raise almost $750 million in *change*, smashing all-time records for campaign contributions. That's more than both candidates for President combined in 2004. Who gave him $750,000,000 anyway? What do they expect in return? How did he raise that kind of money in the worst economy in our lifetime? Does this ring any alarm bells in your mind? When Obama promised to "spread the wealth around," to whom was he promising to give *your* money?

When Obama institutes "carbon taxes" on U.S. businesses in the name of global warming, thereby dramatically raising the cost of utility bills, gasoline, and home heating oil for middle-class homeowners, will he be looking out for "the little guy?"

What about Obama's "Windfall Profits Tax" on Big Oil? Is that looking out for "the little guy"? Once sworn in as president, Obama quietly decided to drop the Windfall Profits Tax because oil had fallen below $40 per barrel. Obama's decision makes sense only to a liberal who understands nothing about business or risk and reward. When the price of oil goes down, thereby hurting oil company profits, Obama agrees to leave the oil companies alone. When the price of oil goes up, he believes that we must *punish* the oil companies—even though they take all the risk and lay out billions of dollars for exploration without knowing what the price of oil will be tomorrow.

Let me go out on a limb with a specific prediction. As I write this chapter, oil has plunged to less than $40 per barrel and gas at the pump is just less than $2 per gallon. I predict that under President Obama a barrel of oil will rise dramatically. Maybe not for a year or two—it might be held down for the near future by a deep worldwide recession. But within a relatively short period of time, after Obama kills the idea of offshore drilling and announces draconian new measures to combat global warming, oil will rise to new heights. I wonder how the little guy will feel about that?

The media blamed President George W. Bush for $4 per gallon gas, even though his policies had no direct effect on the rise in the price of oil. I wonder if that same biased liberal media will blame Obama (whose policies *will* have a direct effect) when gas at the pump blows by $4 per gallon? And when that happens, Obama will immediately blame big oil and reintroduce legislation for a Windfall Profits Tax to punish them because the price of oil rose higher due to *his* policies. You almost have to laugh to keep from crying.

When Obama eliminates secret ballots in labor votes, thereby empowering union goons and bullies to intimidate employees into voting for the union, will he be looking out for the little guy?

When Obama raises capital gains taxes (by simply letting the Bush tax cuts expire), thereby raising taxes for *every* U.S. citizen who owns stocks in their retirement accounts, and dramatically raising taxes on the sale of your home, will he be looking out for the little guy?

When Obama hires millions of new federal government bureaucrats with bloated salaries, pensions, and health benefits, in order to create jobs for Democratic voters, will that help the little guy?

None of this will help the taxpayer, that's for sure.

Obama comes from the Chicago political machine—a modern day Tammany Hall. The same machine that produced Governor Blagojevich. Obama not only supported Blagojevich for governor (twice), he never in his entire political career stood up to the machine. Not once. Yet he calls himself a "reformer." Funny how Obama never found a single reform candidate to support, in all his years in Illinois politics.

The pattern continued after Mr. Obama went to Washington. He talked a lot about cleaning up Washington's culture of corruption. He talked about getting rid of the influence of lobbyists. Within days of being sworn in as president number 44, his choice for commerce secretary Bill Richardson had to step down over a criminal investigation into a possible "pay for play" scandal as governor of New Mexico. His health secretary candidate Tom Daschle admitted he had a tax problem (he didn't pay them) and a lobbying background (he made millions from the very health companies he was asked to oversee by Obama). Treasury Secretary Tim Geithner had a tax problem (he didn't pay them). Obama appointed a lobbyist for the fourth largest defense contractor in the United States as the Deputy Secretary of Defense. Obama's Chief of Staff Rahm Emanuel made over $300,000 in one year serving on the Board of Freddie Mac (the mortgage company that helped to destroy the mortgage industry). Is this change? Has Obama "reformed" Washington, DC? The list goes on and on. I'd need a second book to list all the people Obama appointed with ethics problems.

Just saying "change" doesn't make you a man of change. Just talking about "reform," doesn't make you a reformer. If you think Obama is a man of change, you poor thing—you are certainly a battered voter.

■ ■ ■

Do you see a pattern? Both parties take care of their friends—read that as contributors and cronies—while fleecing you, the taxpayers. They just happen to have *different* agendas and friends. Republicans promise smaller government and more freedom from Big Brother. But once elected they bring us bigger government and more power over our personal lives and private decisions. Republicans expand government in order to help their friends—defense contractors, oil companies, pharmaceutical companies, and billion dollar agribusiness conglomerates. The small business owners that Republican politicians talk about at election time are thrown overboard in favor of corporate lobbyists.

On the other hand, Democrats promise to take care of the little guy. But once elected, they too throw the little guy overboard and hand the country over to their friends: trial lawyers, teachers unions, federal and state employee unions, radical environmentalists, and entitlement addicts. Democrats swear they will raise taxes only on the rich in order to spread the wealth around. But once elected, *you* become "the rich." The reality is that Obama wants to spread the wealth around from those who work hard, achieve success, and create most of the jobs . . . to those who don't work hard and expect government handouts. Why would he do that? Because those are his voters. His economic philosophy isn't about "fairness," it is simply about *bribery*.

■ ■ ■

Over the past few years, polls have consistently shown that 90 percent of Americans believe we are on the "wrong track" as a nation. That's the highest rate in history. Yet, if you've been voting for the same two choices, Republican or Democrat, for the last few decades . . . if you've been voting all these years for "the lesser of two evils" . . . perhaps it's no coincidence why we are on the wrong track. *We're on the wrong track because you've been voting for the wrong person.*

Voters who choose the same two flawed choices of Republican or Democrat year after year are starring in *Groundhog Day*. You make the same choices election after election, yet you keep expecting different results. You fall for the same deceptions, lies, and fraud year after year, yet you're shocked that nothing changes. You still believe it when the politician claims to offer *change* without evaluating the politician's track record, and asking exactly what is the change that he or she is proposing, and how are we going to pay for it? If you vote for politicians who offer change without a clear plan for what that change is and how it will be implemented, *you are a battered voter.*

But there is another choice. There is a way out. There is a *right* train on a *right* track. The Libertarian Party promises to end the abuse. As "America's Third Party," we offer you an honest, fair, and loyal relationship with your government. We really do support smaller government, reduced spending, lower taxes, school choice, and more freedom. We do not support special interest pork-barrel spending, government handouts, bailouts, or corporate welfare. Those aren't campaign slogans trotted out on Election Day for us—those are principles we live by. We don't just talk about these principles of limited government. We don't just trot out actors (known as "candidates") to portray a love of these principles every election day. We *live* these principles every second of every day. And once elected, Libertarians at the local level have a proven track record of doing what we said we'd do—cut government, make it more efficient, and give more money back to the taxpayers.

Unlike certain campaigns referenced earlier in this chapter, our Libertarian Presidential 2008 campaign wasn't bought or paid for by special interests or large corporations. As a political party that opposes corporate welfare, union payoffs, and big government, it is not surprising that Libertarian campaigns do not receive funds from these bureaucratic organizations. And our campaign certainly was not funded with your tax money. So, while we don't owe anyone *anything*, this lack of funding prevents us from getting our message out to you.

That is why the message in this book is so important. The message couldn't be clearer—Libertarians are only interested in you, the U.S. taxpayer. If we can get this message out, I believe we can win elections and facilitate the necessary overhaul of governmental programs and policies. And once U.S. taxpayers and voters see that we keep our promises, that we govern just as we promised during our campaigns, then there will be no stopping this citizen revolution.

Although November 4 was an end to the 2008 presidential campaign, it was only the beginning of my long-term vision to give power back to the citizens. My goal is to empower U.S. voters to recover from battered voter syndrome. Stop accepting the battering and abuse. Stop accepting the lies and deception. There is a way out. You can change the self-destructive pattern by not wasting your vote on the two parties that 90 percent of U.S. voters agree have led us in the wrong direction. It's never a wasted vote to choose a candidate who you really like, instead of someone you neither like, nor trust. The truth is, you do have a choice. A *third* choice—the Libertarian Party, America's Third Party. That's why I wrote this book—to prove to you that you are not trapped. Like Libertarian solutions to most problems that plague the United States, the answer is freedom, choice, and competition.

We don't batter our voters. We *better* them.

Chapter 6

The Citizen Revolution

The Army of Rebels with Pitchforks

The spirit of resistance to government is so valuable on certain occasions that I wish it to be always kept alive. It will often be exercised when wrong, but better so than not to be exercised at all. I like a little rebellion now and then. It is like a storm in the atmosphere.

—THOMAS JEFFERSON

For the past 20 years, virtually my entire adult life, I've been the United States' most successful odds maker and prognosticator. My accurate predictions and instincts have made me successful, well-known, and in-demand as a TV media expert. I've appeared on all the major networks to talk about my career and make predictions: FOX News Channel, FOX Business, ABC, CNBC, MSNBC, CNN, ESPN, FOX Sports, and so on. Today I make a powerful prediction—one that literally screams from my gut, and from every cell of my body. *There is a political revolution brewing—a "Citizen Revolution."* The two-party system is failing. Never before in modern U.S. political history has the time been more right (excuse the pun) for a third party to successfully do battle with the two major parties. More U.S. citizens identify themselves as "independents" than ever before. One size no longer fits all.

I believe a majority of U.S. citizens are exactly like me—fiscally conservative, but socially moderate and tolerant. I believe in both economic freedom and personal freedom. I want government out of both sides of my life—and I'm not willing to compromise. I believe that a large portion of the electorate wants government out of their lives, too—out of their wallets *and* out of their bedrooms. Winston Churchill put it best when he said, "If you're under 20 and you're a conservative, you have no heart. If you've over 30 and you're a liberal, you have no brain." Only one party allows voters to be both conservative on economic issues and tolerant on social issues. Only one party allows voters to think for themselves and retain common sense on a variety of issues. Only one party allows Barry Goldwater and Ronald Reagan conservatives to feel at home. Only one party allows voters to rebel against Big Brother in all areas of our lives. Only one party stands for both economic and personal freedom. Only one party stands for personal responsibility and individuality. Only one party believes, as the Constitution clearly demands, that power belongs to the people, not to the politicians and career bureaucrats.

That party is the Libertarian Party. And I encourage you to pick up your pitchfork and join this citizen revolution.

■ ■ ■

In the 2006 and 2008 elections, voters certainly moved toward the Democratic Party. But the Democratic victories in 2006 and 2008 were simply a rebellion against the corruption, arrogance, and incompetence (a very bad combination) of the Bush years. The United States is a center-right nation. Always has been, always will be. Liberal Democrats like Obama do not think anything like the majority of people in this center-right nation. Remember that in both elections, the same voters who pulled the lever for Obama and a Democratic Congress, voted against initiatives on state ballots that promised to raise taxes. Americans did not vote for Obama, the liberal crusader. They voted for Obama—*the personality.* They voted for Obama—*the celebrity.* Americans are so entranced by reality television shows, that voting for a president now feels like voting for the winner of *American Idol* or *Dancing with the Stars.* Obama was simply the fresh, young, dynamic new guy on the scene . . . and the old, boring guy (McCain) had little chance. Congratulations Barack, you just won *American Idol.*

But the thing to remember is that while U.S. citizens may fawn over their celebrities and even elect one as president, socialist-at-heart liberal Democratic politicians actually think the very *opposite* of the "Silent Majority" of taxpayers on important issues like downsizing government, reducing spending, cutting entitlements, cutting taxes, eliminating the death tax, protecting the rights of property owners, ending affirmative action, allowing offshore oil drilling, enacting tort reform, ending welfare and entitlements for illegal immigrants, ending English as a second language in schools and voting booths, gun owner rights, supporting the death penalty, ending affirmative action—the list goes on and on. U.S. voters are center-right on most, if not all of these crucial issues. Up until now, the Silent Majority that supports smaller government had no other choice but to vote for the GOP—that same Republican Party that is only slightly more Libertarian on fiscal and economic issues, yet in some cases even more pro–Big Brother than Democrats on social issues.

I now believe that our voting choices are beginning to expand in a dramatic way. The time has come for change—and for *choice.* I believe that most U.S. voters are now open to voting for a credible, common-sense third party candidate who can explain, debate, and defend a fiscally conservative/socially tolerant position. If this lifelong Republican was willing to make the move, I'm confident that millions of other U.S. voters are ready to pick up their pitchforks and join the citizen revolution. Politics as usual is not working. The "one size fits all" structure of our two major political parties just doesn't feel right anymore. Electing Obama as president might mean more personal freedoms, but it certainly will also result in reduced economic freedoms. One size fits all is nothing more than a big disappointment and a big fraud.

True change will only happen if each of you personally stands up and says "I'm mad as hell and I'm not going to take it anymore."

True change will never happen if you continue to choose to vote for the Republican or Democratic candidate you dislike the least. I encourage you to think of how you can produce dramatic change in this country by joining the citizen revolution. *It really is that easy!*

■ ■ ■

So who, typically, is going to fight this citizen revolution? And how can this citizen politician spark a citizen revolution in a country that barely recognizes the existence of life outside the two-party system? The answer is simple: with a "Citizen Army" made up of several unique constituencies that feel angry, betrayed, and abandoned by Republican and Democratic officials alike. An army of rebels with pitchforks— made up of citizens who believe in limited government, God, guns, gambling, school choice, and tax cuts! And, of course, any American who strongly believes in economic, personal, and religious freedom.

To build a majority that can facilitate necessary change and elect a Libertarian to the White House, first we must cobble together a base— a foundation of constituencies of U.S. voters who are tailor-made to support the citizen revolution. I have identified and targeted nine constituencies.

1. *Independent-minded small business owners, entrepreneurs, and independent contractors.* Small business owners and independent entrepreneurs are the natural constituency of a Libertarian conservative presidential candidate, in particular, *this* candidate, who happens to be a small businessman himself. Within this category, I include any hardworking person who earns his or her compensation via performance-based commission, rather than through a safe, steady weekly paycheck. As mentioned previously, there are approximately 27 million small business owners in the United States, who vote and contribute in far greater numbers than the general electorate. This constituency pays a huge portion of the taxes in the United States—remember, small business provides a majority of nongovernment jobs, and creates 75 percent of new jobs. Small business owners don't ask for much; we simply want to be free to run our own businesses and live our own lives without government interference or bureaucracy. The only thing we ask from government is to be

left alone. Democrats see small businesses as a target—that's where they get their tax funding from to fund all their big government programs and handouts. Republicans aren't much better. They have talked a good game and acted like a friend to small business for many decades. But the reality is they have done next to nothing for this group.

Well, the buck stops here. I've been a small business owner my entire adult life. I'm the son and grandson of small business owners. I understand the unique issues and concerns of small businessmen and women. In my first run for president, and then as the 2008 Libertarian Party vice presidential nominee, almost every dollar that I raised came from self-described small business owners, independent contractors, and entrepreneurs. This audience will certainly provide the base of the citizen revolution.

2. *Home-school parents, plus millions of parents looking for education reform, parental choice, and more freedom to choose alternatives to our failing public schools.* There are more than 2 million home-school parents in the United States (and growing rapidly every day). But the audience for school choice and parental freedom is far bigger. A recent Nevada Policy Research Institute (NPRI) study in my home state of Nevada (reported in the *Las Vegas Review-Journal*) asked parents to choose—if they had the freedom—what kind of education they would want for their children. According to the *Las Vegas Review-Journal*, a whopping 89 percent of Nevada parents chose either private, parochial, charter, or home-schooling for their children. That means 89 percent of parents chose something *other* than public schools. Remarkable. If only they had the choice. If only they had the freedom to determine their own child's future. If only the parents had control of their own children's education, instead of bureaucrats and teachers unions.

Education clearly demonstrates the contrast between Wayne Root and Barack Obama. I'm not against public schools. I'm not a fan of only home-schooling. To the contrary, I simply support freedom and choice—something as American as apple pie and freedom of speech. I simply support allowing parents to take their own property tax money (in the form of a voucher) and use it in any way that they feel is best for their child's education and future.

This choice could be home-schooling, charter schools, private or parochial schools. Or it could be public schools. I believe very strongly that when vouchers are offered, they encourage true competition in education and public schools greatly improve. All I ask is that parents have the choice. I simply feel that parents know what's best for their own children—not government bureaucrats or teachers unions.

Now contrast my views on education with those of President Barack Obama, who opposes school choice or vouchers, yet chooses to spend $60,000 per year to send his two little girls to the best private school in Washington, DC. What limousine liberal hypocrisy! His kids have the choice of the best education money can buy, while Obama chooses to condemn poor and middle-income children to a bleak future stuck in the worst public schools in the United States. I'll talk more about education and school choice in a later chapter. I consider school choice one of the greatest civil rights issues of the 21st century. Democrats are (ironically) against school choice and vouchers, while Republicans have talked a good game for decades, but accomplished nothing. I believe that parents seeking alternative education will become a strong part of the citizen revolution.

3. *Online gaming and poker enthusiasts.* The online gambling community is estimated by the media to number 10 million to 12 million. One organization alone, the Poker Players Alliance (PPA), has more than one million members. I am a celebrity and high-profile name to this crucial audience. They've watched me on TV for more than 20 years. They've read my books. They've even taken photos in front of my granite star on the Las Vegas Walk of Stars (in front of the ESPN Zone at New York New York). More than 2 million of these sports and gaming fans have called for my advice as a professional odds maker and sports prognosticator. This is a group tailor-made for the Libertarian Party (LP). They simply want to be left alone by government. They want the freedom to choose their form of entertainment. These are consenting adults whose choice doesn't bother or hurt a single soul in the world. Whether they choose to play poker or make a wager on Monday Night Football on their own computer in the privacy of their own home is the business of no one but themselves.

I can think of no issue that exemplifies Big Brother and the Nanny State more than the ban of online poker and gaming. No, gambling is not a big issue in a world filled with war, death, and taxes. But it is what a government ban on online poker *represents* that is crucial to all of us—*freedom*. If our government thinks it has the right to ban our choice to play poker on our own computer, in our own home, with our own money, can you imagine what else our government wants to control in our lives? Can you imagine what other powers government wants to seize? It's time to draw a line in the sand. Millions of U.S. poker enthusiasts will stand on my side of the line—*the freedom side. This group will certainly support the citizen revolution.*

4. *Conservative voters.* This isn't your father's GOP. There is little doubt that today's Republican Party has abandoned the conservative principles of Barry Goldwater and Ronald Reagan. This presents an opportunity to gain the loyalty of millions of conservative voters, especially during the next four years of an ultraliberal, big-government administration. If Republicans continue to move to the center (which really means *standing for nothing*) and willingly go along with Obama's expansion of government, you will see a further exodus from the GOP. That will be the ultimate final death spiral. The good news is that the GOP's loss is the Libertarian movement's gain. The even better news is there is no limited window of time to capture these disenchanted conservative voters. They started leaving the GOP in small numbers during the Bush administration. The exodus accelerated during the McCain campaign. I have no doubt it will become a tidal wave during the next four to eight years of the Obama administration. I am a long-range planner. This isn't a sprint, but rather a *marathon.* The Barry Goldwater/Ronald Reagan constituency will certainly support a citizen revolution.

5. *Ron Paul supporters.* Because of my dynamic energy and speaking style, I've been called "Ron Paul . . . *on steroids.*" I'm a younger, more enthusiastic Ron Paul—with one big difference. A quarter of a century from now, I'll *still* be younger than Ron Paul is today. I hope to lead the LP and "freedom movement" for many years to come. What Dr. Paul accomplished is truly remarkable. He attracted (against all odds) more than one million votes in the GOP primaries in 2008,

and raised more than $35 million—both totals far higher than Rudy Giuliani, the man many media experts pegged as the frontrunner. Ron Paul is truly a hero. I hope to finish what Dr. Paul started.

My plan is realistic and doable. Bob Barr and I built a Libertarian base in 2008. We attracted the second highest vote totals in Libertarian Party history (37 years). We attracted a record number of new LP members, with as much as 50 percent increases in memberships in many states. From this base, let the battle begin. By 2012 I will aim to dramatically increase vote totals to the 2 to 5 million range. By 2016, I will pose a legitimate third party threat to the two-party system, attracting Ross Perot–like numbers of voters. By 2020, I aim to become your first Libertarian president. Along the way, we will elect Libertarian local candidates from the top down: water commissioners, school board members, councilpersons, mayors, Congresspersons, and governors. It all starts with having a dynamic, youthful, credible (and patient) communicator and messenger at the top.

But here's a warning: Building a credible third party in U.S. politics is not easy. Many have failed. Our ace in the hole is that the LP has been around since 1971. It has achieved 45 to 50 state ballot access for decades—something no other third party has achieved consistently in modern U.S. political history. There will be setbacks, but I am relentless like another of my heroes Winston Churchill. As Churchill said, "Never, never, never, never, ever give up . . . and when you find yourself in Hell, keep on going." We will soldier on like Churchill. That attitude saved England (and eventually the entire free world) against hopeless odds from the threat of Nazi domination during World War II. Our battle has just begun. I happen to like our odds. If you doubt our success, please read Chapter 2 about the long but successful journey of my parent's party—the New York State Conservative Party. Ron Paul fans and supporters certainly will form the backbone of the Citizen Revolution.

6. *Young voters and college students.* Ron Paul proved that young voters can be motivated to think, vote, and contribute to Libertarian candidates and causes. He did that despite being 72 years old. *Quite an achievement.* But I believe that a passionate, high-energy, youthful candidate, who has a young family himself, can move the bar even higher. This is the one audience that most appreciates energy,

enthusiasm, passion, and a dynamic, colorful speaking style. Like it or not, the MTV generation appreciates style.

Also, keep in mind that the issue that gets college students (especially men) excited is online poker. Millions of college students play poker in their dorms and online. My career as the "King of Vegas" makes me a counterculture celebrity to that huge audience. Many of them watched my television show *King of Vegas* on Spike TV (the network of young males). I hope to do for the Libertarian movement in 2012 and beyond what my college classmate Barack Obama has done for the Democratic Party—excite and mobilize younger voters.

But it isn't only college students who will appreciate a Libertarian message. I believe there is a target audience of millions of 25- to 39-year-old, college-educated professionals and entrepreneurs who are moderate or tolerant on social and personal freedom issues (like stem cell research, medical marijuana, and online poker) who have voted for Democrats based on those issues, but who favor traditional conservative economic views (lower taxes) because they earn high incomes and don't support government stealing their money in the name of fairness. This group of younger voters will now have a third choice in future elections.

7. *Healthy and holistic living enthusiasts.* We spend more than $30 billion per year on alternative medicine and unconventional therapies. A remarkable one out of every two Baby Boomers chooses *unconventional* medical therapies. Here's an eye-opening statistic—more people now visit alternative health care practitioners than traditional MDs (628 million visits versus 385 million visits).

U.S. consumers spend more than $25 billion on vitamins and nutritional supplements alone. Organic food sales produce more than $15 billion per year. One health food supermarket chain alone, Whole Foods, produces revenues of $6 billion per year. Not surprisingly, its chairman and CEO John Mackey is a dedicated Libertarian. The entire idea of "organic, holistic, alternative, and unconventional" comes straight from the Libertarian playbook. The ideas of choice and health freedom are certainly out of the Libertarian playbook. Libertarians don't just follow rules blindly. We choose to search for the best possible answers to any issue—without worrying what the government says is best or acceptable, without worrying about what society says is "conventional" or the "norm." We understand that not all solutions in life fall under the category of conventional. Sometimes you have to walk the road less traveled to find the answers that change or improve your life.

You may be surprised to hear my background is tailor-made for this trend toward healthy living and health freedom. I credit all of my success in life to my foundation of holistic and organic health. I am what you might call "a health nut." I consider the balance of body, mind, and spirit to be the key to achieving success at anything in life. I eat organic, workout to the max, practice meditation, prayer, and yoga daily, and take 100 vitamin and nutritional supplements per day. That is my natural source of energy, enthusiasm, passion, vitality, and focus. Earlier in my career, I took online courses in holistic health and natural healing that resulted in my achieving a master's and PhD in holistic health. I'm not a big believer in flaunting online degrees, so I've never called myself Dr. Wayne Root. I took those courses not to become a doctor of letters, or give health advice to others, but rather to increase my understanding of my own body and the role of nutrition in keeping me young, healthy, and balanced. I've probably spent 10 percent of my income for the past 20 years on health, fitness, vitamins, diet, and, of course, Whole Foods supermarkets. I certainly hope to be the favorite candidate of any U.S. consumer who demands the freedom to choose organic, holistic, or unconventional diet, lifestyle, and medical treatments. And, of course, I should naturally (excuse the pun) be the favorite candidate of John Mackey and a whole generation of Whole Foods' customers. Neither Democrats nor Republicans have ever made health freedom and alternative therapies a focal point of public policy. I will. This group should therefore become a centerpiece of the citizen revolution.

8. *Gun rights enthusiasts, hunters, and gun owners.* I've saved perhaps the most passionate and dedicated constituency until now. I am a proud member of the NRA (National Rifle Association), GOA (Gun Owners of America), and JPFO (Jews for the Preservation of Firearms Ownership). As a Jewish American, I think I have a special and unique understanding of the need for gun ownership.

Millions of my fellow Jews died in the Holocaust. Their government took them away from their families, stole their businesses, imprisoned them, tortured them, enslaved them, and murdered them. I can think of no more horrific and gruesome story in the history of humankind. How did it all start? Hitler passed a law in 1938 that banned the manufacture and ownership of guns by Jews. Before he could imprison, enslave, and murder more than 6 million of my people, he first disarmed them.

The famous saying in Israel is "Never Again." That is why Israeli citizens are armed to the teeth. No one—not a Nazi, not an Islamic extremist, not a terrorist, not their own government—will ever again disarm Israeli Jews. I feel the same way, even in my beloved country of the United States. Gun laws only serve to disarm innocent civilians and law-abiding citizens. Choose any major urban city in the United States with strict gun laws—crime (and in particular, murder) rages out of control. Have strict gun laws prevented crime? Or have they simply disarmed law-abiding citizens, thereby encouraging crime? These laws have emboldened vicious criminals who know that a disarmed citizen is a helpless target. No gun law will ever disarm a criminal—they will always be able to buy guns on the "black market." But now travel to rural and suburban towns where guns are welcome, if not encouraged. In places like my home state of Nevada, Montana, Wyoming, Idaho, Alaska, Arizona, and Utah you find lots of guns, but very little crime. Wherever citizens carry guns, crime is low (if not nonexistent). Strange coincidence.

I believe our Founding Fathers understood best that an armed citizenry cannot be imprisoned, enslaved, or murdered by its own government. Adolph Hitler understood that idea, too. That is why he chose to disarm Jews before he put "the final solution" in play. I support the right of all U.S. citizens to bear arms: *period*. I believe that all citizens have a right to defend their lives, their families, and their properties. As Charleton Heston often said, "You'll take my Second Amendment rights from my cold, dead hands."

The GOP has done much damage to their support among gun owners—just as they have done among so many other groups—by not standing strongly for gun owner rights. The GOP has moderated (i.e., *watered down*) their pro gun ownership message as best exemplified by the nomination of John McCain in 2008, a luke-warm (at best) supporter of gun rights. The opportunity exists during the next four to eight years to bring this large and passionate crowd of gun rights enthusiasts into the Libertarian fold.

Obama promised not to touch our guns. Obama is good with words. You have to watch people who are good with words very carefully. Obama may not try to disarm gun owners, but he is already leading the charge to take away the ammo (or at the very least discourage the purchase of ammo) with the Ammunition Accountability Act. You see, the words of politicians can be used to distort intent. If government takes the ammo away, or makes it so expensive as to be unaffordable to the average person, or creates a Big Brother–like database listing the owner of every bullet, it serves the same purpose as disarming the citizenry.

I think one of my heroes Thomas Jefferson put it best:

The strongest reason for the people to retain the right to keep and bear arms is, as a last resort, to protect themselves against tyranny in government.

I will strongly support the rights of gun owners. I do not support any attempt to create a database to monitor the sale of every bullet in this country. I believe that gun owners will become a strong base of support for the citizen revolution.

9. *Locally elected officials across the United States.* There is one more group that I plan to target, but they are not a constituency of voters. They are politicians already serving in office across the United States. I will target primarily local officeholders disenchanted with the Republican Party. Once again, I am following a proven model—the Republican Party originally came to power by getting elected Whig Party officials to defect to the GOP. That's how they built the Republican Party into a national powerhouse. Every person reading this book needs to buy multiple copies to give to your elected officials. You are my citizen army. You need to convince your local elected officials that the two major parties are a lost cause when it comes to true reform of government, and personal and economic freedom. They are merely *big and bigger, dumb and dumber.*

You can give your local elected officials an incentive to switch—a promise from you to volunteer on their next campaign if they make the switch. One by one, we'll get elected officials across the country to make the switch. These elected Libertarian office-holders will become our "farm team" to get the message out and build name recognition and credibility. Nothing energizes a movement like tangible success. Elected Libertarians actually serving in office will attract more converts. This will become our grassroots management team—these are the folks who already understand how to run for office and *win*. Want proof that this goal is realistic? As I wrote this book, Indianapolis City Councilman Ed Coleman announced his switch from Republican to Libertarian in the 12th largest city in America. Coleman is now a proud Libertarian representing over 800,000 constituents.

■ ■ ■

Those are the constituencies that I believe can supercharge a Libertarian presidential run. Cobble those groups together and you come close to reaching a majority of U.S. voters. But those are specific constituencies. My case is best made on a more general basis by a recent Zogby International poll as reported by the Cato Institute (a Libertarian think tank). The poll asked a simple question: "Would you describe yourself as fiscally conservative and socially liberal?" Forty-four percent of U.S. voters answered *yes*. That means that almost half of all Americans are willing to label themselves as libertarian (with a small l) based on the definition above. That's one heck of a start. That is our message—fiscally conservative mixed with socially tolerant. That's a base to build toward victory.

But I believe Zogby made a big mistake by using the word "liberal" in that question (or any definition of Libertarian). The United States is a center-right nation. To get elected Obama had to moderate all his views, stay away from the "L" word, and morph into Ronald Reagan by promising tax cuts for 95 percent of all Americans. The description of "Libertarian" as fiscally conservative and socially liberal turns off millions of conservative and religious Christian voters simply because of the word "liberal."

I believe the proper definition of "Libertarian" is "fiscally conservative, socially tolerant, pro freedom, pro constitution, standing for more rights for the individual, and reducing the size, scope, and power of government." Word it that way and the LP has the potential to attract a majority of U.S. voters.

Virtually every political poll in the United States indicates that people are desperately searching for a viable third party option. Yet they don't vote that way—*yet*. The Libertarian Party has so far done a poor job of reaching those voters with our message. Very few voters have ever heard a passionate, dynamic Libertarian message. That's all about to change. This is the role I was born to play—the messenger

I believe that in our fast-food, sound-bite, attention-deficit-disorder, television-obsessed society, the messenger is more important than the message. The proof comes from both the right and left of U.S. politics. My hero Barry Goldwater had the perfect Libertarian conservative message. Yet he lost in a presidential landslide in 1964. Ronald Reagan, a former actor and one of the great communicators in political history, came along in 1980 and won two massive presidential landslides—*with the exact same message*. The only thing that changed was the way Reagan said it. The right message became a success when delivered by the right messenger (excuse the puns).

George McGovern (like Goldwater) was not a talented communicator. He preached the most liberal message in modern political history. And he preached it poorly. Not surprisingly, McGovern lost in a presidential landslide in 1972. Now fast-forward to 2008. Barack Obama has similar leftist views to George McGovern. The *National Journal* rated Obama the most extreme left-wing politician in the entire U.S. Senate in 2008. That makes the actual (factual) voting record of Obama more liberal than Ted Kennedy, John Kerry, Hillary Clinton, or even avowed socialist Bernie Sanders. Obama defines "extreme left" in a center-right nation. Yet Obama took McGovern's message and produced a smashing presidential victory. The difference between a Democratic landslide loss in 1972 and a Democratic landslide victory in 2008 wasn't the message, it was *the messenger*. Obama is a Reagan-esque communicator and a world-class salesman. Perhaps the *Wall Street Journal* put it best when describing Obama's upset victory over Hillary Clinton for the Democratic nomination, "With no disagreement on policy, Democrats opt for a top salesman . . . if you are selling a dream you need the best possible salesman to make it seem somehow possible. They found him in Barack Obama."

Both Reagan from the right, and Obama from the left, prove that what the Libertarian Party and the Ron Paul freedom movement need is simply a messenger: a talented communicator who can take the right message and sell it. I happen to know a certain *citizen politician* who is perfect for the job.

Chapter 7

God and Government

Be Careful What You Wish For!

A government big enough to give you everything you want is strong enough to take everything you have.

— THOMAS JEFFERSON

B efore I move onto the next part of this book, I want to briefly discuss the issue of God and government and its relationship to the Libertarian revolution. I included God in the subtitle of this book for good reason. This revolution cannot happen without the support of God-fearing religious Christians—the biggest faction in the conservative movement. But before you can join this citizen revolution, as Joan Rivers might say, "We need to have a talk."

God is the foundation of my life. I start and end each day with prayer. My children start and end each day—as well as each meal—with prayer.

I believe in the power of prayer. I think that anyone and *everyone* can benefit from prayer.

With all the violence, sex, and drugs rampant in our schools, we could all do far worse than start each school day with prayer. It could only help. It can't possibly hurt.

The overwhelming majority of people in the United States believe in God. Many of us—myself included—accept as the truth that the United States owes its remarkable success and prosperity to our belief in God. In other words, God has blessed the United States of America, and many of the values that religion teaches us, such as honoring our agreements and not harming others.

As a God-fearing and loving nation, it is perfectly understandable why pious Americans would want to demonstrate love and loyalty to God by enacting laws that enforce His will on others.

But that would be a mistake.

You see, Christians (and religious people of all kinds) are making a terrible error when they try to inject God into government. One of my heroes, Thomas Jefferson, said it best, "A government big enough to give you everything you want is strong enough to take everything you have." I might put it a bit differently: "A big government religious enough to give you all you want can also turn against your religion, and take it all away."

■ ■ ■

Like most people, I am comforted by the idea of our electing public officials who are religious God-fearing and loving men and women. That is generally good for the United States because moral people are less likely to bring about a corrupt government. But my religious views should not allow me to use government as a hammer to smash those views down your throat. I want to explain to Christians who support all my fiscal views of smaller government, less government spending, lower entitlements, lower taxes, and more freedom, that asking for government to enforce our religious and moral values is in fact *big government*. And it's also a *big* mistake.

You can't say that you're for smaller government when it comes to fiscal issues, and then turn around and support Big Brother and "the Nanny State" when it comes to social issues. You can't support smaller government when it comes to your business, but bigger government when it comes to the bedroom. Those views are inconsistent, hypocritical, and, to be blunt, dangerous. That is precisely where the hypocritical GOP lost the votes of millions of U.S. citizens.

Once you allow government to grow big enough and powerful enough to control our lives, determine our moral values, and enforce personal morality, you've opened up a Pandora's Box from which we can never escape. Either you want government in our lives, or out. It's that simple. You can't pick and choose the spots where it's convenient to give government great powers and control. If you do, where will it end? History proves that once government has a foot in the door, you cannot get it out. It will only expand from there.

When most people think about what government should and should not do, they imagine *they* will be the ones writing the rules. They imagine that they are benevolent dictators. But life doesn't happen that way. Even if your dearest friends can get control of the reins of government today, they won't be in control tomorrow. Imagine the very worst, immoral people in Congress—yes, I'm being redundant—and imagine granting them power over religion. Your own right for you and your family to practice religion in a manner compatible with your values will be compromised.

Here's an example: marriage. After the abolishment of slavery, some states began licensing marriages in order to prevent blacks and whites from marrying each other. Prior to this, marriage was a religiously defined institution. It wasn't until 1964 when the United States Supreme Court decided in *Loving v. Virginia* that the state had no right to deny a marriage license to an interracial couple. But the Court made the wrong decision. They should have declared that government had no right to license marriage at all. Now, because we continue to allow government to be involved with marriage, we are now forced to deal with the issue of whether a same-sex couple should be entitled to a marriage license.

To demonstrate the absurdity of government involvement in religion, imagine for a moment that you had to get a license to call yourself a Christian and that you were granted special tax or inheritance privileges as part of the package. Now, let's suppose that an atheist argues that he wants to be licensed as a Christian because he wants to be afforded equal treatment and protection under the law. There's the fundamental problem. If you allow government to *define* religious institutions, you will eventually make them meaningless. You'll also probably wind up (down the line) fighting laws created by government (with the power you gave them) that damage or destroy all you hold dear.

It's simply too risky to have government assert itself into the realm of religion. And it's not even effective. You can't make someone adopt your religious beliefs at the end of a gun. That was the wisdom of our brilliant Founding Fathers. They did not create a religious state. They created a country based on religious freedom—the freedom to practice any religion (or not) you chose—without government interference. Our Founding Fathers wanted to avoid the creation of a religious state, such as the country (England) they risked their lives to escape from.

All we can and should do is live our own lives in a positive way, so that others might model our behavior. In other words, it is not government's job to define morality. But it is most certainly (if you choose) your right to show others the way. It is your right to educate others as to what you believe is moral, or not. It is your right to advertise and promote your religion and your moral code. It is your right to protest. That behavior all falls under "Free Speech." People exercising free will can adopt our way or not. That's their choice in a free country like the United States. To force people to adopt our choice of religion or morality is exactly what happens in countries controlled by intolerant religious groups such as the Taliban. I have no interest in having the United States emulate the Taliban.

It is true that our brilliant Founding Fathers were religious men. So am I. But these same wise men made sure that while the Constitution and Bill of Rights protected religion, it also separated church and state. I believe in the Constitution. Don't you?

Believing that someone has the right to act contrary to your religious views does not mean that you condone the behavior. If I believe someone has the right to practice Buddhism, does that mean I advocate that particular religion? Of course not.

Living in a free society requires that we take ownership of our own values and not relinquish them to others. If you don't like violence, sex, or foul language on TV, *change the channel*. If you don't like the views being expressed on talk radio, *change the channel*. If you don't want to see pornography on your computer, I have more good advice—*don't go to any porn sites*. You have complete freedom on the Internet to go, or not go, wherever you want. If you want to protect your children from adult sites on the computer, *install parental controls*. If you don't like magazines like *Playboy* with photos of naked women, don't buy *Playboy*. No one is putting a gun to your head in a free country like the United States. You have the freedom to choose. To enforce your version of morality is to take that freedom away through the force and power of government. To enforce your version of morality is to take choice or free will away from others.

Eventually, those groups that oppose you will gain power and use that same power you've willingly given to government to enforce their views on *you*. They will find an excuse to ban religious television or programming. They will ban conservative talk radio in the name of "fairness." If you are a devoted Christian (as the majority of U.S. citizens are) please think long and hard about what I'm saying here. My Libertarian philosophy makes sense for people of all religions, as well as atheists. These issues are private and personal—they are none of the government's darn business! Don't give government the power to enforce your beliefs because it is guaranteed to come back to haunt you.

■ ■ ■

The one thing we must be careful *not* to do as a society is to give big government the power to ban something because we don't like it, or we object, or it offends our definition of "moral decency" or "moral values." If you're a religious Christian, and you don't like those things, and you want to fight to change them, I won't disagree with you or fight you. *I'll say bravo!* I applaud you for teaching your children those positive and religious moral values, just as I do for my children. I applaud you for teaching your family to make the right moral choices. I applaud you for bringing your children to church on Sundays. I applaud your decision to install parental controls on your TV and computers. I have no problem with any of that. Those are well within your rights in a free society. Those are your personal choices. I happen to agree with those choices. I've made many (if not all) of those same choices for my family.

Technology allows us all to define and enforce morality in our own homes, on our own computers, on our own television sets. You are the king of your own castle. But you have no right to define those choices for others. Or worse, you have no right to ask government to define those choices for others on your behalf. There is a huge distinction between creating laws that prevent people from harming others, or abuse children (laws I wholeheartedly support), versus creating laws to prevent consenting adults from voluntarily enjoying (or perhaps, in your opinion, harming) themselves.

A liberal or atheist may tell you to "shove it" over your moral or religious views. Or they may scream that you're an "ignorant religious fool." But I'm a God-fearing and -loving spiritual person just like you. Let me take a moment to toot my own horn. My wife Debra and I have done an exemplary job as parents. We've raised *great* kids. You'd love my 17-year-old daughter Dakota. She is a fine young lady—respectful to adults, never a bad word to her parents, she never utters profanity, she has high moral standards, she is intelligent with grades and ACT/SAT scores that place her among the top 1 percent of students nationwide. She has a black belt in martial arts, and is one of the top young competitive fencers in the United States. To top it off, she is gorgeous (inside and out). She recently traveled to Germany and Austria to represent the United States as a champion fencer at World Cup fencing events. She's quite a young lady. She takes after her mother, my wife Debra, who is a former Miss Oklahoma, as well as a strong religious Christian. Any parent in the United States would be proud to have a daughter like Dakota.

Then there's the rest of our brood—Hudson Franklin (named after my wife's great, great, grand Uncle Benjamin Franklin), Remington Reagan (named after one of my heroes, Ronald Reagan), and our new baby Contessa Churchill (named after another of my heroes, Winston Churchill). They are the greatest children a parent could hope for: healthy, bright, and respectful to their parents. They bring joy to their parents every hour of every day. There's a reason for our success as parents—we're home with our kids all the time. I'm here for breakfast with them every morning. I play football with my two boys almost every day. I'm home to kiss them goodnight and say bedtime prayers most every night. That's how you raise good kids. It does *not* take a village; it simply takes loving, caring parents.

The job we've done raising our children speaks for itself. I may be a big talker, but this is one case (family) where actions speak louder than words. And I'll give odds that if you are reading this book, you possess the moral character to raise good children too.

Now, contrast that with many politicians who every day preach family values and moral values, yet they have had multiple divorces, dysfunctional families with teenage children addicted to drugs or alcohol, or pregnant, or getting poor grades in school. Worse still, many of these family values politicians have no relationship at all with their kids. From my experience, *most* politicians I've met have done lousy jobs of raising their kids. So I guess that what I'm saying here is to watch what a person does, and how they act, rather than what they say. Talking about moral values, or demanding Big Brother laws to enforce moral values upon the citizenry does not make you a good moral person (or politician). Living a moral life by example does. You don't need to enlist government to force morality down people's throats at gunpoint, if you win them over by being a good role model.

But, you ask, "Won't some parents do a bad job raising their kids? Won't some parents fail to teach their children the values of hard work, good manners, thrift and delayed gratification?" Some will. But, at least the damage is limited to only those families. But to the extent we allow the government to raise our children, the damage affects *every* family. Remember, you are the ones who are going to care the most passionately about the future of your own children. Children tend to model the folks who raise them. So, who should raise your children and teach them moral values? Should it be you, or the folks running Washington, DC? If you choose "we the people" (and parents), then stop voting for big government to get more and more involved in our lives—even if it supports your views (today). Because tomorrow the tables could turn.

What I believe, and what I teach my children, is no one else's business (especially government bureaucrats). That is between my family and me. Morality and religion are *personal* issues. No law or government can enforce morality. They can try, but they always fail miserably and create a police state. Or what I call a Nanny State.

As an example, I choose to not smoke or drink or do drugs. I have never tried marijuana in my life. I haven't drunk a sip of alcohol in 25 years. Yet I would never try to prevent you from enjoying a martini, or beer, or cigarette. I would never deny you the right to use medical marijuana. As long as you are not putting others in harm's way, that's *your* business—not mine. Now if you get in a car while under the influence of alcohol or drugs, that's a completely different story. Then you are putting my life and my safety at risk. Then you have committed a crime by putting the lives of others in danger. But what consenting adults choose to do to themselves, while not harming or involving me, is none of my business, and none of the government's darn business.

I have a right to preach about my moral values to others. I have a right to teach a Sunday school class and educate others. But I have no right to get government involved to force you to live your life the same way I choose to live mine. If you want to smoke, drink, use medical marijuana, or play poker online—none of that is any of my business. Now keep in mind, it's my right to not want to party with you. It's my right to not want to be your friend. It's my right to avoid you. It's my right to keep you away from my daughter. People tend to befriend like-minded people. So in this great country of freedom and free speech, a churchgoing, God-fearing Christian can choose to befriend other religious Christians and avoid gamblers, drinkers, and wild partiers, and vice versa. That choice is as American as apple pie. But asking the government to ban their choices of entertainment— now that's not fair or proper or cool or American. It won't work; people do what they want to do, whether it's legal or not. And eventually government will get around to banning your choice of entertainment or religion if you give them that power.

You have no right to stop me or anyone else from enjoying our chosen form of entertainment in a free society. Last I checked, Prohibition was the biggest failure in U.S. political history. It made a mockery of the law by turning otherwise law-abiding adults into criminals, by preventing very few people from drinking, and by literally creating organized crime (Al Capone, Meyer Lansky, and Lucky Luciano were all made rich and powerful by Prohibition). Whatever government chooses to ban, quickly becomes "in-demand" and goes up in value. It becomes an instant hit on the black market. Government stops *nothing* with the ban, but loses out on billions in tax revenues. Pretty dumb, huh?

Do you know what ended Prohibition the last time? There was a public outcry, but that was not the main force of change. The main determiner was that the government desperately needed tax revenue during the Great Depression. So liquor was once again legalized and taxed—and the United States did not fall off the edge of the universe. To the contrary, that tax revenue helped us pay for World War II. I'd venture a guess that taxes on liquor pay quite a few important bills today, too. For all of you who don't think alcohol or gambling should be legal, I'd love to see how big our national deficit would be without alcohol or gaming taxes.

A recent study estimated that if the United States legalizes online gaming (or even just poker), we bring in an extra $50 billion in taxes over the next 10 years. That's $50 billion—*with a B*. These are taxes on citizens who choose to play a game of poker on their own computer, in the privacy of their own home, with their own money. They don't hurt anyone else—to the contrary, there is no way for even their best friends or next-door neighbor to know that they are playing online poker. It doesn't affect another human being. It is none of your business. It is none of my business. It is none of the federal government's business. It is a personal choice of entertainment. It affects no one, but the person playing poker. Yet it will create $50 billion (or more) to pay down our deficit, or improve education, or pay for homeland security. The ban of online gaming could be the single dumbest thing I've heard of—at least since the infamous Prohibition of the 1920s, which also failed dramatically. This twenty-first-century Prohibition will fail miserably. People will ignore the silly ban. As a matter of fact, millions of us are playing poker on their computers *right now*. People learn to disrespect the law. And taxpayers miss out on an opportunity to save at least $50 billion in taxes. That's the Triple Crown of ignorance and idiocy.

The point of all this is that asking government (any government—federal, state, local) to enforce morality (or your definition of morality) is a big mistake. It's going down a slippery slope that no Christian or any religious person should want to consider. It's inviting Big Brother into our lives. We all know from experience (and history) that once we let government get involved in any aspect of society, it will never go away. It's giving government far too much power and authority—and that power will only grow stronger and become more invasive. It's turning the United States into a police state.

A conservative and religious administration (think Bush) might choose to oppose or ban stem cell research, assisted suicide, medical marijuana, sex and violence on television, the sale of *Playboy* on the newsstands, and gambling (poker) on the Internet. You might approve. But if you give a conservative government the power and authority to do all that, I promise you that tomorrow when a more liberal, or atheist, or anti-Christian, or simply anti-religious administration takes power, they may choose to use that same power and authority to ban TBN (Christian television) or religious web sites, or religious free speech, and implement "The Fairness Doctrine" (banning conservative talk radio).

■ ■ ■

The point of this entire book is that government should be stripped of the power to ban anything that is voluntary. Government has no right to determine what we should watch, or surf on the Internet, or what form of entertainment we choose, or what magazines are sold on the newsstand. Those are personal issues that the government has no business regulating. They are issues of freedom, personal choice, and free speech in a democratic society. That is the price we pay for freedom—sometimes you won't approve of how the other guy chooses to live his life. But that's not your business. And as soon as you make it your business, or government's business, suddenly *your* choices of how you choose to live your life are under scrutiny (or banned) as well. Your personal freedom is threatened as well.

I wrote this chapter for my many religious Christian friends, fans, and voters. I'm one of you. We need you to support the Libertarian "Citizen Revolution." It is a conservative revolution that should appeal to every Christian American. Reducing the power of government, getting government out of your way and out of your life, is the very definition of conservative. Ending the Nanny State is conservative. It's in your best interest to reduce the government's power. It's in your best interest to dramatically lower government spending and taxation. In the end, whether you are religious or not, as our Founding Fathers understood, *smaller* government is better for the individual. As a Christian, you need to support reducing the size, scope, and authority of the federal government. Even if you're religious, you need to defend the right of others to play online poker and buy *Playboy* at newsstands (and on military bases). You do not need to support these choices, but you need to defend them. You cannot possibly support government banning *anything*.

Because today's ban on *Playboy* and poker becomes tomorrow's ban on the sale of the Bible, or religious web sites, or religion itself.

The only ban we all need to support is a ban on government. We all need to support getting government out of our private lives and personal decisions. I'm the perfect political figure to lead this fight because of who I am. I'm not an atheist. I'm not a liberal. I'm not anti-religion. To the contrary, I'm a proud family man and patriot who strongly supports God, religion, and prayer. It's not that I endorse gay marriage. It's not that I endorse the right to die. It's not that I endorse medical marijuana. Whether I choose to allow those things to happen under my roof is my private business. If I choose to live a Christian life and preach how negative those other choices are, that is my business. Education is good. Preach to your family. Preach and protest to the rest of the world. In a society that allows free speech that is your right.

But do not ask or demand that the federal government impose your choices and values on the rest of us. That violates my freedom. That violates my free speech. That violates my ability to enjoy my life in a free society. I simply want to get government out of my business, out of my bedroom, and out of my life. I don't want government defining marriage, or anything else. Let churches define marriage and marry couples. It's simply *none* of the government's business.

Attempts to use the government to instill virtue and piety will eventually boomerang against you. One example: Many decades ago, the government sanctioned mandatory prayer in schools. Now, I'm certain that those who originally lobbied to impose mandatory prayer did so with the noblest of intentions. I certainly want my kids to pray each day. But look at what eventually happened. Because we granted this power to the government, there are those in power today who have completely turned this around and are now attempting to prohibit even *voluntary* prayer. The lesson learned is that giving the power to government simply because you believe they are on your side is a dangerous decision. Because today they are on your side, tomorrow they can (and often do) turn against you. Why give government the power in the first place? You would never trust the government to feed your children. Why would you trust them to educate them?

Discuss these morality and personal choice issues with your pastor or rabbi, and with your children. Enforce the morality you want in your own home. But don't ask government to enforce it, or to force it upon your neighbor. Your version of morality today may come back to haunt you tomorrow. Less power for government will in the long run be positive for religion, Christians, Americans, and *all* people. And a truly free society is the foundation of a virtuous society.

Now that that's out of the way—*let's go start this revolution!*

Part Two

LET'S TALK MONEY *AND* POLITICS

Chapter 8

The Nevada Model

Showing America How It's Done!

Do you know the difference between Las Vegas and Washington DC?
In Vegas the drunks gamble with their own money.
    —OPENING OF WAYNE ROOT SPEECHES ACROSS THE U.S.A.

Although I discuss political, economic, and social issues in this book, *The Conscience of a Libertarian* is primarily about money—how to cut the budget, cut government, and cut your taxes. This chapter provides the perfect model for all of the United States—my home state of Nevada. We're not perfect by any means, but we do keep government small and taxes low. That could be why we have been number one in the United States in virtually every economic category possible for the past quarter of a century. And the U.S. Census Bureau predicts we'll stay number one for the next quarter of a century. Like the rest of the country, we are having our problems during this economic tsunami. But Nevada has always recovered first in any recession and I'm betting we will lead the way again. Yes we've lost thousands of jobs, but within months, several new casino-resorts will open in Las Vegas, adding thousands of new jobs. Yes, we've had thousands of foreclosures, but residential real estate sales are dramatically up as I write this chapter. I'm betting Las Vegas will be the first major city to recover from this economic tsunami. Yes, our population growth has slowed, but we've had 100,000 new citizens a year move into Nevada for a decade now—we were due to slow down and breathe for a minute or two. The fact that we've slowed down, after adding a million new residents in the past decade, is certainly not terrible news considering that our next door neighbor California has lost more than 1.3 million U.S. residents over the past decade (although they've added hundreds of thousands of illegal immigrants to balance the numbers). By comparison Nevada is still doing great. Because of smaller government, lower taxes, and more personal freedom, Nevada will undoubtedly lead the way for our country's economic recovery.

As mentioned previously, I am proud to have no prior experience as a politician, as well as no connection of any kind to government. I am also proud to be a commonsense, no-nonsense "Citizen Politician"—the first small businessperson and home-school father on a presidential ticket in modern political history. But most importantly, I am proud to be the first Nevadan ever on a presidential ticket. I believe that it is time for the "Nevada model" to be adopted by the entire country: smaller government, lower taxes, free enterprise, rugged individualism, self-reliance, personal responsibility, individual rights, and *freedom*—both economic freedom and personal freedom. Here is the Nevada story.

■ ■ ■

We pride ourselves as the state that allows individuals the freedom to be individuals. We showcase both economic and personal freedom in Nevada. In direct contrast to the big-government, big-spending, big-tax, Nanny State career politicians of the DC Beltway, Nevada has zero state income tax, zero business income tax, zero inheritance tax, no capital gains tax, and property taxes limited by law to 3 percent per year increases, with a citizen initiative proposed to lower them further. Through initiatives, our

Nevada voters put into law a restriction that a tax increase can only be passed with a supermajority, two thirds or more of our legislature. As you might expect, even in Nevada this had to be passed directly by the voters over the howls and protests of the legislators, unions, and state bureaucrats.

The obvious advantage of lower taxes is the additional money you have to support you and your family. But, just as important, and what many people forget is the peace of mind and privacy that you gain when government is not intruding in your life. When you have no state income taxes or business income taxes, you also have fewer rules, regulations, and bureaucracy, as well as no Gestapo-like state tax authority. Therefore, it's not just the money you save, it is also the ease with which you can open and grow a small business in Nevada. That is undoubtedly why Nevada has led the nation in small business creation and "Brain Gain"(college graduates moving to Nevada) for most of the last two decades. How important is the creation and success of small business? Small business now produces 75 percent of new private sector jobs. Small business is the economic engine of the United States.

Is this freedom from government harassment really such a big deal? Let me tell you a personal example. I moved to Nevada almost a decade ago. That means that I have not lived in California since the late 1990s. Yet, I am still harassed by the California tax collector, otherwise known as the California Franchise Tax Board. Every year, like clockwork, California sends me bills in the mail demanding $10,000 or more for phantom taxes that I don't owe. How do I know I don't owe them? Because I don't live there! Can you imagine? They bill me annually for taxes even though I'm not a resident of California (and haven't been for a decade). I have my accountant send them a letter every year, sometimes multiple times a year. But their tax bills just keep coming. And each time my accountant writes a letter, I get stuck with a $500 bill. Do you realize the cost of this kind of bureaucratic waste? Figure I've spent at least $5,000 just in denying that I owe anything to the state of California in the decade since I left—a complete waste of $5,000, simply to respond to phony bills. Four things are obvious:

1. California believes in fraud and harassment. They assume that if they send enough $10,000 bills, some taxpayers will pay a few thousand to simply make them go away. And I'm sure many do.

2. California thinks that once you've paid taxes in their state, you are a prisoner for life. They believe that they can follow you, hound and harass you, and bill you for taxes in a state in which you no longer live.

3. The state of California couldn't care less about the facts, or what it forces taxpayers like me to waste on paying accountants to answer their false claims.

4. If a businessperson or CEO like me conducted business like this, the state of California would prosecute me for fraud. Why isn't government held to the same standards as private industry?

Now can you imagine how the state of California tax authorities harass taxpayers who *do* live within their state? Can you imagine how wonderful my life is in Nevada simply because there is no state tax authority to hound and harass me? When I think of what I've gone through with the California Franchise Tax Board for almost a decade, the privacy and peace of mind that results from having no government tax authority in Nevada may be more important to my quality of life (certainly my stress level and mental health) than the lack of taxes in Nevada.

But as much as my story proves that lower taxes (or in this case, no taxes) leads to mental freedom, they also lead to *economic freedom*—the freedom to keep more of your own money and make your own decisions on how to spend or save it. I believe that individuals always make better spending decisions than government bureaucrats. Often that decision is to start their own small business, which in turn creates more jobs, more tax revenues, and fuels the economic growth of our country.

In addition to economic freedom, the Nevada Model has created a unique, Libertarian form of *personal freedom*. In a recent issue of *Reason*, Las Vegas was rated the number one major city in the United States for personal freedom, out of 35 big cities examined on a range of issues.

■ ■ ■

What does Nevada's rare combination of economic and personal freedom really mean? It means remarkable success. People are voting their approval with their feet and their assets. For 21 of the past 23 years Nevada has been the number one population growth state in the country. The U.S. Census Bureau projects Nevada will be number one for the next quarter of a century. That kind of long-term success and growth can only be described as amazing. But we are not perfect. Because of our dependence on tourism, Nevada is experiencing a deep economic crisis, just like every other state in the union. But as always, because of our economic and personal freedoms, we are poised to recover from this deep recession first and more powerfully than high-tax states like New York, California, Michigan, or Illinois.

That is provided, of course, that our own entrenched bureaucratic politicians and state government employee unions don't destroy the goose that is laying the golden eggs. And believe me—they are trying. The Nevada Teachers Union has already pushed a new tax on hotel rooms to raise education spending. Once again, this new tax is a prime example of the ignorance and greed of government employee unions. First, those taxes on tourists threaten to hurt our leading industry, the one that pays so many of our taxes. Second, those increased tax revenues will not go to "the children." The word "education" as used by teachers unions merely means higher salaries for teachers, principals, and entrenched bureaucrats. It means that the education bureaucracy will hire more educators and bureaucrats so that the union has a bigger budget and more power, and, of course, a reason to give raises to union leaders. The desire for growth of government and higher taxes is always about the same thing: enriching government employees, strengthening government employee unions, and making the bureaucracy more powerful and controlling. It always means taking more money from *you*, the taxpayer, and giving more power to *them*, the entrenched bureaucracy. It always means more and more taxation without representation. Government bureaucrats are trying to raise taxes every day in Nevada. But as of the writing of this book we are still the second lowest-taxed state in America (behind only Wyoming).

How has Nevada been able to keep its taxes and government bureaucracy under control, at least compared to the other 49 states? Simple. Our Nevada founding fathers, in their infinite wisdom, limited the damage that politicians can do by creating a part-time "Citizen Legislature." Our legislators meet for only four months every two years, making it difficult, although not impossible, for politicians to damage our economy, complicate our lives, and violate our freedom.

Remember my story about the Congressional Effect Fund? Their research proves that the more time politicians spend doing their job, the more damage they do to our economy and our lives. So the key to the survival of taxpayers is to limit the time politicians spend at the office. Every hour these "dedicated public servants" spend working on our behalf, is an hour we are being damaged and taxed to death. So, Nevada got it right. We limit *by law* the time that politicians can meet. They still do plenty of damage, but not as much as in states like California, New York, Illinois, or Michigan.

Why are so many people moving to Nevada? It's simple. When you keep more of your own money, you achieve a better life. Every dollar that you save from the clutches of government and tax collectors is money you can use to enjoy a higher quality of life, provide a better life for your children, or retire earlier to enjoy your sunset years. Every dollar you give to the government tax collectors is a dollar you won't have for retirement, or your children's private school education, or your children's college education, or buying your dream home, or taking your dream cruise to celebrate your wedding anniversary, or starting your new business.

Politicians (especially liberal politicians) and the biased liberal media claim taxes "enhance the quality of life." Really? Whose quality of life do they supposedly enhance other than bureaucrats and government employee union members? The fact is, I don't think high taxes enhance a *damn thing*. Want proof? I lived in New York State for over 25 years and then in California for over a decade. New York and California taxpayers pay some of the most onerous taxes in the country. But they're not alone. Just look at New Jersey, Massachusetts, Connecticut, Maryland, and Illinois. These unlucky taxpayers are stuck with obscene local property taxes, sales taxes, state income taxes, and even additional city taxes for those living in New York City and other big cities like it. In New York City just the taxes add up to 20 percent of your cell phone bill. *Twenty percent! That's before you've paid your income, sales or property taxes.*

Finally I got smart and *escaped* to Las Vegas, Nevada. I'm not alone. Thousands of taxpayers flee high tax states like New York, California, and Illinois to escape to Nevada. Nevadans are living proof of the biggest lie of all—that taxpayers get something in return for high taxes. As someone who has lived in New York, California, and now Nevada, I can tell you that I am missing *nothing* in Nevada. So tell me what I got in return for all those years of paying substantially more out of my earnings to state and local government? There is nothing any politician, bureaucrat, or liberal do-gooder can point to that is different, or missing in my life. All those poor taxpayers in New York, California, and all the other states like them are working extra hours every day to pay more taxes—and do you know what they get? They get to have less time to enjoy life. On an income comparable to Nevadans, they get to have smaller homes, cheaper cars, smaller retirement plans, enjoy fewer vacations, and provide a lower quality of life for their families. And what do they get for this in return? *Nothing.* Well, I will concede that Southern California does have better weather. But it doesn't beat the weather in Hawaii in the winter or Park City, Utah, in the summer where I am able to take my family on vacation with the money I save by living in Nevada.

Are you high-tax state residents feeling sick right about now? You should. But, wait, it gets worse. I can afford a 7,000-square-foot home on a world-class golf course in Las Vegas because of the taxes I *don't* pay to the state of Nevada. That extra 10 percent or more of my income and much lower property taxes that I save literally pays my mortgage. So in effect my home is paid for by the taxes I *don't* pay to the state of Nevada. Join me in Nevada and you, too, can get a *free* home!

You see, it isn't taxes that are "fair." It is taxes that make life *unfair* for residents of high tax states. Does it seem fair that the residents of New York and California are forced to endure a lower standard of living just to pay higher taxes? Their hard-earned money is being wasted, burned, literally thrown down a sewer to never return. When a businessperson rips off consumers, that's called fraud. When the Mafia demands "protection money" for doing nothing, that's called extortion. But, when the government demands half of your money and provides little or nothing in return, that's called taxes! Government certainly has a way with words.

Not only can I live a better, wealthier life because of lower taxes, my children benefit for the rest of their lives as well. Lower taxes mean that I'll save more money, so my kids can afford to go to any college in the United States because I can afford it (Harvard, Columbia, Princeton, or Stanford), instead of a cheaper state school, which could translate into a better job and bigger paycheck for the rest of their lives. And when I die as a Nevada resident, my kids will collect a larger inheritance, because I saved extra money over the years by not paying state income taxes and, of course, they'll inherit more simply because as a Nevada resident

I pay zero state inheritance tax upon my death. Every step of the way, my life and my family's lives are improved by paying lower taxes in Nevada. So now you can clearly see the biggest lie told by politicians, bureaucrats, and big-government proponents—quality of life is *not* enhanced by high taxes. It is destroyed by taxes. That old adage "you get what you pay for" does not apply to taxes. Residents of high tax states get *nothing* for all those taxes. They are simply being ripped-off by government solely for the benefit of the entrenched bureaucrats and their cronies who feed from the trough filled by *you*, the hardworking, trusting (but naïve) taxpayer.

Now, here's a question for you to ponder. If I got nothing for all those years of paying high taxes in New York and California, except a lower quality of life, what exactly do you and I get for paying high *federal* income taxes? Does it not occur to all of you reading this right now, that if we paid lower federal income taxes, our quality of life would improve even more? Does it not occur to all of you that we'd be missing nothing, just as I miss nothing by living in Nevada versus New York or California. The simple fact is, taxes are not fair or good or natural. They destroy your quality of life every day. They prevent you from buying a bigger home or better car. They prevent you from sending your kids to private school, instead of the dangerous, failing, hellhole government schools that we call public schools. They prevent you from saving for retirement so you'll be forced to work your fingers to the bone until the day you die.

Oh, taxes do help someone. They help politicians, career bureaucrats, and government employee unions. In addition to taking good care of them and their families, your taxes provide the money they use to keep enough voters dependent on government handouts, by making sure that taxpayers don't have enough money to own their own home, start their own business, or ever become a member of the "investor class." Never forget that every dollar you pay in taxes is a dollar that robs you of the life, family, and retirement of your dreams. It's one dollar less to start your own business (and tell your boss to "shove it"). No, high taxes are not fair. They are not fair at all. To the contrary, they are the enemy of the people—at least the people who work hard, create jobs, invent products, build businesses, and achieve success.

While I've always paid what the government claims is my fair share, that doesn't mean that I'm happy about it. It doesn't mean I won't fight to reduce my tax burden with everything I've got. I fight liberal politicians and bureaucrats every day to create a better tax system. The current system does not work. It is not fair. It punishes those who are successful, who work harder and smarter, who do everything right, who follow the rules of society and make something of themselves. Sadly, it rewards those who don't. The best way to fight high taxation is to move to a place where taxes are legally lower. Nevada is the "Monte Carlo" of the United States, a legal tax haven where guns are welcome (for law-abiding citizens), personal freedom is allowed, government is smaller, and income taxes are barred by the state constitution. I call it home. It is as close to heaven as exists in the United States. I believe that Nevada is the model for the entire nation. Nevada is no place for old liberals.

■ ■ ■

I want to spread the Nevada model of economic and personal freedom from coast to coast. The only way to make a change from Big Brother and bigger government to more power for the people, is to elect anti-establishment, anti–status quo, anti-politicians from outside the Beltway. We need to elect politicians who understand that the best government is that which governs least. It is time to elect politicians who will downsize and dismantle government—politicians who are not afraid of limiting their own power and influence. It is time for a political Hippocratic Oath: *Above all else, do no harm.* Perhaps it is time for a small businessman, home-school dad, citizen politician from Nevada to show the country how it's done—*the Nevada way.*

Chapter 9

The Anti-Politician

Why We Need a Small Business
Owner in the White House

The legacy I want to leave is simple and straightforward. I want to be known as the man who took the power away from the government and gave it back to the people. Who cut government down to size. Who took the side of the individuals versus big government. Who let the taxpayers keep more of their own money. Who rewarded the people that produced all the wealth, started the businesses, took the risks, created the jobs, made the payrolls, and paid the taxes. Who cared about the rights, freedoms and liberty of the citizens—instead of the politicians, lobbyists, lawyers, unions, bureaucrats, back-room deal makers and DC insiders.

—WAYNE ALLYN ROOT

I've just shown you the kind of state that should serve as the economic model for the United States: Nevada. Now it's time to show you the kind of job that should serve as the ideal model for our next president: *small business owner.* I know I'm a bit prejudiced, but

I stand before you as Exhibit A. Let me show you why our country needs a small business owner to lead the way.

■ ■ ■

As evidenced from my commentary throughout this book, I'm certainly a very different kind of political candidate. Not too many Presidential or VP candidates become new fathers during the campaign. My lovely wife Debra gave birth to our new daughter Contessa Churchill Root during my campaign for the Libertarian presidential nomination (which eventually resulted in the vice presidential nomination). It was a new start on the second half of my life. Becoming a father again often gets you thinking about your life. Just a few days before Contessa's birth, I appeared as a guest on FOX News Channel. I explained to the host that I was a unique presidential candidate—a son of a butcher and small businessman. The FOX host looked at me like I was certifiably insane. I could see his mind working as we spoke—he was thinking, "A small businessman running for president? Fat chance."

But you see that's the whole problem with the political process. The media has a preconceived stereotype of who should be president. If you don't meet that stereotype, the media writes you off, disregards you, ignores you. Trust me, that will not be happening to this future presidential candidate. I'm many things, but "ignored" is definitely not one of them! The national news media has no idea what's about to hit them. The fun has just begun.

I believe that my life has been the perfect preparation for running the greatest economy in the world. It's a wonderful and exciting time in my life. Yet it's also a scary time. You see I'm just like any other person with four young children—worried about the future. The economy of not just the United States, but the world, is melting down as I write this chapter. The global economy is declining at a pace not seen since the Great Depression. Eastern Europe is teetering on the verge of a deep depression, thereby pulling European banks (who loaned those countries hundreds of billions of dollars) into a financial disaster that may be too big to fix. It all looks rather bleak. But I saw all this coming 12 months ago. When the Federal Reserve Chairman Ben Bernanke was saying to Congress that we were not technically in a recession, and still might avoid one, I was publicly calling our crisis a depression. As a small businessman, I felt the start of this tsunami like the proverbial canary in the coalmine. I understand how deep a hole we've dug. I understand how long this crisis will last. We are in for a protracted battle.

Against that backdrop, how could anyone not be concerned about the future? Just like any other person, I'm worried about bills. Worried about my big mortgage. Worried about paying for the home-school education of my four children. Worried about how I'm going to pay for four college educations over the next 25 years (and perhaps graduate school, too). Even worse, I'm worried about how I'm going to pay all the taxes—property taxes, sales taxes, income taxes, business taxes, and payroll taxes for my employees. The worries are endless. And, of course, the biggest worry of all for a small business owner like me—how will we pay all the additional taxes being put on our shoulders by President Barack Obama. Those tax increases will kill jobs and force businesses to close.

I don't know where I'm getting the money to pay all the bills and taxes listed above, let alone even *higher* taxes. In the midst of the worst recession of my lifetime, most small business owners I know are either taking a cut in salary so they can pay their bills, or worse, taking no salary. Some (like me) are even cutting into our life savings to make payrolls and keep our businesses going. For many it is too late—our businesses are closing, forcing our employees to the unemployment line. So where on earth would a small businessperson find extra money to pay the higher taxes that Obama thinks we can afford? It's enough to keep me from sleeping at night. Four kids add up to a lot of joy—but also a lot of bills and a lot of worries!

The good news is that this makes me the first candidate to run for president who has all the same worries of a typical U.S. voter and taxpayer. I am a small businessman. Every week for a decade, I've had a payroll to make. I have been personally responsible for the payroll taxes of each of my employees. I have been responsible for the health insurance for each of my employees. And, of course, my biggest responsibility of all has been to my wife and four children. It's a lot of responsibility. In a big company the CEO has a lot of help—other executives, junior executives, middle managers, support staff, including executive assistants dedicated to just the CEO. In a small business it's just the owner. The weight of the world is on my shoulders.

I am proud to be a small businessman. I guess that makes me unqualified to be president, according to the national media and the political pundits. They laugh at small businesspeople. We're meaningless to them. We can't afford to hire lobbyists and powerful, connected DC lawyers. We can't afford to contribute tens of thousands of dollars in political contributions to each and every politician. We don't control corrupt union pension funds. We don't employ thousands of people to go door to door to get out the vote. So to politicians and the national media we are meaningless, insignificant, and *invisible*.

Yet politicians, pundits, and the liberal media are missing the big picture. Today the epicenter of the twenty-first-century U.S. economy is *small business*. We now create the majority of the U.S. jobs. We pay billions in taxes. We are single-handedly responsible for making the U.S. economy go and grow. In 2007 alone, small business created 1.9 million net new jobs. There are today almost 27 million small businesses fueling the U.S. economy. If each one employs only three people on average, that's about 100 million votes we represent. Just one category, female-owned small businesses, numbers 6.5 million businesses producing $940.8 billion in revenues. There are 1.1 million Asian-owned small businesses. There are 1.2 million African American–owned small businesses. There are 1.6 million Hispanic-owned small businesses.

Small business now employs a majority of this nation's private, nonfarm workforce. The days of big corporations and big unions dominating the U.S. economy are over. But the politicians in DC haven't figured that out yet. As usual, they are behind the curve. Because big corporations and big unions are the ones with the lobbyists, they get all the attention from the media (and the DC politicians).

It's a new world out there—a world dominated by small business. I call small business owners the heroes of the business world. They are the "fly boys"—the guys with the mirror sunglasses and leather bomber jackets flying multimillion dollar jets. They take the big risks with their own money, based on their own ideas, live and die based on their own decisions—they are the CEOs of their own little worlds (just like jet pilots).

Each small business has someone like me running the show. A guy or gal with two or three or even (gasp!) four kids, big mortgages, big bills to pay, college educations to fund, employees to feed, nonstop taxes to pay. Each small business owner runs his own little eco-system—his or her own little economy. Millions of dollars are created, spent, and pumped into the economy by each small business. We need a president who understands small business and the unique problems, bills, and taxes that each small business owner faces. Name someone running for president in the two major parties who has any experience with these issues and problems? Who has any connection whatsoever to small business? Drawing a blank? *That's because I'm one of a kind.* I am not just a small businessman. I'm the son and grandson of small business owners.

It is not a cliché to state loudly and proudly that the United States really is the land of opportunity. But we need to change our definition of who is "qualified" to be President of the United States. I believe the time is past due for a small businessperson in the White House. I'm certain that the liberal national media thinks a small business owner with fewer than 100 employees is unqualified to run the government of the United States of America. But remember—I have no intention of running the government. *I aim only to cut government.*

For that job, a small business owner is perfect. I understand how to cut budgets to survive in a bad economy. I understand how to run a business on fewer dollars, on fewer employees. I understand how to cut bureaucracy and empower employees to take personal responsibility. I understand how to pay bills when funds are short. I understand how to "make do" without automatic annual increases in funding. I understand how to earn a living based on performance, without a safe weekly paycheck. I understand how damaging and deadly the combination of bureaucracy and high taxation are to the creation of jobs and businesses. And most importantly, I've never requested a government bailout for any of my businesses. Some of my businesses have succeeded, some have failed. But I've never asked government for a thing. "If it is to be, it is up to me." That's something the big-shot zillionaire CEOs of Wall Street and the banking world cannot say.

Therefore, the day that I take office, I plan to start the process of handing power back to the people—where it belongs. I believe that government's job is not to run the country, it's to get out of the way of the individual. I believe that government belongs to the people, not the politicians. I believe that your money is your property, not the property of government, bureaucrats, IRS tax collectors, or politicians. I intend to downsize government. I intend to limit its power, size, and scope. I intend to cut spending dramatically. I intend to lower your taxes dramatically. I intend to increase the rights and freedoms of the individual. It's time for a change in the way we think about government. It's time for a big change in how we define "qualified" for the job of president. I think a small businessperson is just the person for the job.

■ ■ ■

Now let's look at how my background differs from the typical president and presidential candidate in recent times. President George W. Bush was born into wealth, power, and privilege. He had all the necessary connections from his day of birth to lead a comfortable, effortless life. Eventually he became owner/general partner of the Texas Rangers. That's the closest he got to small business: owning a major league baseball team with a $50 *million* payroll.

How about the leading contenders for president in the 2008 election? On the GOP side, Mitt Romney was born into wealth and privilege—his father was governor of Michigan and CEO of American Motors. Worth more than $400 million, he is "big business" all the way. Mitt Romney has never known a worry about money or bills in his life. John McCain was the son and grandson of powerful Admirals who ran the United States Navy. He is literally a prince born to the kings of the military class. Rudy Giuliani was a powerful prosecutor and mayor. The closest he ever came to business was putting businesspeople in jail to build his name recognition. Only a few years after leaving office, Rudy is today worth about $100 million, just another out-of-touch man of wealth and privilege without a clue about surviving on a tight budget.

The only 2008 Republican presidential contender with middle-class roots was Mike Huckabee. But to my knowledge, he also never ran a small business in his life, never created a job, never risked his own money to start a business. As a pastor, Huckabee never had to worry about taxes (churches don't pay them—no property taxes, no taxes on contributions). Can you even imagine how easy it is to run a business if all the money that comes in is tax free and you can tell your customers that any checks they write are fully tax-deductible? Huckabee is a good man. I respect him and like him. But he went straight from pastor to career politician (who has consistently supported big government and the Nanny State).

On the Democratic side we had a really interesting group—wall-to-wall lawyers. Hillary Clinton is a lawyer who has spent most of her adult life either holding government jobs (or married to someone who did). As far as understanding the middle class, she was paid a reported $8 million advance for her biography. Today she and her husband are worth more than $50 million. Government service has been very, very good to the Clintons. So much for "sacrifice for the good of the people."

To my knowledge, Clinton has never risked her own money on a business, never created a job, never run any business of any kind. Ditto for my Columbia College classmate Barack Obama—another lawyer *squared* (he's married to a lawyer). And then there's John Edwards, the lawyer who earned his $50 million fortune by suing doctors. He, too, never created a business or a job; worse, his lawsuits damaged businesses and destroyed jobs. Edwards campaigned as a man fighting for the under-privileged and condemned U.S. companies sending jobs offshore. All the while he reportedly asked $50,000 per speech, paid $400 for fashionable haircuts, and was paid a salary of $500,000 dollars per year by an *offshore* hedge fund. But wait, it gets even better—Edwards railed against greedy banks that foreclosed on homeowners, while his own hedge fund fore-closed on thousands of homeowners. You couldn't make this stuff up if you wrote fiction novels—readers would call it too unrealistic.

These were the 2008 presidential contenders who the national media declared "qualified." No wonder our country is in such trouble. These are the people who have run our country into the ground—career politicians, career bureaucrats, career lawyers who know nothing about how business works, and spoiled brats born into wealth. What do any of them know about running a business? Or creating jobs? Romney is the one exception, but what does he know about starting a business without millions in the bank to start with? Not one of them has a clue how to start a small business, run a small business on a tight budget in a challenging economy, or pay the bills and taxes that come with such a responsibility. In a country and economy now dominated by small business, isn't it time for a change?

By the way, I hope I've written a book that is timeless. I hope U.S. citizens will be reading this book in 2012, 2016, 2020, and beyond. Don't let the names of presidential contenders that I've listed above fool you into thinking this book is dated. The names will change in 2012 and beyond. But the storyline will be the same. Whoever the new presidential contenders are at the moment you're reading this book, they'll be carbon copies of the politicians I've named above—lawyers, career politicians or bureaucrats, or spoiled brat lucky-sperm-club members. As Barry Goldwater proved, nothing ever really changes. The same politicians will be running in 2012 and 2016 and 2020 and beyond—it's just the names that will change.

■ ■ ■

Now, let's take it one step further. Let's compare me with President Obama. Let's discuss the stories of two young men who graduated from Columbia University on the exact same day in 1983. It is the opportunity of a lifetime to clearly contrast the stark differences in the paths we've each taken in the past 25 years since college graduation. No two political opponents have ever been able to point so clearly to how their philosophies and political visions have changed their lives.

Both of us were children of nonprivileged backgrounds. Barack, a product of biracial parents, grew up as the rare black kid in Hawaii. As the blue-collar son of a butcher, I grew up the rare Jewish kid in a virtually all-black public school on the Bronx borderline in Mt. Vernon, New York. Both of us later benefited from attending exclusive private schools (in both cases with help from our grandparents) that prepared us for entrance into Columbia University. That, however, is where the eerie similarities in our lives end. Obama and I took very different paths after graduation from Columbia. Those paths will illuminate the value of the Libertarian conservative economic message.

I chose the path of an entrepreneur and small businessman. I've started businesses, funded businesses, risked my own money on business ideas to achieve the American Dream. I've created jobs; pumped tens of millions of dollars into the U.S. economy; made hundreds of payrolls so that my employees could raise families, pay mortgages, and share in the American Dream themselves; and paid health insurance and payroll taxes for my employees. Like most entrepreneurs, I've also failed a few times. Perhaps that's the problem with politicians—they've never risked or lost their own money. Many of our country's smartest venture capitalists actually choose to invest only in businesspeople who have failed before (and learned valuable lessons from those failures). Perhaps that should also be a litmus test for politicians who want to run the most powerful economy in the world. In a modern world where small business now creates the majority of U.S. nongovernment jobs, I believe it's time for a small business owner to fight on behalf of the small business constituency and ultimately occupy the White House.

Contrast my 25 years since graduation with Obama. He has spent the quarter century since his graduation from Columbia as a law student, law professor, lawyer, community activist, and career politician. To my knowledge, he's never started a business, never funded a business, never run a business, never risked a dime of his own money on a business, never created a job, and never paid anyone else's health insurance or payroll taxes. And he's never had to face the endless stream of government regulations that interfere in the running of a business either. To the contrary, he's spent his life suing, protesting, and pontificating against the very people who create the jobs and grow the economy.

Barack has lived off a safe weekly paycheck provided by the taxpayers for more than a decade now. He's far from being a fly boy (an entrepreneurial risk-taker). And as a U.S. Senator, he'll never have to worry about Social Security like the rest of us—he'll live off a taxpayer-funded pension for the rest of his life. The reason his pension will be so much richer than Social Security is because government employee pension funds can do what Obama opposes for the rest of us—invest in stocks. Like I always say, watch what a politician does, not what he says.

Obama fights privatization of Social Security tooth and nail, yet his pension is structured the exact same way. He opposes school choice, yet his kids go to the best private schools that money can buy. He supports much higher taxes on U.S. citizens earning $150,000 to $500,000. He calls them "rich." Yet he'll never have to worry about those higher taxes—once he retires, he'll be offered $20 million for his autobiography and $250,000 per speech across the globe. To the filthy rich (of which he'll be a member after leaving office), tax rates are insignificant. When you make $250,000 per year, every dollar you save from taxes is priceless. When you make $20 million (or more) per year, it just doesn't make much difference if you pay 35 percent or 37 percent tax rates.

As further background to the small business owner versus big government lover, let's examine where we have each chosen to live. Barack is an Illinois resident. Illinois has among the highest tax rates in the country. Income tax, business tax, sales tax, and property taxes that are so high they're driving residents by the thousands out of state. Illinois is a prime example of the folly, fallacy, and failure of big government and big taxes. Small business owners are overwhelmed by taxes in the state that Barack calls home. The result is a dramatic loss of jobs, businesses, and residents. It's a vicious cycle caused by liberal tax-and-spenders.

The higher the taxes and entitlements, the more that forces successful people (business owners, job creators, high income earners, retirees with nest eggs to protect) to escape to states (like Nevada) with lower taxes. The result is, of course, a loss of tax revenues for high tax states. And who is therefore left behind in high tax states like Illinois? The less productive citizens, who can't afford to move, and who often depend on entitlements from government. So taxes must be raised *again* to compensate for the loss of producers—the very residents who create the jobs and pay the taxes. Illinois is a dying state because of the ultra-liberal tax-and-spend policies of politicians.

But if you agree that Obama's business credentials are not good news for the economy, sadly President Obama's new "Dream Team" of economic advisors may be even *worse*. The new Treasury Secretary is Timothy Geithner, who as head of the New York Federal Reserve was a key supporter of the trillion dollar bailout-to-nowhere. Lawrence Summers is head of the National Economic Council. Check out his resume—Summers is an egghead who has spent his life reading about the economy in big thick books and teaching it at Harvard. But he's never run a business himself. Then there's a multitude of economic advisors appointed by Obama who are all disciples of Robert Rubin (from the Clinton administration). Rubin sat on the Board of Citigroup as the company literally self-destructed and required a $40 billion bailout from the federal government to survive. As I write this chapter, Citigroup appears headed for disaster (even with all the bailout money). It will most certainly require even bigger bailout funds, or be nationalized by the federal government.

Just what the U.S. economy needs—more of Robert Rubin's strategic thinking. Let's turn the entire U.S. economy into one big Citibank. On second thought, perhaps it's not a bad idea—think of what you or I could do with a $40 billion handout from Uncle Sam.

Problem number one is that there are too many chiefs, not enough Indians. Obama's actions are typical of a big-government liberal—to try to solve a problem by appointing layers of bureaucracy. But with all these economic heavyweights no doubt having a diversity of opinions, who will pick the right solution to our economic woes? Obama answers that question confidently—he says that he's the chief and his word is final. Great, *just what I'm afraid of.* The guy who I just described as never having run a business or created a job in his life, is firmly in charge of choosing the right (or, in this case, left) economic plan to save our country.

Problem number two—Obama and his cabinet members have never run a small business and consequently are out of touch with the problems and issues that affect the people who create the majority of U.S. jobs. What do any of the people discussed above know about creating or running a small business on Main Street? A big shot that runs Goldman Sachs or Citigroup has no clue what to do to help out the pizzeria owner in Long Island, New York, or the real estate agency owner in Henderson, Nevada, or the plumbing company owner in Columbus, Ohio.

I'm sorry to report the facts, but the very people considered "qualified" to run our country by the DC establishment are the guys that got us into this mess. It's time for a change. But not President Obama's version. When he says change, it's because by the time his first term is over, all you'll have left in your pockets is *change*.

The story of Obama versus Root presents a terrific opportunity to contrast the stark differences in our political philosophies, choices, and visions. Barack Obama liberally uses the word "hope." Yet our contrasting personal stories and choices prove that only my Libertarian vision offers true hope. People have already voted for my Libertarian vision— they've voted with their feet—out of Illinois in record numbers, and into Nevada in record numbers. They've already chosen the right path. Now Libertarians just need a candidate to communicate to voters why they need to make the right choice for president.

Chapter 10

The California
Nightmare

*Why California Leads the Nation in Deficit,
Debt, and Out-Migration*

*The problem with socialism is that you eventually run out of other
people's money.*

—Margaret Thatcher

The California Dream of the 1960s (as sung by the Mamas and Papas) has morphed into the *California Nightmare*. The whole point of this book is proven by examining the economic crisis occurring (at this moment) in California—or as some call it "The People's Republic of California."

The real problem is that the entire country is moving toward the California model. Government is far too big, spends far too much, and hires too many at every level, in every state. But as usual, California leads the nation. Remember my favorite description of Republicans and Democrats: Big and bigger, dumb and dumber. Well, California breaks the mold. Everything in California is bigger and dumber. California is arguably the most liberal, big spending, big government state in the entire United States of America (with New York fighting for the lead). Yet, after decades of spending like there was no limit to taxpayers' money, California is mired in a deep economic crisis, and poised to turn into economic Armageddon. The reality is that the state of California is bankrupt. Actually, far beyond bankrupt—California is so bankrupt that there is no amount of money available anywhere in the world to pay off their debts and bankruptcy attorneys have no words to describe the depths of this disaster.

How much has California spent? According to California's own governor, treasurer, and state legislature, in early 2009 the state had an expected budget deficit of at least $41.8 billion (over the next two years). That was a bigger deficit than any state *ever*. That was a bigger deficit than most countries. Later in the Spring of 2009, the state legislature tried to solve the deficit by raising taxes (a lot) and cutting spending (a little). But on Tuesday, May 19th, California voters rejected the tax increases, leaving California with a $21 billion dollar deficit. Panic set in. Media across the country suddenly reported what I'd been saying for a year—the state of California is *insolvent*.

Here are the facts, plain and simple:

- California leads the country in spending on government employees (according to Adrian Moore. "California highest spending state in nation by a LONG ways." November, 27, 2008. Reason Foundation. www.reason.org/blog/show/1005018.html).
- California spends twice as much as the national average on education—with dismal results (according to an editorial entitled "Golden state for teachers: California teachers the highest-paid in U.S." Orange County Register editorial, March 8, 2009. http://capoliticalnews.com/blog_post/show/1471).

- California spends almost $200 million per year on free college educations for *illegal* immigrants—no that's not a typo (according to Teri Sforza. "Lose college tuition subsidies for 'illegals,'" OC Register. August 9th, 2008, http://taxdollars.freedomblogging. com/2008/08/09/if-you-could-cut-one-thing-from-the-budget-chuck-devore-ponders/25/).
- California has the most draconian anti-business rules and regulations in the nation. The result is that California is the most costly place in the United States to do business (according to the Milken Institute's business cost index).
- California is heaven for trial lawyers and hell for small businesses, which could be why so many major employers have left the state (according to *Investor's Business Daily*).
- California has either the highest, or second highest income tax rates in all of the United States (California and New York are constantly switching places). And it is among the nation's leaders in virtually every tax category possible—income taxes, business taxes, sales taxes, property taxes, taxes on real estate transactions, taxes on stock transactions, capital gains taxes, workers compensation taxes, the list is endless. (according to Chuck DeVore. "More Tax Hikes Seen for California." Human Register. August 27, 2008. www.humanevents .com/article.php?id=28203).

The results:

- As of the writing of this chapter, California is facing (according to the governor) a budget deficit of more than $40 billion over the next 18 months—and that may prove to be *conservative*.
- California is reduced to begging the federal government for a bailout. There is no other solution on the table. But the fact that the federal government will hand billions over to California as part of Obama's economic stimulus bill, and California will raise taxes by billions, and cut some spending, all adds up to nothing more than a temporary Band-Aid. One or two years after a federal bailout, the state will undoubtedly be tens of billions of dollars in debt again. Obama's stimulus is a one-time only billion-dollar bonus baby, but the spending it pays for, and the government employees whose jobs

it saves, will have to be funded for years to come. Where will the money come from?

- California has been given the lowest bond ratings of any state in the United States (soon no one will dare loan a penny to California). That little problem costs California's taxpayers millions of wasted dollars per year in increased interest costs.
- In the 1970s California led the nation in job growth. Since 2000, California's job growth is 20 percent lower than the nation. But it's not just *any* jobs that California is losing. According to the California Manufacturers and Technology Association, the state has lost 440,000 high-wage jobs. California's unemployment rate is now the third highest in the nation.
- In the 1970s California was among the nation's leaders in population growth. Last year, more than 135,000 more people left California than moved in. That was the fourth straight year of *out*-migration. Overall, in the last decade more than 1,000,000 U.S. citizens left California (yet the population growth figures don't reflect that because so many non-U.S. citizens moved in). Why is that important? As more and more high income and high-net worth individuals move out, homes will drop in value, small businesses will fail (as they lose customers), and taxes will rise on the remaining citizens (to replace the taxes paid by those who have left). Those who remain, or move in, are "high-need" residents who depend on government to survive—thereby raising taxes (and debt) for everyone left behind in a vicious cycle.

This is a lesson for the rest of the country about what happens when you spend too much and tax too much.

Do you get the picture? The proof is in the pudding: out-of-control big-government spending leads to economic disaster. When your state (or country) is run by government employee unions—teachers unions, trial lawyer unions (the Bar Association), auto unions (who demand billion dollar bailouts from politicians they supported)—and special interest groups, the result is financial Armageddon.

And there is no way out for California, short of bankruptcy.

■ ■ ■

So, what specifically has caused California to reach this lowly place? You guessed it—bloated out-of-control government spending. The problem, of course, is "California Dreamin'." It sounds nice to pay government employees (like police officers, firefighters, nurses, and teachers) huge salaries and pensions, as well as lifetime health benefits (as much as 60 percent higher than similar jobs in the private sector). It sounds nice to mandate a "living minimum wage." It sounds nice to enforce tough rules and regulations on business. It sounds nice to offer generous welfare benefits to the poor. It sounds nice to take care of the homeless. It sounds nice to let anyone sue his or her employer for virtually anything. It sounds nice to make it virtually impossible for business owners to fire an employee. It sounds nice to mandate fines for whatever government thinks is beneficial for society (recycling, carbon taxes, greenhouse gases). It sounds nice to spend more money on education "to benefit the children." It sounds nice to offer free breakfast and lunch (as well as courses taught in Spanish) to poor students at public schools—even if they're here illegally. It sounds nice to pay for the college education of illegal immigrants. It sounds nice to defend animal rights. It sounds nice to ban offshore oil drilling. These Californians are really nice people! They are generous. Except for one problem—they're generous with other people's money—money the state doesn't have.

The lesson here is that "nice" may sound wonderful and fair in theory. It might work out well in some kind of utopian dream state. But in the real world nice doesn't pay the bills. Nice doesn't pay the mortgage in the real world—and California has a very big mortgage. All the liberal do-gooding in the world only leads to one thing: high taxes that productive citizens are unable or unwilling to pay, huge deficits that lead to the bankruptcy of your state, and a massive exodus of taxpayers who have the assets or incomes to allow them to escape. Nice but naïve liberal policies have turned the California Dream into a nightmare.

And with this nightmare, comes high taxes—well, at least for those who earn high salaries. As the state that boasts the second highest income tax rates in the country, California imposes an additional "millionaires" tax surcharge on the people who earn the highest incomes. The top-earning 1 percent of the California population pays 50 percent of the entire state's income taxes. In 2005, the top 14 percent of taxpayers (those earning $100,000 or more) paid 83 percent of the income taxes in California. The 2009 budget solution agreed to by the governor and state legislature in February 2009 raised taxes again—by $14 billion. Yet another surcharge was added to punish high-income taxpayers. Could there be a connection between these taxes and the mass exodus of productive people (like me) out of the state? I escaped to Nevada a decade ago for these very reasons. The California Nightmare of big government, big taxes, and big spending drove me away. My loss has cost California dearly—in the way of millions of dollars of lost tax revenues to the state. But in the real world that's what happens when you choose to treat the people who create the jobs and pay the taxes badly—they choose to leave. The result: California gets none of my money. As the soup store owner in Seinfeld might have said—"Now you get *nothing* from me!"

California proves once and for all that taxes are not too low. The out-of-control deficit in California has nothing to do with taxes. California has a *spending addiction*. It just doesn't matter what the tax rates are. Whatever tax revenues flow into government coffers, the spendthrift politicians and bureaucrats in California find a way to spend it all—*and then some*. The actual total is irrelevant. Give them $1, and California politicians will spend $1.50. But raise taxes and give them $2 (thereby bankrupting small businesses and forcing them to flee your state) and they'll spend $2.50. The rate of taxes is irrelevant because no rate is high enough to satisfy a spending addiction. There's always some "worthy" program or disadvantaged group of citizens to spend it all on, when you entrust billions of dollars of tax revenues to a government bureaucrat or politician looking to keep a job for life. Keep in mind, in many cases, these government bureaucrats are people who couldn't even get or keep a job in the private sector. Now they are getting revenge on all of us in the private sector who wouldn't hire them, by taxing us to death and trying to manipulate, intimidate, and control our lives. And of course, by paying themselves more than taxpayers in the private sector make in comparable jobs.

■ ■ ■

This is where I differ from your typical politician who complains, but provides no solution. I've always believed if you have no solution, you are part of the problem. So here in this book, I'll do more than rant and complain. I'll provide commonsense solutions. How do we stop the insanity? Simple—*stop spending!*

Let's start with state and federal employees' salaries. No sane state (or taxpayer) can justify paying government employees compensation packages 40 percent to 60 percent higher than the private sector. On what grounds? Have you ever been to the DMV office? Are you satisfied with the service? Is the service better than what you'd find in the private sector? Do DMV employees work more efficiently than employees at Neiman Marcus or Saks Fifth Avenue or the Apple Store? Do they treat you better than those private sector employees? Of course they don't. So why are the government union employees paid 60 percent more? Why do they get gigantic pensions and health benefits for life? Do these government employees deserve to retire at age 45 or 50 (or younger), while you work until the day you die (to pay all the taxes necessary for their huge pensions and unlimited health benefits)?

Education is another place to start cutting spending. "Spending more on education" is one heck of a sound bite. But what it sounds like and what it means are completely different things. Educators always argue that "the spending increases are for the kids." Well, that certainly pulls on every parent's heartstrings. But a raise in "education spending" has little or *nothing* to do with spending more money on our kids, or improving their futures. It merely means spending more money on the bureaucratic educational system. When the government gives the board of education money, where do you think they spend it? On new books or supplies? On after-school programs? Nope. They spend it on themselves. With this new taxpayer money, they invariably hire thousands of new administrators who will never pick up a book, grade an exam, or teach a course. This does nothing for the kids.

Or, they raise teacher salaries too far above the national average. None of this helps the kids (just look at California for the proof). It does, however, increase union dues for the teachers union. It does fund more bureaucrats. It does multiply the population of the teacher's union, thereby giving it more clout and more reliable votes (in order to vote themselves more raises and pension increases).

Giving teachers tenure (job security for life) doesn't help the kids either. Giving teachers bigger pensions and allowing them to retire at age 50 (after 25 years) to enjoy a pension for *life* doesn't help the kids one iota. But if that teacher lives to age 85, collecting a big pension for 35 years, it is guaranteed to overwhelm taxpayers and bankrupt your state budget. It all sounds nice and seems like "the right thing to do." In reality it's a one-way street leading to deficit, debt, and eventually bankruptcy and default. There just aren't enough taxpayers, nor is there enough money in any state or country, to allow government employees to retire at age 50 (or younger) and collect pensions for more years than they worked. The numbers just don't add up, unless you expect the rest of us to pay 80 percent tax rates until the day we die to pay for this "privileged class" of federal and state employees.

The consequences of higher government spending do not affect just taxpayers' pocketbooks, but also their professional lives and personal welfare. For example, business owners are one group that has suffered the dire consequences of California's "punish the successful" tax policy. In turn, these consequences negatively impact the well-being of the citizens of the entire state.

First, if you raise taxes on business owners, the result will be a mass exodus by big business, small business, and doctors. They will flee your state by the thousands, thereby reducing the tax base and requiring more tax increases for those who are left. Not to mention, the state will lose its valuable and needed services (such as doctors).

Second, most jobs and tax revenues are created by thousands of small business owners—not by big business. Small business is hurt far more by high taxes and workers compensation rates. Third, contrary to what liberals think, business (even big business) isn't all bad. The reality is that business pays the bills for all these bloated government programs. Government (and all the people living off government) desperately needs business to be successful, or government ceases to exist.

Punishing successful businesses and chasing them away is therefore counterproductive.

As an example, I'm an animal lover. I've always loved my dogs and treated them like my own children. So I understand how animal lovers think. To me, a dog is a member of my family. But any good thing can be taken to extremes. Fighting on behalf of the rights of defenseless animals sure sounds like "the right thing" to do. Unfortunately, when you extend animal rights to chickens, and create draconian new laws that require more humane treatment of chickens by farmers, the results can be disastrous. In the case of California, where voters just approved new laws governing the treatment of chickens, the entire egg industry may be forced to leave the state.

Radical environmentalism sounds nice, too. Saving the beaches by banning offshore drilling, making it virtually impossible for new oil refineries to open within your state borders, requiring special formulations in the gasoline sold in your state, and mandating draconian new greenhouse gas rules that will add billions of dollars to bills paid by business and consumers all sounds wonderful, *until* you get your latest utility bill. When you see your gas bill the next time you fill up at the pump; when you realize every product you buy at the store is now more expensive, then you realize that these government mandates result in more energy dependence on foreign nations that support terrorism. The result is that Californians are treated to the highest energy costs in the country—35 percent higher than the national average. That's before California passes new laws to combat global warming. When utility bills are 100 percent higher than the national average, how will Californians afford to stay in their homes? They won't—they will choose to move.

This reliance on big government, big unions, big taxes, and special interests is a toxic brew that has poisoned the future of California, its citizens, its taxpayers, and future generations. The California Dream has turned into a toxic nightmare.

Now it's coming to a city, county, or state near you. Instead of running from Armageddon, we're *embracing* it. We're electing more big government proponents, more bureaucracy (more agencies with hundreds of thousands of employees like Homeland Security), more draconian government rules and regulations (in the name of global warming), more government involvement in our everyday lives (universal health care), more foreign aid, foreign entanglements, and wars across the globe, more powerful unions (our bailouts of the Big 3 automakers will prop up bloated auto union contracts), more corporate welfare (by handing taxpayer money to wealthy companies through trillion dollar bailouts), more government economic stimulus packages that waste hundreds of billions of dollars in the name of "doing something" when in fact doing nothing would be better for the economy, and higher energy costs that will make owning a home unaffordable.

In reality the best way to stimulate the economy is not for government to spend more. It is not for government to choose winners and losers—by giving away the taxpayer's money through bailouts, corporate welfare, or stimulus giveaways. It is not for government to hire millions of new government employees. Do you realize that we cannot pay the pensions for those that already exist? The best way to stimulate jobs and economic growth is getting government out of the way. It is best accomplished by dramatically cutting the taxes of those who earn the money and create the jobs. My solution is to allow the taxpayers to keep more of the money they already earn, so that they can spend it as they see fit, thereby automatically pumping more money back into the economy. Now that's a stimulus.

Allow me to give you a personal example. Even a *failed* business is good for the economy. I started a business back in 2000 based in California. High taxes chased me out of California. I relocated the business in Nevada. That business failed in 2009. But in the nine years that it lasted, my business spent more than $60 million. So whether we succeeded or failed was immaterial—either way the business I started pumped more than $60 million into the U.S. economy. Think of where all those dollars went: to landlords, electric companies, phone companies, furniture companies, computer companies, banks, lawyers, health insurance companies, credit card companies, media companies (because I spent millions advertising on TV and radio), web designers, my employees, and, of course, to government, too (in the form of payroll taxes and fees).

Now think of how many people benefited from all that money for almost a decade. Every one of my employees turned around and spent the money that I paid them on homes, groceries, meals at restaurants, vacations, contractors, and so on. And every one of the companies that I spent money with hired people with that money—who, in turn, bought homes, groceries, enjoyed meals out with their families, vacations, and so on. I believe every dollar a business adds to the economy is spent 10 times over (or more). So over almost a decade one business idea from one small business owner pumped more than $600,000,000 into the U.S. economy. That was all produced by a small business that eventually failed.

Think of how much money and how many jobs California lost by chasing me away with high taxes? Now think about the results if high federal taxes prevented me from ever starting the business in the first place. Society would have lost $600,000,000 of productivity, spending, and taxes. That's the cost of hindering one single entrepreneur. The California economic model is forcing thousands of businesses to close. It is forcing thousands more to relocate to lower tax, smaller government states (like Nevada). And worst of all, it is preventing tens of thousands of would-be-entrepreneurs from ever opening businesses in the first place. What a tragedy. What a terrible cost to society in jobs, spending, productivity, and taxes *lost*.

We're headed in the wrong direction. Instead of running from the train wreck of California's economic model, we are *embracing* it. With Obama as president, now all of the United States is closer to turning into one big California with crushing debt, limited job growth, out-migration, failing schools, higher energy costs, higher business costs, bigger legal bills, failing businesses, and a drastically poorer quality of life. *California Dreamin'* has turned into our national nightmare. The Mamas and Papas must be rolling over in their graves.

So are Barry Goldwater, Ronald Reagan, and Thomas Jefferson.

Chapter 11

An Impending Disaster

A Toxic Brew of Big Government, Big Bureaucracy, Big Unions, and Lots of Lawyers!

In general, the art of government consists of taking as much money as possible from one party of the citizens to give to the other.

—VOLTAIRE (1764)

From reading the quote above, it sounds like Voltaire knew Barack Obama. We've just handed over our country to a man with no experience as a businessperson or government official—simply because we all disliked George W. Bush and wanted ABB (Anything But Bush). I can certainly understand that feeling. Bush joins Carter on my list of the worst presidents in modern U.S. history. But now that the ABC (After Bush Celebration) is over, it's time to face reality. What have we done? We've now elected a man to govern the United States whose entire experience of governing is serving less than four years in the Senate, during which time he never put his name on *one* bill of any significance, and never held a meeting for the only committee that he chaired. Obama simply arrived in Washington as a celebrity and spent the next three years running for president. Then in the fourth year he ran for president. That's quite a resume of accomplishment. Worse, he now takes over the White House during the worst economic crisis of our lifetime.

People across the country naïvely say they hope and believe Obama will solve this economic crisis. With what? *Voodoo?* How can he solve it, when he knows nothing about business? He's never started a business, run a business, or risked his money on a business idea. During the campaign, he talked about creating millions of jobs—well, the first job that he creates as president will be the first one of his life. He's already started to lower expectations. During the campaign he was shouting about the millions of jobs he'd create. Once elected, he downgraded his promise to creating only 3 million jobs. Then he changed the wording overnight to "creating and *saving* 3 million jobs." Lately he talks only about "saving jobs." Now that he's elected, it appears that President Obama is not so confident about creating jobs. It's no wonder—look at his sum total of experience. He's never paid an employee's payroll, payroll taxes, or health insurance. Yet his supporters, fans, and voters think he holds the magical solutions to a crumbling economy. How frightening is this scenario?

I feel like a father who has fallen ill and has to hand over the keys to his business empire to his 16-year-old son, whose entire prior business experience is running a lemonade stand at age six. That's what we've just done to the entire U.S. economy.

But it gets worse. Far worse.

■ ■ ■

It's not just that President Obama knows nothing about business. Obama is a lawyer, and lawyers think they know *everything* about business. If there is anything worse than knowing nothing about a subject, it's not knowing how much you don't know. As a small business owner, I can tell you from firsthand experience that lawyers destroy almost every business deal they get involved with. Why? Because of a deadly combination of big ego, combined with a lack of knowledge about business. Lawyers learn absolutely nothing about business in law school.

If they learned about business, it would be called "Business School." But in law school, they only teach future lawyers how to sue businesses. There are no courses offered on how to run them.

Lawyers are also taught in law school a thousand ways that any deal can go wrong. So with this negative mentality, they go out into the business world and charge exorbitant fees to lecture businesspeople about all the things that could go wrong with a deal. They scare everyone involved with the deal half to death with all this negativity, thereby killing most deals. It's amazing a deal ever gets done once a lawyer is involved. After years of dealing with lawyers, I've learned to appreciate one of the great lawyer jokes: What is the most amazing trait of lawyers? *They can quote their fees without smiling.*

Lawyers are also taught in law school about the importance of control. They demand to be involved in every aspect of their client's business and try to influence every important decision, because that's how they justify their fat fees and important title. This is where lawyers get their early training and preparation for politics. Did you ever notice how politicians desperately want to control every aspect of our lives? Now you know where that deep-seated desire comes from. It starts in law school.

Therein lies the problem of government. It's made up of lawyers. Not just any lawyers, but lawyers with egos so big that they are hated by other lawyers. It's no wonder that once in political office, these lawyers-turned-politicians then try to get government involved in *everything*—whether they know a thing about it, or not. Why? First, because they want to be in control to justify their political power and important political titles. Second, because politicians (like lawyers) need to create the image that they are invincible, infallible, and all-powerful. They need to create the image that they have the answer for everything. That's how they get elected—by convincing voters that they have all the answers. Once elected, that's how they convince the citizens to hand them unlimited power over our lives.

Now that these lawyers have the important and powerful title of mayor, or Congressperson, or U.S. Senator, or worst of all, President of the United States, do you think they'll ever admit that government doesn't have the solution for any problem? How can they admit weakness? If they admit that, they ruin that invincible and infallible image they've worked so hard to create. They will decrease their power and control over the people. They want you dependent on government (and them).

If there is a problem in society, lawyers-turned-politicians will always try to prove their brilliance and assert their power by trying to solve it—even if government can only make it *worse*. That is a far better choice to a lawyer than admitting that he or she doesn't know the answer. Obama's economic stimulus plan was a great example. It was rushed through without debate, even though almost a trillion dollars was involved. It was passed even though none of the Congresspeople had time to read it. And it was passed despite the predictions from Obama's own CBO (Congressional Budget Office). The CBO reported that whatever slight uptick in jobs and economic activity it produced in the first year or two would be negated over the long term. The CBO predicted that the debt created by the stimulus package would decrease GDP (Gross Domestic Product) over the next decade—that is, *damage* the U.S. economy. The CBO actually said the economy would be better off if we simply did nothing. But no lawyer or politician could possibly do nothing. We're better off doing something, even if it's bad for the economy—that's the politician's credo.

So what's the first thing a lawyer with a huge ego and no knowledge of business will think he should do as president? Of course, he will try to use the power and money of government to *fix* the economy. He'll choose to create more laws. He'll add more regulations. He'll raise the minimum wage (even if it forces businesses to close and jobs to be lost). He'll pass "card-check," thereby erasing the right of privacy for union votes (instantly creating an environment of intimidation and manipulation, which can result in a wave of unionization across the country). He will nationalize banks. And since none of our Congresspersons had time to read the details—it will become law. Exhibit A is the $19 billion in the bill for developing a national digital repository of health records. But no one read the chilling details until after the bill passed. One billion or so will be spent to study the effectiveness of medical, surgical, and pharmaceutical options. Government bureaucrats will then determine what regimens or procedures work and which ones (in their opinion) don't deliver enough improvement for the cost. Think of the implications. Government bureaucrats will now tell doctors what protocols and procedures are "allowed" and which ones are not. Patient's lives will be at stake. Doctors' licenses will be at risk. Medicare and Medicaid bureaucrats could one day use this information to deny or withhold treatments and ration health care to older or terminally sick people. This is just one "small detail" in the Obama economic stimulus bill that Congress passed without reading, discussing, analyzing, or debating. It sends chills down my spine.

Obama believes in the power of government to change and control our lives. He believes only government can fix our economy. Therefore, he will choose to raise taxes dramatically on the most successful entrepreneurs, business owners, and job creators in the United States—in order to provide government with more money to *fix* the economy. He will create millions of new federal government bureaucrat jobs (thereby increasing the size and power of government employee unions). He will give billions of dollars to state and local governments so that no state and local government employees lose their jobs (meanwhile in the private sector, millions are losing theirs). Not only will this stimulus money shield government employees from job losses, but in many states across the country, they will get *raises*. New York just raised taxes by billions under the guise that "everyone must sacrifice." Yet New York State government employees got a 3 percent raise. Where is their sacrifice?

Obama will spend billions on education, thereby increasing the power of teachers unions—even though all the billions we've already spent have made public schools a gigantic failure—among the worst (if not the worst) in all of the industrialized world. If you doubt me, just look at the last chapter on California. They spend double the national average on education only to produce dramatic failure in their public schools. Washington DC spends $14,000 per student, the highest in the country, to produce failing public schools.

And, of course, Obama will redistribute the wealth from taxpayers to union members by bailing out the Big 3 automakers. Automakers will use almost every dollar of bailout money to continue paying bloated salaries and pensions to auto union members, thereby perpetuating a failing business model. Yes, it was George W. Bush who started the auto bailout, but Obama will make Bush's government intervention look small.

Obama will use this economic crisis as an excuse to radically and dramatically expand government (as his Chief of Staff Rahm Emanuel said, "Never allow a crisis to go to waste"). The stimulus program will raise the baseline for government programs to the highest levels in history. But while the stimulus funds will run out in a couple of years, the newly established baselines will keep growing for decades, thereby expanding government and bankrupting taxpayers.

Incidentally, I wrote this chapter back in November and December of 2008 (when I first started writing this book). As I make the final edits of this book in the early spring of 2009, it has all happened exactly as I predicted above. I don't need to see Obama's next move—**I already know the script**.

■ ■ ■

Only a lawyer could possibly dream up this agenda to "save" the economy. Save it from what? *From capitalism?* Obama won't rest until we become . . . France. The stagnant French economy is dominated by big unions and big government. There are few entrepreneurs or business owners in France—with taxes so high, there is no way for individuals to ever save enough money to open a business. And even if they did, the onerous taxes, government rules, and regulations would destroy their chances of success. There are only two viable career routes in France: Work for government, or join a union and work for a big corporation. Is that what the United States wants our economy to become? Do we want Europe's version of big-government social capitalism? Where does it all end? That's the subject of the next chapter on "The Big Auto Bailout Adventure."

Chapter 12

The Big Auto Bailout Adventure

When a private enterprise fails, it is closed down. When a government enterprise fails, it is expanded.

—Dr. Milton Friedman

The Big 3 automakers quietly received $25 billion (with a "B") during the infamous banking crisis during the fall of 2008. The general public barely noticed amid the distraction of the dramatic stock market meltdown (and the backdrop of a presidential election). Soon the Big 3 automakers were back for a repeat performance—asking for another $30 billion weeks later. And back again in February of 2009 for $20 billion more. Guess where all that money will go? To pay for the same outrageous union compensation plans, pension plans, and lifetime health care that bankrupted the Big 3 automakers in the first place. Our government is simply subsidizing failed union contracts that have destroyed the U.S. auto industry, wiped out the city of Detroit (which also recently requested $10 billion from the federal government) and turned Michigan into the state with the worst performing economy in the United States. Sounds like good business practice, huh? But of course, there is no choice for Obama and the Democratic Congress—they each received millions of votes and tens of millions of dollars of contributions from auto unions and autoworkers. Now the unions want payback. This is exactly why 90 percent of voters think our country is headed in the wrong direction. It's all because politics is about payback—"Scratch my back and I'll scratch yours."

Government giving away billions of dollars more to GM, Ford, and Chrysler makes absolutely no business sense. Because of their outrageously overpaid union contracts, the Big 3 automakers can never successfully turn their companies around. They are twenty-first-century *dinosaurs*—GM, Ford, and Chrysler are literally walking dead, they just don't know it yet. Their entire business plan is based on a failed business model. Bankruptcy would be the best thing that could happen to them. Bankruptcy would allow them to restructure, throw out union contracts, and create new labor agreements at much reduced prices. So why are we continuing to loan them billions of dollars? The answer can only be the corrupt politics of Tammany Hall (or in this case, the Chicago machine). Or perhaps it is the fear that letting automakers die would cost more than keeping them alive. Short term, letting the automakers fail would certainly be expensive, but long term it might turn out to be far cheaper to taxpayers. Investing billions of dollars in economic losers is certainly *not* what made the United States great.

The U.S. Big 3 automakers remind me of the state California. As I said earlier, in California everything they do is bigger and dumber. Well, the same can be said of the Big 3. Just as the country's 50 states are experiencing economic and political problems, automakers across the globe are in trouble. Sales are tanking to historic lows for every automaker. But it's not even close—the Big 3 are the ones facing imminent death. The Big 3 are the ones drowning in debt. If the Big 3 were a state, they'd be California. Big and bigger, dumb and dumber.

The Japanese automakers are hurting, yet they are still in the enviable position of building brand-new plants across the country. Where are they building them? In nonunion states only. They are filling these plants with nonunion employees. The same week that the Big 3 pleaded for handouts in DC, a Japanese automaker christened a gleaming, sprawling new plant. A nonunion plant. The Japanese automakers are hurting, but they are in no danger of failing. They will survive this economic tsunami while our Big 3 could not without government intervention (and they *still* may very well fail, even with bailout money). The difference is simple: *unions*. The Japanese automakers are able to beat the Big 3 U.S. automakers simply because they pay their nonunion employees $20 to $30 per hour (or less) versus the $70 per hour (in total compensation over the life of the contract) the Big 3 must pay to their union employees.

Is it fair to pay tens of billions of dollars in bailouts (and counting) to the Big 3 automakers while companies that have successful business models ask for nothing from the federal government? Why would we reward failure, incompetence, and greedy unions? Oh, I forgot, that is Obama's entire business model. Spread the wealth around, punish the successful, and reward those looking for handouts. I guess he thinks if handouts and entitlements work so well for his voters, why not utilize the same game plan for big business? Let's make big business dependent on government handouts, too. *Pass the drugs around.*

An important question comes to mind: Who will pay for my bailout? I'm a small business owner. I'm in trouble, too. Virtually all of my small business owner friends are in big trouble amidst this economic crisis. We are struggling to survive because U.S. consumers have stopped buying anything. Small business creates the majority of nongovernment jobs in the United States—as well as 75 percent of all new jobs. Aren't we too important to the U.S. economy to fail? Who is bailing us out? If we create more jobs as a group than the Big 3, why isn't there a Small Business Bailout plan? Is it simply because we aren't unionized? Is it because we did not give huge donations to certain government officials and members of Congress?

■ ■ ■

Allow me to present the free market alternative. It's simple: Get government out of the way. Any money government gives to the Big 3 (or banks or Wall Street firms) is money taken away from the private sector.

Any money given to failing automakers is money that could be better spent on small businesses struggling to survive. Any money wasted on Big 3 bailouts is money not available to start-ups. Why are we investing in the past, instead of in the future of the country? Any jobs that government creates are jobs taken away from the private sector. Any money doled out by government to solve this crisis, is money taken away from the tax-payers who create most of the jobs. Any money given to the Big 3 is a gigantic waste of taxpayer money used to prop up failing companies with no hope of ever succeeding. It is a legal bribe to corrupt unions that ruined these companies in the first place. Only two things are certain about more multibillion dollar bailouts of the Big 3. First, they'll be back for more money—soon. Second, the handouts and bailouts will *never* end.

The free market alternative is to let the automakers go bankrupt. Does bankruptcy mean that they'll they go out of business? Not necessarily. If they can convince a bankruptcy judge to shed their union contracts, they will emerge as leaner, meaner, more successful companies able to compete with Toyota, Honda, and Nissan. If they can't, they'll go out of business and be replaced by new auto companies with better business models (without unions). Both of these scenarios are far better options than throwing good money after bad. (As I edited this chapter for the final time in May of 2009, my predictions for the automakers appear to have been "on the money." Chrysler just entered bankruptcy, and GM appears likely to do the same in a matter of weeks. We could have saved the taxpayers billions of dollars by making them enter bankruptcy from the start.)

Did the airline industry as we know it end when TWA went out of business? Of course not. Instead, Southwest Airlines emerged as a new airline business model. And it works—they actually arrive at their des-tinations on time, have never lost my luggage, charge lower fares, and manage to make a profit. No one wanted TWA to fail, but their demise turned out to be a good thing for consumers. By bailing out TWA there may never have been room for a bright star like Southwest Airlines. What we need right now is Southwest Motors for the auto industry—a far bet-ter alternative than a bailout that allows failing companies to continue to pursue a disastrous, reckless, bloated business model at taxpayer expense.

Or let's take a look at the television business. When Zenith went out of business, did U.S consumers lose out? Did we even notice? Zenith's demise hasn't stopped U.S. consumers from buying televisions—we've just bought better televisions at cheaper prices from Sony and Mitsubishi (among others). What if GM, Ford, and Chrysler really did go out of business? Would life as we know it in the United States end? Or would U.S. consumers just keep buying cars from Toyota, Nissan, Honda, Lexus, Acura, Volvo, Volkswagen, Mercedes, BMW, Audi (and other foreign car makers who manage to make a profit—*without* unions)? Perhaps we'd buy better cars at cheaper prices. Perhaps we'd drive safer cars. Perhaps we'd drive cars that are much more fuel-efficient, thereby reducing gas consumption and pollution. Perhaps we'd wind up better off as a country.

Most importantly, all of this money the federal government is giving away has to come from someone. It is being stolen from taxpayers without explanation, discussion, debate, or permission. I say "stolen" because I do not believe government has a right to take my money (in the form of taxes) and redistribute it (in the form of bailouts) to failing companies that just happen to make huge campaign contributions to the very politicians supporting and voting for the bailouts. This scam sounds a lot like the one that goes on between politicians and government employee unions (more on that in the next chapter). Nor does the federal government have a right to take my money (when I don't have a pension or health care benefits for life) and use it to prop up union contracts which provide bloated pensions and health care benefits for life.

Bailouts are a recipe for disaster. Anyone who now wants government to create more regulations and take more control over Wall Street and banks has learned the wrong lesson from this crisis. Government is incompetent. Government knows nothing about economics or finance. Government doesn't care about taxpayers. When government needs money, taxes are increased or more money is printed (which dilutes the value of the U.S. dollar). When government wants to create jobs, taxes are raised on some of us, to create unnecessary jobs for others.

Why would we want the same government that has produced an almost $2 trillion dollar budget deficit, a $10 *trillion* national debt (and counting), 9.7 trillion in bailouts, and as much as $100 trillion in total debt (when including the unfunded liability for Social Security and Medicare), to take *more* control of our financial system? Why would we want the people who have managed Social Security and Medicare to the brink of financial ruin to take more control of our financial system? Why would we want the same people who regulated Wall Street, and therefore presided over this catastrophe, to now create more rules and regulations? Shouldn't we be taking power *away* from these people?

Why would we want to elect politicians who call tax increases "fair" and a "national sacrifice"—so that they can use the additional tax money to bail out their biggest (and richest) campaign contributors, dramatically increase spending, and give raises to government employees? What exactly is fair about that?

■ ■ ■

The only lesson to be learned from the great financial crisis of 2008–2009 (and beyond) is to take the power *away* from government. We must make government smaller. We must give politicians less power and control over our lives and finances. We must lower spending and taxes dramatically to allow our economy to recover from this crisis. More taxes and regulations will only deepen the crisis. We must ask government to get out of the way. We must leave free markets *free* to profit and to fail. And if we want to avoid the next financial crisis, we must stop rewarding those who caused this crisis with their irresponsible decisions. We must stop bailing out and handing out taxpayer's money to those with the most powerful and expensive lobbyists and lawyers. Handing AIG or GM more of the taxpayers' money when they fail is not the solution. The only real lesson in this tragic story is that government doesn't have the solution. *Government is the problem.*

I'm not a fan of never getting government involved, but if we are going to give taxpayer money away, I'd much rather look to the future than the past. I'd rather spend government money on loans to startups (the next generation of great ideas), than to bailouts (failed companies wasting money on archaic ideas and models). There is no upside in loaning money to GM, but there is a big upside for taxpayers to loan money to the next Microsoft or Apple. If government is going to give trillions of dollars away, then we should be providing venture capital to entrepreneurs with innovative and creative ideas. Let's fund the next generation of winners, not the last generation of losers.

Republican and Democratic politicians across the spectrum are on record as supporting bigger government, more regulation, more power, more control over private markets and the U.S. economy. The Democrats just happen to favor more government on the fiscal side, while Republicans favor more government on the social (or personal freedom) side.

Where does it end? It ends when we stop electing the same politicians from the same two corrupt political parties, making the same promises, building, expanding and retaining power by giving away bribes with our taxpayer money. It ends when we stop allowing the politicians to rob us. It ends when we demand accountability, responsibility, and transparency. Obama talks nonstop about holding CEOs accountable and responsible. *But who holds government accountable?* Yes, capitalism had one bad year in 2008 and lost a lot of money. Yes, CEOs should be held accountable for those failures. **But government has *never* had a profitable year**. Virtually all government agencies and programs have lost and wasted mindboggling amounts of money every single year of their existence. Who holds these government agencies accountable for losing all that money every year? Who pays for all these losses? We—the taxpayers—do in the form of higher deficits and higher taxes every year.

If government is so successful, how come the federal debt obligations of the U.S. government are now larger than the entire world GDP (Gross Domestic Product)? Does that sound like success to you? These aren't the million or billion dollar losses of Wall Street, mind you. These are trillion dollar losses of government. So who is Obama firing over all those trillion dollar losses?

When Nancy Pelosi promised that the economic stimulus bill would be available on the Internet for taxpayers to see before the vote by Congress, and it wasn't, who held her accountable? Why wasn't she fired for failing to deliver the promised transparency? Not only didn't the taxpayers get to read the stimulus before it passed, *Congress didn't get to read it!* It only arrived at their offices at midnight of the night before they voted. Do you honestly believe any of our Congresspersons or Senators knew what was in the bill they were voting for?

How much money was given away in that economic stimulus bill? If we spent $1,000,000 per day from the day Jesus was born until today, it still wouldn't equal $800 billion. That's how much money we gave away—without *one* Congressperson reading the details. Is this what Obama calls success? Is this what he calls accountability? If CEOs operated like this, Obama would put them in prison. Yet government gets a pass every time. Why?

Why can government loan billions to automakers, yet when the automakers come back to beg for billions more, no one in government is held accountable? Why does no one point out the obvious conflict of interest when Obama and Democrats receive millions of dollars in contributions from auto unions, then give billion dollar loans to automakers with failed business models, in order to prop up bloated union contracts? Where is the accountability there? Why aren't politicians getting fired?

Big Brother doesn't bother to ask taxpayers about our opinion of the bailouts. The arrogant government doesn't say please or thank you—even though it's our taxpayer money they are throwing at their friends in high places. There is no national discussion or debate. There is no vote of taxpayers. Yet it is our money, yours and mine. It will keep our children, grandchildren, and great grandchildren enslaved to bigger government, bigger unions, and higher taxes for generations to come. But then I'm beginning to think that's government's plan in the first place. What do you think?

Chapter 13

Government Employee Unions Gone Wild

My reading of history convinces me that most bad government results from too much government.

—THOMAS JEFFERSON

A s I sit writing this chapter on New Year's Day 2009, it occurs to me that I've worked all day. *On a national holiday.* From 6 A.M. until 10 P.M. I've run my business, phoned a few key business associates and employees to talk about our plan of attack for 2009, mapped out my political plans for the coming year, prepared for numerous media interviews booked for the next few days, created a business plan to present to potential investors for a new business that I'll be starting in the new year, and now I'm spending my evening writing a chapter for this book. These are the things you do when you have a private sector job. Unlike government employees, in the private sector there is no job security or tenure. You earn your keep, you produce, or you lose your job. It's that simple. No one's job is safe—not even the CEO. From morning until night, you make phone calls, send e-mails, attend business meetings—anything and everything to survive and *thrive*. That includes working on New Years Day.

Even more extreme is the workday of the entrepreneur or business owner. When you work as a business owner, independent contractor, or in sales (real estate, stocks, bonds, insurance, mortgages, automobiles), there is no such thing as an "off day." Those of us who work without a guaranteed weekly paycheck are *always* open for business. We work early mornings, late evenings, weekends, holidays, birthdays, anniversaries, often during our kid's ballgames and dance recitals (not all of them, thank goodness—sometimes we actually get to sneak away and attend). You see, no matter how big our paycheck was last week, we always start the next week with a big fat 0 on Monday. Until we literally manufacture new clients and new deals, we stay at 0. We either produce or we don't eat next week. That's why private sector workers are so ambitious, motivated and hungry: Our lives depend on it. Our jobs are on the line every week.

And the thought of "early retirement"? Well, it's just not in the cards for ambitious professionals. If you're employed in the private or professional sector, I know you understand exactly what I'm talking about. But if you're a federal, state, or local government employee, this kind of work schedule is something you can't even begin to understand (or accept). Why? Because you have a guaranteed job for life. And as soon as you retire (at age 45 or 50) you have a guaranteed pension and health care benefits for life. Your performance never enters into the equation. A bad government employee gets the same pension as a good government employee. That is exactly the problem. A huge problem. A cancer upon our nation. This growing divide between private and public employees is perhaps the biggest crisis facing our nation today. It is driving our country toward insolvency and bankruptcy.

■ ■ ■

There is a war brewing in this country. I'm not talking about the Iraq war. Nor the Afghanistan War. Nor the threat of any war with Iran. I'm talking about an economic war that threatens to bankrupt our cities, our states, and our country. A war that threatens to burden our children and grandchildren with debt they can never hope to pay off. It is a war of government employees and their unions, versus all of us who work in the private sector. President Obama never mentions this war. He never mentions this divide that has created two Americas—the America where you and I work our fingers to the bones in the private sector to pay the huge taxes necessary to support that second America—a "privileged class" of government employees.

We have created a monster—government employees who think they are *entitled* to a better deal than rest of us who don't receive our check from Uncle Sam. As taxpayers, these people essentially work for us, yet many of them think they deserve better than us. They act as if we work for *them*. They think that while the country is in recession, they deserve guaranteed jobs, guaranteed pensions and health benefits for life, and here's the truly amazing one—guaranteed annual *raises*.

Are you aware that government employees across this country get guaranteed cost of living and step up (longevity) raises? Even in a national economic crisis, they refuse to give up these raises, while private sector workers are losing hundreds of thousands of jobs per month. More importantly, these raises aren't based on performance. They aren't reserved for the best and brightest. They aren't merit increases. They are given out to every government employee based on the amount of years they've worked for government. If you're the worst government employee in the world, you get this salary increase *automatically* every year. As long as you have a pulse, you get your raise . . . in a depression. This is the very definition of entitlement. Government employees think they are entitled to jobs for life with benefits few of us in the private sector will ever see. So where exactly is the "shared sacrifice" that President Obama talks about incessantly? This government privileged class is not sacrificing a thing.

While small businesses are closing left and right, while big businesses are at death's door, while private sector employees are losing their jobs in droves, guess who *isn't* cutting back spending? Guess who isn't laying off employees? Guess who isn't reducing salaries, or pensions, or benefits? Guess who is getting *raises*? I'll give you three guesses.

Local government. State government. Federal government.

A study released in the fall of 2008 by Moody's www.Economy.com reported that 49 states were either in recession, or on the verge of falling into recession. But Washington, DC, was thriving. The 50th state by the way, not in recession at that time, was Alaska (because of oil prices). Now that oil prices have collapsed, it is safe to say that all 50 states are in deep recession. But not Washington, DC. How can one district continue to grow while the rest of us are in economic crisis? How is that possible? It's actually pretty simple. No matter how bad your business gets, no matter how low your income drops, no matter how low your stock accounts fall, no matter how low your home value sinks, government just keeps spending and hiring (with our tax dollars). They have guaranteed salaries—every week for life. They have guaranteed cost-of-living increases. They have guaranteed pensions and health care benefits. And they have zero risk—they cannot be fired (except under the most extreme circumstances). On top of all that, they get "bonuses" when the government hands out stimulus checks. Why? Their incomes haven't dropped. Their jobs aren't at risk. Their personal economies are fine. Why do they need stimulus checks? I'd call their guaranteed weekly paychecks for life "stimulus enough." *This is truly insanity.*

Best of all, government can't fail. No matter how broke governments go, no matter how underfunded their pension plans are, taxpayers are on the hook to make up the difference. Not enough money to pay the wages for local or state employees? Raise taxes. Not enough money to pay federal employees? Raise taxes. Not enough money to fund pensions and health care for retired government employees? Raise taxes. President Obama's almost trillion dollar stimulus package includes plans to create millions of new federal government jobs.

How could we be doing this? In the deepest recession of our time, while private sector companies are closing or laying off large segments of the workforce, Obama's plan is to create millions of useless new government jobs? I say useless because we survived just fine without those government jobs yesterday and today. So why do we suddenly need them tomorrow? Keep in mind the danger here—these are not temporary jobs. No government job is temporary. These are jobs for *life*. Once we hire these unnecessary new government employees, taxpayers are responsible for their bloated wages, pensions, and health care for *life*. They retire at age 50 after 25 years on the job to pensions of 70 percent (or more) of their last year's bloated salary (with overtime). And guess what? That's not the end. Now government fills that useless job with another person, and rewards them with 40 percent higher pay and 60 percent higher benefits than comparable private sector workers. So taxpayers are now paying for two salaries for each job. The tax burden for all these jobs never ends. But since virtually every one of these government union employees will vote Democrat for life, President Obama is thrilled.

So local, state, and federal governments want *more* money during the worst recession of our lifetimes. Bigger budgets. Higher taxes. More money spent on education (which translates to higher teacher salaries). Hire more employees who couldn't get a job in the private sector. Hire more employees we don't need. Higher cost of living increases. Bigger pensions. More health benefits. Can you even imagine the gall, the stupidity, or the arrogance? Are the U.S. taxpayers asleep while our money is being confiscated by a "privileged class" of government employees? We are being fleeced—and it's a *multiple* generation fleecing. Do you realize that your children will be paying for 30 years for the pensions of the same employees (once retired), who had their salaries paid for by you and me for 25 years. It's madness.

■ ■ ■

It should come as no surprise or shock that unions have had a devastating effect on the economy. It's obvious that the greed of government employee unions threatens to bankrupt the United States, in much the same way that autoworker unions have bankrupted the U.S. auto industry. Auto unions certainly played a starring role in wrecking the biggest companies in the world—Ford, Chrysler, and GM. Unions certainly played a supporting role in the destruction of the economies of Detroit and the state of Michigan. More people move *out* of Michigan (percentage-wise) than any other state in the country. I wonder why? It's pretty obvious—you either have a government job or bear the tax burden to keep all of these people employed. So those who didn't get awarded a job with the privileged class are running for their lives. The movie should be called *Escape from Michigan*. It is a horror film. But if you're one of the lucky ones who manage to escape, it has a happy ending.

This has all been a long time in coming. Auto executives of the Big 3 saw this financial Armageddon coming back in 1977 when the *Wall Street Journal* quotes a United Auto Workers leader as saying how flabbergasted he was at the number of younger workers (55 and under) retiring with full pensions. The U.S. auto industry was destined for destruction and bankruptcy on the very day three decades ago that it agreed to let autoworkers retire with full pension and health benefits after 30 years on the job, regardless of age. That was the day that Detroit died. The autopsy should read "Death by Suicide."

It doesn't take a brain surgeon or Harvard economist to understand that if an employee enters the workforce at age 18, works for 30 years, retires at age 48 with full pension and health benefits for life, and then collects their pension and benefits for more years than he or she actually worked, the company will not survive. Well, it has all happened according to plan. This is not a surprise. The automakers and politicians saw it coming, but no one did anything about it. Why do I point all this out in a chapter about government employee unions? Because the *exact* same scenario is currently playing out with government employees. Except this disastrous business model doesn't affect only three auto companies. It effects (and ruins) the United States economy.

Local, state, and federal government employees are retiring at young ages, with union contracts that allow them to collect giant pensions and full health care benefits for life. Many retirees will collect these gigantic retirement windfalls for more years than they actually worked for government. Government employee unions have the same business model as auto unions. Can you guess the ending to this story?

It is no coincidence that Michigan is a strong pro-union state and now has the single worst economy in these United States of America. Michigan makes California look good by comparison . . . well, at least slightly better. These unions won't rest until all of us in the private sector slave away eight or nine months a year to meet all their demands, to pay all their obscene salaries and pensions and health benefits. They won't rest until the whole United States is one big decaying, depressed, economic relic like Detroit. The city council of Detroit recently voted to ask the federal government for a $10 billion dollar bailout. But didn't they hear? Our federal government is bankrupt, too. You know why? Because the federal government owes more than $5.3 trillion in unfunded liabilities for the pensions and health care benefits of government employee union members. Sound familiar?

The U.S. federal government is kept alive by transfusion—the Federal Reserve just keeps printing money. Here's the game plan: Unions bankrupt the Big 3 automakers; then they demand a bailout for their failing business model (so they can keep paying bloated union wages); next the city of Detroit needs a bailout to survive this train wreck; and, of course, Obama's stimulus plan gives over $100 billion to the bankrupt states (like Michigan). But now the federal government is busted. So who pays off the trillions of dollars in debts owed by the feds? You and me. Remember, someone has to pay the bill. Lovely. We have unions to the right, unions to the left, unions in the middle. *And bankruptcy all around*.

■ ■ ■

If you doubt how big this crisis really is, please Google the *Los Angeles Times* cover story of Sunday, June 10, 2007, on this economic tsunami headed our way. The normally ultraliberal *Los Angeles Times* reported that California will surely go bankrupt sometime in the near future under the weight of unfunded public employee liabilities. The *Los Angeles Times* reports that health care benefits alone for retired California public employees will grow from $4 billion today to $31 billion by 2020. That's just the *health care!* That doesn't include a penny for the pensions for these same state government employees. There is no possible way to pay for it all. It is a looming disaster for every state in the nation. But the bleeding-heart liberal, "People's Republic of California" is the perfect test-tube, poster-child for the disaster headed our way.

That article was "the canary in the coal mine." It was written two years ago. It is no coincidence that Governor Arnold Schwarzenegger spent this past winter pleading with the federal government to loan California billions of dollars. The chickens have come home to roost. You can't pay government employees 40 percent higher wages than employees in the private sector—at least not if you want to survive economically. California now has the highest taxes in the country. Those two are no coincidence. In order to pay one privileged class a "decent living wage" (as liberals like to call it) you have to redistribute wealth away from those who actually earn it (by risking their own money).

In other words someone has to pay for all these bloated salaries and pensions for government employees. So taxpayers get fleeced. The result is that successful business owners (and anyone with assets) are leaving (or should I say *escaping*) California in droves, just as I chose to escape a decade ago. Tax revenues are therefore going down, not up, due to this exodus of brains and talent to lower tax states like Nevada, Arizona, Utah, Wyoming, Colorado, Texas, and Florida. That could be why those states are all on the fastest-growing list.

The problem exists all over the country—although on a smaller scale (simply because California is that much bigger, more liberal, and obviously more ignorant of simple mathematics). The *Los Angeles Times* article entitled "Public sector reels at retiree healthcare tab" (June 10, 2007) reports that "local governments will soon be overwhelmed. It will be impossible to meet their financial obligations. The only possibilities are bankruptcies, or death by a thousand cuts in services to the public." That's a direct quote from the ultraliberal *Los Angeles Times*. The situation is *that* grave.

That prediction of being overwhelmed "soon" is obviously referring to *today*. My prediction is that over the next four years, hundreds, if not thousands of U.S. cities will declare bankruptcy in order to get out from under their government employee union contracts. Bankruptcy will give them the leverage to lay off government employees and renegotiate more reasonable (some would say "sane") deals with government employee unions. This all comes at the same time that Obama is pledging to hire millions of new federal government employees. This can best be defined as economic suicide.

The *Los Angeles Times* quotes nonpartisan studies that report wages for state and local government workers are 40 percent higher than private employees, and retirement and fringe benefits are a whopping 60 percent higher. But in California, government employee wages are the highest of all states. That could explain why California is the furthest in debt of all states. No coincidence there. The liberal media bombards the public nonstop about the "divide between rich and poor in America." But this chapter describes the true "fairness divide" the media has up until now completely ignored (or hidden): the obscene, outrageous, bloated compensation and benefits lavished upon public employees (who happen to vote virtually 100 percent Democratic just like the media), versus private sector taxpayers.

■ ■ ■

Why do public employees deserve so much more compensation than those in the private sector? Based on what? Small business owners like myself take massive risks, often put their life savings and homes on the line as "personal guarantors," create jobs, make payrolls, pay millions in taxes (payroll, state, and local, federal, sales taxes), and pay for health insurance for our employees. We make it possible for others to live the American Dream.

Entrepreneurs and private sector workers rarely get to retire early. I have yet to meet a business owner retired at age 50. Not one. Yet we in the private sector have no guaranteed paychecks (actually we often pay ourselves nothing in order to make employee payrolls when things are tight), no tenured jobs for life, no pension of any kind, and no one to pay our health insurance after retirement. Heck, we have no idea if we can *ever* retire.

Why do public employees (who have guaranteed jobs for life, guaranteed weekly paychecks, and don't have to risk a dollar of their own money on a business) deserve higher compensation than private sector employees? Why do they get to retire early on an obscene pension for *life*? Why are they allowed to include overtime in that last year's salary used to determine their pensions for life? Why do they deserve health care for life? No one I've ever met in the private sector has health care for life. Think of the dollars this all adds up to and you'll start to understand why our country is going bankrupt.

Why do government employees deserve to get the day off for New Years and weekends and sick days, when small business owners who create the majority of jobs in the United States don't? There simply are no "sick days" when you own your own small business—you either show up, or you lose your customers (and your business). There is no time to get sick when you own your own business, so you just *don't*. I haven't missed a day of work due to illness in 25 years, a quarter of a century.

My father owned a small butcher store. He, too, never missed a day of work in his adult life until he found out he had cancer. He closed the store to begin cancer treatments and died five months later. That was his retirement. No watch, no pension, no good-bye party.

My grandfather owned a butcher store for 50 years. He never missed a day of work, until he had a heart attack. The doctor recommended retirement as his only option at age 86. He closed the store and retired. He died (of boredom) a few months later. That was his lengthy retirement. The truth is that no country (or company) can afford to pay big pensions to retired employees for 20 or 30 or 40 years. Pensions or Social Security were never meant to support people for long retirements. Social Security was originally set up to support retired U.S. citizens for just a few years (based on life expectancy at the time). The system must be radically reformed. No one working for government can expect to retire and be paid a huge pension for decades. The costs are burying U.S. citizens in debt.

Let's look at a real-life example that illustrates the problem: A public employee retires after 25 years on the job. Since they started at age 25 (or younger), they can retire at age 50. If they live to 85 years old, they'll be collecting close to full salary for *not* working for the next 35 years. If thanks to medical technology they live to 95, you and I will be paying for their almost full salary (and all medical bills) for 45 years. That's just shy of half a century. For *not* working. To replace that retired employee, we must also hire another overpaid government employee to take their job. This is sheer madness. *Stop the insanity.*

But in the private sector or small business, none of this exists. My father and grandfather retired, they died, and no one was left on the hook for a dime . . . let alone for 30 years of paying someone a full (or close to full) salary.

Why is this gigantic divide between public sector employees and private sector taxpayers "fair"? The answer, of course, is it is *not*. And it is time for a citizen revolution to end this travesty of justice—simply because the rest of us can't afford to pay for this government "privileged class" anymore.

Tens of millions of U.S. taxpayers are going to start asking these four crucial questions:

1. Why should we in the private sector take all the risks, and labor under the burden of ever-higher taxes, so we can pay for the lavish salaries, pensions, and benefits of public service employees?
2. Why do we work 12 to 14 hour days, while government employees work 9 to 5? Why do they get to leave at the stroke of 5 P.M. on workdays, while we often have many hours of work still left to go?
3. Why should we slave away at work until the day we die, so we can pay for the early retirements at age 50 (or younger) of public employees who get to play golf for the rest of their lives with pensions of

70 percent (or more) of their last annual working salary, plus full health care for life?

4. Why should the private sector taxpayers be stuck with this burden? Who are these government employees that they should be paid so much better than the typical taxpayer?

Can you feel my passion and energy right through the pages of this book? I'm one of the most passionate, excited, energetic, and fiery individuals on this planet. I get up each and every morning excited to take on the world. Have you been to the DMV (Department of Motor Vehicles) recently? Now compare my energy and passion to an employee of the DMV. Are you laughing? Now you get it.

That's the problem with government. Give someone a job for life, guarantee them a fat pension, and I guarantee that they'll spend their entire career looking at their watch waiting for retirement. A small businessman like me has to have infinite energy. I have to be a ball of fire. I have to be more creative than the next guy. I have no choice. No one has guaranteed me a job for life. No one has guaranteed me a safe weekly paycheck. I have no pension. *I'm on my own.* I have to move fast to make things happen.

That's precisely why government employees often move slowly. Because they get their paycheck every week come rain or shine, good performance or bad, whether they work fast or slow. Motivation and ambition are missing ingredients in the lives of anyone guaranteed a safe paycheck, a job for life, all health care benefits for life, an early retirement, and a bloated pension.

Are government employees bad people? Of course not. Most are nice people, just like you or me. Some are the best and brightest who could have made a fortune in the private sector (if they'd chosen to). Some are heroes (policeman and fireman instantly come to mind). Some deserve a higher wage or "step-up bonus" for the risks they take (police officers and fire fighters instantly come to mind). In the military, soldiers get a bump up in compensation for "combat pay." If they are sent into the combat zone, they are paid a bonus. I agree that policeman, law enforcement, and fireman who are "in the combat zone" (active in the streets) deserve bonuses and higher pay than other government employees. But those groups make up a small percentage of government employees.

More importantly, the reality is we cannot afford the current system as it is structured. We just can't afford to be more generous to government employees than private sector taxpayers—even if they are nice people. Government employees may be wonderful people, but they certainly are often overpaid people. And their unions certainly are bankrupting the United States and fleecing the taxpayers.

Are there reasonable steps we can take short of firing a large percentage of government employees, or taking their pensions away? Sure. First, institute a hiring freeze on government employees. Second, change the compensation, pension, and health care benefits for all *future* government employees hired. Eliminate forever the "defined-benefit pension plans" which fleece the taxpayers. And mandate that government employees (if they want to receive their full pensions) must work to age 65—just like the rest of us (the exception being high-stress, fitness-oriented jobs like police or firefighters). Eliminate automatic pay increases and raises. Award them only for superior performance or "combat pay" for law enforcement and firefighters. Suspend any automatic raises in times of economic crisis. And we must put a stop to the use of overtime to determine the size of pensions. By just instituting these few commonsense changes, we can dramatically reduce government spending, while at the same time protecting the deals of current government employees (and continuing to reward the true heroes of society—police and fire personnel).

■ ■ ■

Unfortunately, the real issue is not whether the overwhelmed taxpayers and small business owners can pay for it or not—we cannot. The real issue is what happens when the unfunded liabilities come due? California and the other 49 states are facing bankruptcies and economic crises of epic proportions. Meanwhile the real heroes of the U.S. economy—the job creators and risk takers—will be forced to work from January to October just to pay the 70 percent to 80 percent taxes that will be necessary to save this country from economic disaster. And even with those high tax rates, it may still be impossible to pay off our staggering national debt. The looming economic disaster is *that* bad.

Is there a way to peek at the future? To see what happens when public employee unions dominate your economy? Yes, it's called *France*. That's why our U.S. economy is so successful year after year, when compared to the stagnant French economy. It's because the United

States (with lower tax rates) encourages and rewards entrepreneurship, ambition, and personal responsibility, while France (with much higher tax rates) encourages a welfare state where those lucky enough to join a union have a guaranteed job, guaranteed medical care, four weeks of guaranteed vacations, and guaranteed pension for life. The rest of society is out of luck. The result is high unemployment, high taxes, and shared misery for all. There is only one way out of the economic crisis we are in—entrepreneurs and small business owners are the answer. Free market capitalism will get us out of this gigantic hole. More government employees will certainly worsen the crisis.

Brave politicians (if there are any left) must deal head-on with this looming economic crisis now, *before* public employee unions destroy the greatest economy in world history and bleed taxpayers and private industry dry. History proves that great democracies are always destroyed when too many citizens believe that they are entitled to feed off the public dole. When one of five (or more) citizens works for the government, and many more live off companies that do business with the government, and even more citizens depend on government handouts, our economy is in deep trouble, our quality of life is threatened, and our taxpayers are drowning in debt. Barry Goldwater saw it coming way back in 1959. It has gotten far worse in the half century since then. It will get far worse in the years to come, unless we make radical changes now.

Worst of all, this current system encourages and legalizes political bribery and extortion. It allows unions to say to politicians, "Pay me more, increase my pensions and benefits; and I'll vote for you, support you, contribute to you, and my union members will man phone banks and walk door to door on your behalf." Why should government employee unions that donate millions of dollars to politicians (usually Democratic politicians) and thousands of hours working on their political campaigns, then be allowed to negotiate with those same politicians for obscene pay increases? No wonder every time that a union requests a raise in pay or pension, the answer is a quick *yes*. No wonder one class (private sector taxpayers) shoulders all the burden of another class (entitlement junkies and government employees). It is pure and simple a culture of corruption and conflict of interest.

Our Founding Fathers created our Constitution to keep the government out of the lives of the citizens. That Constitution clearly gives the power to the people—*not* the government. But if a majority of U.S. citizens live off of, and work for, the government, then the tables have turned. These same people who work for the government, depend on the government, and pay their bills and mortgages with government paychecks, desperately *need* the government to grow ever larger (to protect their jobs, benefits, and entitlements). It is a vicious cycle leading to dependency and bankruptcy.

The more government keeps hiring, the more employees are automatically available to join the government employee unions. And therefore more union members are available to contribute to union political action funds, to vote for union-friendly politicians, and to work on phone banks, or walk door to door to campaign for union-friendly politicians. These same union organizers and "community organizers" (as Obama calls them) can therefore be counted on to rig the system to continually fleece the taxpayers and benefit themselves—with the full cooperation of the corrupt politicians they helped elect.

I'm sad to say that this war being waged today is all about the same issues as the American Revolution of 233 years ago: freedom, excessive taxes, and taxation without representation. But today it isn't rebels and barefoot peasants fighting against the corrupt, greedy British Empire. Today it is a war of government employees versus the rest of the United States (the taxpayers who create all the jobs and pay all the taxes). Today the war we fight is between the private sector and the government employee unions. No lives are being lost in this war. But taxpayers are fighting for our economic lives—and the future of our children and grandchildren. There is no blood spilled. But taxpayers are sacrificing blood, sweat, and tears to toil all day, every day, in order to pay the heavy taxes required to feed this privileged class.

When the ultraliberal *Los Angeles Times* makes it a front-page story, the crisis is bigger, closer, and more devastating than we ever imagined. That was two years ago. We move ever closer to disaster. The time to act is now—*before* the people working for and depending on government outnumber the individuals who depend on themselves and want government out of our lives.

■ ■ ■

My New Year's Day is now over. I've been working on and off for 16 hours. I'm going to sleep. I have to be up at 5:30 A.M. again tomorrow ... and the next day ... and the day after. Remember, I have four young children, a big mortgage, no guaranteed weekly paycheck, no pension, no guaranteed job for life, no health care benefits for life, and no early retirement on the horizon. I'm 47 years old, yet for me, it's "off to work I go" for the next 30 years (or more). For those of us who aren't members of the privileged class, there is no rest.

Chapter 14

The PSTA—Private Sector Taxpayers of America

Stoking the Citizen Revolution by Unionizing

The democracy will cease to exist when you take away from those who are willing to work and give to those who would not.
—THOMAS JEFFERSON

I've been inspired by all this talk of unions and taxpayer rip-offs. I think it's time for the business owners, job creators, private sector employees, and U.S. taxpayers to start our own union, hold our own protest, and take our own important day off from work. Let's call our new union the *PSTA—the Private Sector Taxpayers of America.*

■ ■ ■

For years I've been saying that the group that Nixon defined as "The Silent Majority"—educated, law-abiding, married-with-children, job producers, business creators, taxpayers, private sector professionals and executives, and owners (homeowners, business owners, stock investors)—should form our own union. The members of this union are highly paid and heavily taxed (punished) simply because they make good money—therefore, they are obvious targets for politicians like President Obama looking to find more tax revenues from someone/ anyone. And because this group doesn't work for government, government loves to tax them. But the media rarely presents the side of the argument that supports these taxpayers—that we don't earn our money by mistake or coincidence. *We earn it.* Why does the media ignore us? Because we tend to be fiscal conservatives, and the media is liberal. Plain and simple—they are biased against us.

According to facts presented by the Tax Foundation (founded in 1937) the top 1 percent of taxpayers pay 39.9 percent of all taxes. The top 10 percent pay well over 50 percent of all taxes. The top 25 percent pay virtually *all* the taxes in the United States (86.3 percent to be exact).*

If you want to see one group *prove* that they matter to the United States . . . one group grind the United States to a halt . . . try the TOPS (Taxpayers of the Private Sector). Or better yet, try a day *without* TOPS.

But our new President Barack Obama has no interest in rewarding these producers. To the contrary, Comrade Obama seemingly wants to *punish* success. He actually wants to give a new welfare payment to the 40 percent of U.S. citizens that pays no federal income taxes—and he brilliantly calls this socialist entitlement scheme "a tax cut." Obama certainly has a way with words. I give him that much. How can it be a tax cut if you didn't pay any taxes in the first place?

It is amazing how we have allowed liberals (and in Obama's case— *socialists*) to define the words used in the U.S. media. Liberals call tax

---

*Prante, Gerald. Summary of Latest Federal Individual Income Tax Data. Fiscal Fact No. 135. July 18, 2008. www.taxfoundation.org/news/show/250.html

cuts "a giveaway to the rich." Well, how can it be a giveaway when it's our money in the first place? When you allow a taxpayer to keep a little more of his or her own money, how is that a giveaway? You can't give someone back their *own* money and call it a handout. Yet those same liberal politicians want to give away our hard-earned money to those who didn't earn it, nor pay any taxes in the first place, and call that a "tax cut." Amazing. The gall, the arrogance, the hypocrisy is almost too much to fathom.

Please allow me to set the record straight. It is not a giveaway to allow a taxpayer to keep more of his or her own money. Remember, it's our money in the first place. It is not greedy to want to keep more of our own money. Remember, we earn it fair and square. It is in fact a giveaway to take our money and redistribute it to people who do not earn it, and who are laying around with their hands out. Hence the term "handout." *Taking money from those who earn it, to give to others who don't, is in fact the very definition of a giveaway.*

It is those who demand redistribution of wealth and choose to accept money from government without working for it, who are the ones guilty of greed. It is jealousy, greed, and envy—all sins in the Bible—that cause a person to want what someone else has, without working for it. When you give a payment to someone who didn't pay taxes, it is *not* a tax cut or refund, but rather a welfare payment, entitlement, or handout. It is time for taxpayers to aggressively take back those definitions. Liberals have lied and distorted the record for far too long.

Obama says that he is not a socialist. But for someone who isn't a socialist, Obama's views on taxation happen to match exactly with how a socialist defines "spreading the wealth around." Tax successful people to death . . . then tax them again on capital gains (which is money they've invested in the United States *after* already paying taxes on their earnings) . . . then tax them some more *after* they die . . . and then have the government (Big Brother) give all that money to people who don't work, don't create jobs, don't pay taxes—in the form of a national welfare check—and call it a "tax cut." Brilliant.

■ ■ ■

I have argued for years that it is a terrible strategy to trade income tax cuts for successful people, in return for taking a large portion of low-income people off the tax rolls altogether. This trade is the very reason most people no longer rate taxes as a top issue in political campaigns. If you no longer pay taxes, why would you care about them? If you don't pay them, why would you care if they are raised through the roof on others? The reason so many citizens no longer seem to fear federal tax increases is because so few actually pay them. Taxes have become so foreign to certain people that I feel the need to give them a crash course in where they come from. Taxes are a form of money that people—like Obama supporters—think falls off trees. Taxes are that mysterious thing that pays for their roads . . . their public transportation . . . their children's free public education . . . their entitlements . . . their hospital bills. Where do they think it comes from?

It comes from one place—from the PSTA—the Private Sector Taxpayers of America.

Funny how many U.S. citizens nowadays think that money is easy to make. And that it's easy for that "other guy" to pay higher taxes. Any time liberal politicians like Obama find the need for a new billion dollar program, they simply think the solution it is to raise taxes on "the rich." Well, if money is so easy to make, why don't Obama's supporters just make some of it themselves? Perhaps they should pay for their own programs if they think they are so essential. If money is so easy to make, *go make it.* But please stop asking me to make some more money, every time you want something. The very definition of greed is to want something, but expect others to provide it for you. Money is not easy to make, nor can I magically find some every time government decides a tax raise is necessary. It has to come from somewhere—it means I can't invest in that stock, or real estate, or my child's college education, or a new business investment, or I can't spend it (which of course means the economy grinds to a halt). When government takes more of my money, I have less to spend on consumer items or my business. I have to lay off someone, or decide against a new purchase that is necessary for my business.

During the 2008 election Obama showcased his power by asking his voters to take a *paid* day off from work. Well, how about if our PSTA union shows the United States what it's like to be *forced* to take a day off from work—*without* pay?

How about if the private sector taxpayers and business owners who pay for all these government entitlement programs simply decide to hold our own PSTA protest? How about if our union decides to shut down the United States for the day? Instead of the inmates running the asylum, how about if we turned the tables? How about if we organize *the management!*

Instead of the employees shutting down the construction sites . . . how about if the owners of the construction company shut down the construction sites? Instead of the employees refusing to work at the supermarkets and bodegas . . . how about if the storeowners told the employees not to bother showing up for work today? How about the homeowners telling their maids, nannies, gardeners, delivery people, and contractors not to show up for work today? How about the farm owners telling their farmhands not to bother to come to work today? What if business owners across the United States tell their employees not to show up for work today? How about if the real estate brokers, stockbrokers, mortgage brokers, and insurance brokers just decide to stop selling for the day? These groups are the ones that buy, sell, and trade just about everything there is to buy, sell, and trade in the United States. These are the hardworking entrepreneurs that Obama calls a dirty word—rich. *I think it's high time that the PSTA showcase their value to the United States of America.*

But alas, it may be just a fantasy. Because these groups (job producers, business owners, and private sector taxpayers) are the very definition of why capitalism is so successful. We don't waste our time marching, complaining, or protesting. We have families to support, businesses to run, taxes to pay, mortgages due, payrolls to make, future college educations to save for, and bills to pay! Ironically, it's the hardworking U.S. taxpayers who cannot afford to take days off. We have no time to complain. We don't have time to worry about whether life is fair or not. We're too busy paying all the taxes so other people can collect government handouts (and complain).

That's precisely why Nixon called us the Silent Majority. Because the people who march and protest and scream the loudest obviously don't have much to do, or anyone depending on them. They don't have to meet weekly payrolls. They don't have big monthly "nuts." They don't have to write big checks to make a payroll so others who depend on them can live the American Dream.

Those of us who are members of the PSTA do have big (and often overwhelming) responsibilities on our shoulders—and consequently don't have the time to waste. We are the owners of the United States for good reason—we *earned* it! We worked our butts off to own the assets we do. We didn't protest to get them. We didn't ask the government to give them to us. We went out and fought the good battle to earn our assets.

Many of us did exactly what society asked of us: We studied hard, got good grades, worked multiple jobs while attending college, didn't smoke, drink, or do drugs, didn't get anyone pregnant while still a teenager, didn't commit any crimes or join any gangs. No one ever had to give us the day off to vote. We consider voting a cherished responsibility. We vote year after year without being asked, or bribed with a paid vacation. We've always done the *right* things (excuse the pun) and made the right choices (by and large—no one is perfect). And our reward is the American Dream. It's still alive—but only to those who fight for it and work for it and *earn it*. It isn't easy. But the opportunity is there. The United States is in fact the fairest nation in the world.

But here's the honest truth that the ultraliberal administration doesn't want you to hear: You'll have to be *patient*—it takes years of education and climbing the corporate ladder to achieve success. It takes years to build your small business. Sometimes it takes more than one generation. My great grandfather was a peasant who died penniless in Russia. His son (my grandfather Louis Root) was a Russian immigrant who died in the "poor ward" of a Brooklyn hospital. My father David Root was a blue-collar butcher. Today I'm a CEO, business owner, author of seven books, business speaker all over the world, and a former nominee for vice president of the United States of America. It took a century for the Root family to achieve "overnight success." But we did it. We could not have done it anywhere but in the United States. If I lost it all tomorrow, only in the United States could I get it all back. This is a remarkable country, but nonetheless success takes time, effort, blood, sweat, and tears. Those looking for government to change their status in life are going to be waiting for a long time—forever! Government might hand you just enough to survive, or to become dependent on government. But government doesn't ever buy you a beautiful home, or a Mercedes. You have to earn the valuable things in life. "If it is to be, it is up to me."

One thing I can assure you—during the long personal journey of the Root family we didn't achieve success by complaining, marching, protesting, taking lots of paid holidays at the workplace, or playing hooky at either work or school. We never looked to government to provide the answers. We never asked government to take anything away from others. We never expected to earn our piece of the American Dream at the expense of anyone else. We never expected or wanted a handout, only a hand up.

Yes, I think it is time to form our own union—the PSTA (Private Sector Taxpayers of America). Obama adamantly supports unions. I wonder how he'll feel about ours?

Part Three

SOLUTIONS FOR THE MESS WE ARE IN

Chapter 15

The Ultimate Spending Solution

Constitutional Impoundment

I believe that as a practical matter spending cuts MUST come before tax cuts. If we reduce taxes before firm decisions are made about expenditures, we will court deficit spending . . . it is in the area of spending that the Republican Party's performance, in its 7 years of power, has been most disappointing.

—BARRY GOLDWATER (1959)

This book comes out in the early summer of 2009, only a few short months after tax day April 15, 2009. What perfect timing to declare that the buck stops here. This is the ideal time to change the way we think and debate about taxing and spending forever more. This is the perfect time to discuss the most powerful and no doubt controversial (at least to those who support big government) one-two punch in the history of political debate on "taxation and spending." Here is a politician proving he is different. Here is a politician offering more than just the same old, tired, recycled talking points. Here is a politician doing more than complaining. Here is a politician offering real *solutions*.

For years presidents—Democratic and Republican alike—have argued for the line-item veto, a power available to most state governors to cut out unnecessary spending from government budgets. Presidents have claimed they are powerless to stop Congress from spending the money without this powerful and mystical weapon. They were not so powerless after all. It turns out that they are just unwilling to use the tools already at hand.

Congress finally enacted the Line Item Veto Act in 1996. During one year, Bill Clinton exercised this veto power 82 times for $2 billion in savings. Far too little, in my opinion—but nonetheless a positive development for taxpayers. The joy for U.S. taxpayers was short-lived. The U.S. Supreme Court in 1998 declared such a power unconstitutional in *Clinton v. City of New York*.

So, what could a Libertarian president do to stem the tide of spending without the line-item veto? While the legislative branch has the power to appropriate funds, it is only the executive branch that has the power to spend these funds. A Libertarian Root administration will exercise a power that is much stronger than a line-item veto. That power provided for in the Constitution is known as "impoundment." It is the power of a president to seize funds not authorized by (or in violation of) the Constitution, and return the money to taxpayers.

■ ■ ■

Thomas Jefferson (arguably the most Libertarian president in U.S. history) first exercised the power of impoundment in 1801, when he refused to spend $50,000 in appropriated funds for some Navy gunboats. He impounded the money and, remarkably, returned the funds to the U.S. Treasury.

Many presidents have exercised this power ever since, the last being Richard Nixon, who attempted to curb runaway spending. But Congress—at a time when Nixon was weak from his criminal scandals—seized the opportunity to overstep its bounds by passing the Congressional Budget and Impoundment Control Act of 1974, which took away the president's unilateral power not to spend money.

Nixon's argument was based on executive powers, and not on the Constitutional duty of the presidency.

Article II, Section 1 of the Constitution requires that the president take an oath to solemnly swear that he will faithfully execute the office of President of the United States, and will to the best of his ability, preserve, protect and defend the Constitution of the United States.

Paradoxically, most government spending today is in violation of Article I, Section 8 of our Constitution and no Congress can require that the president violate his oath of office. If elected, I would dare to go where no previous president in modern history has dared go. This Libertarian president would invite a showdown with Congress that could go all the way to the U.S. Supreme Court.

This president will impound every last red cent of spending that violates the Constitution.

With this promise a political leader finally offers real hope for beleaguered taxpayers. This is the opportunity to finally prove that dramatic cuts to both spending and taxes are not only possible, but doable. This is the opportunity to prove that a rapid, responsible, and intelligent downsizing of the federal government is possible. States would, of course, be given time to determine if they wanted the option to continue the services not authorized by the Constitution. The money saved will give them all the options.

This is our chance to unleash powerful ideas about the way government should be run (and cut) proposed by my hero Barry Goldwater—first and foremost, the idea that dramatic tax cuts *must* be accompanied by dramatic spending cuts to be effective and successful. And the spending cuts must come *first*.

This proposal on dramatically starving the federal government will be followed by a second chapter with a proposal to eliminate federal income taxes forever more. It is a one-two punch to the very gut of all proponents of big government and their "tax and spend" philosophy. The goal of this small businessman and citizen politician is to lead a revolution to starve the federal government back to its proper Constitutional size—and, most importantly, to give the power (and the money) back to the people (and taxpayers) of the United States of America to spend as they deem fit.

■ ■ ■

Rather than just rant or talk about spending cuts, let me give you some concrete examples. Previous fiscally conservative presidents have *talked* about eliminating the Department of Education; this Libertarian president would refuse to sign the checks that keep the department open. It is time for states to take over the education of our children—just as the Constitution intended. The word "education" is never mentioned in the Constitution because it was never intended as a responsibility of the federal government. Besides, look at the fine job they've done. It's obvious that taxpayers are wasting our $70 billion per year or so that is currently being spent at the federal level on education. States have enough bureaucracy in education as it is. If they want more bureaucrats, then the billions saved by eliminating the Department of Education at the federal level can surely provide it.

All unfunded federal mandates would disappear in a Root administration. My goal would be to get back to basics—in the classroom, and in the government. Education funding and decisions should be made at the state and local level, where the concerns of parents, children, taxpayers, and teachers could be heard loudly and clearly. Perhaps the fine teachers in our schools could finally get back to teaching again. And those teachers who produce tangible results should receive performance-based bonuses or pay increases. I'm not in any way against public schoolteachers. I just want the education system to be run like a business—parents should have the freedom to choose (school choice), competition for our public schools should be encouraged, and teachers should be paid based on performance. But education is just one example. Many of the useless and unauthorized departments of government would serve as the rest of my example.

When this Libertarian president is done, a whole alphabet soup of governmental agencies in violation of the Constitution will die for lack of funding. Imagine a federal government where there is no:

- Advisory Council on Historic Preservation
- African Development Foundation
- Agency for International Development
- American Battle Monuments Commission
- Amtrak
- Appalachian Regional Commission

- Architectural and Transportation Barriers Compliance Board
- Bureau of Alcohol, Tobacco, Firearms and Explosives
- Bureau of Arms Control
- Bureau of Labor Statistics
- Bureau of Transportation Statistics
- Chemical Safety and Hazard Investigations Board
- Commission on Civil Rights
- Consumer Product Safety Commission
- Corporation for National Service
- Drug Enforcement Administration
- Equal Employment Opportunity Commission
- Export-Import Bank of the United States
- Farm Credit Administration
- Federal Accounting Standards Advisory Board
- Federal Communications Commission (FCC)
- Federal Election Commission (FEC)
- Federal Energy Regulatory Commission
- Federal Highway Administration
- Federal Housing Finance Board
- Federal Labor Relations Authority
- Federal Maritime Commission
- Federal Mediation and Conciliation Service
- Federal Mine Safety and Health Review Commission
- Federal Railroad Administration
- Federal Reserve System (the Fed)
- Federal Retirement Thrift Investment Board
- Ginnie Mae
- Institute of Museum and Library Services
- Inter-American Development Bank
- Inter-American Foundation
- International Bank for Reconstruction & Development
- International Labor Organization
- International Monetary Fund
- International Trade Commission
- Legal Services Corporation
- National Aeronautics and Space Administration
- National Archives and Records Administration

- National Bioethics Advisory Commission
- National Capital Planning Commission
- National Commission on Libraries and Information Science
- National Credit Union Administration
- National Endowment for the Arts
- National Endowment for the Humanities
- National Highway Traffic Safety Administration
- National Institute of Mental Health
- National Labor Relations Board
- National Mediation Board
- National Oceanic and Atmospheric Administration
- National Park Service
- National Science Foundation (NSF)
- National Skill Standards Board
- National Technology Transfer Center (NTTC)
- National Telecommunications Information Administration
- Neighborhood Reinvestment Corporation
- Occupational Safety and Health Review Commission
- Office of Federal Housing Enterprise Oversight
- Office of Thrift Supervision
- Organization for Economic Cooperation and Development
- Organization of American States
- Overseas Private Investment Corp.
- Pan American Health Organization
- Railroad Retirement Board (RRB)
- Selective Service System (SSS)
- Substance Abuse and Mental Health Services Administration
- Surface Transportation Board
- Tennessee Valley Authority
- Trade and Development Agency
- U.S. Fish and Wildlife Service
- U.S. Institute of Peace
- U.S. Office of Government Ethics—*Has this agency ever been used?*
- United Nations Information Center
- Voice of America (VOA)
- White House Fellows
- White House Commission on Remembrance
- Women's History Commission

And this list is just scratching the surface. Let's call it a good start. A more complete list would be too long to read. This list does not mean that the government would be completely out of our lives, or that all of these services would no longer be provided to the citizens. It does mean that all of these programs and services would be cancelled at the federal level. Almost every task that is currently performed at the federal level can be pushed back to the states—assuming any state believes it is actually needed. As we said, rapid, responsible, and intelligent transitions will be the order of the day.

Would we be able to close (or defund) every single agency or department above? Perhaps not. But it sure would be fun to try. A Libertarian Root administration would take the Presidential Oath of Office to heart and seriously cut back the size of government in a way that has never been imagined in modern times. If it is not authorized by the Constitution, it will not be funded by this Libertarian president. No unconstitutional program will be left untouched.

When we are done, the U.S. government will be so small that it will be a one-line listing in the white pages of your local telephone directory.

The intent of this chapter and this book is to present a vision of a bold Libertarian future, where the United States is restored once again to its constitutional tradition of limited government, peace, and freedom; a vision where future generations will read and recite how a Libertarian president brought individual rights and economic and personal freedom back to our land. Our Founding Fathers will finally rest in peace. Big and bigger, dumb and dumber will finally be transformed to smaller and smarter.

Chapter 16

Eliminating Federal Taxes and the IRS

The hardest thing in the world to understand is the income tax.
—ALBERT EINSTEIN

O nce we cut spending and the size of government, the next obvious step is to give the savings back to the people paying the bills—the U.S. taxpayer. There are many ways to dramatically cut taxes: a flat tax, a national sales tax (called the FairTax), the elimination of capital gains taxes for those over the age of 55 (discussed in another chapter), the elimination of death taxes (double taxation), or a one-year "income tax vacation" (the best stimulus plan of all). These are all ideas worth exploring.

I am open to any idea that cuts the tax burdens on U.S. citizens—at least the ones actually paying taxes in the first place. As mentioned previously, I'm not a fan of giving those who don't pay taxes a welfare check each year called an "earned income credit" and then calling it a tax cut.

But here's a radically simple idea for eliminating federal taxes and the IRS in one foul swoop. Dream with me for a few minutes. This is going to leave you in a relaxed and giddy state.

Imagine a country where businesses and individuals no longer need to account to the government for their income. Imagine a country where we can be free from the Internal Revenue Service. Imagine in one instant eliminating individual federal income taxes, corporate federal income taxes, payroll taxes, death taxes, the marriage penalty, excise taxes, and even the dreaded AMT (Alternative Minimum Tax)—all of it at once, gone forever.

No, this is not a dream. It can be a reality in a Libertarian Root Administration.

■ ■ ■

My economic brain trust (called "Team ROOT") has crafted an alternative approach that we believe will be attractive to the United States, consistent with our Constitution (isn't that a refreshing surprise), and right in line with our Founding Father's ideals. Our plan completely rids the United States of federal income taxes and the IRS, while at the same time restoring power to the people at the state and local level— just as our Founding Fathers intended.

We propose eliminating the income tax and all other sources of federal tax revenues, including payroll taxes (FICA), excise taxes, and import duties, and replacing it with only one tax: a tax on each state in proportion to its population, with each state deciding for itself how to raise its share of the money.

Not only would this eliminate taxes on income by the federal government, and end the IRS forever, it would likely reduce or eliminate taxation on income in virtually all states in this country. Most states calculate their own income taxes starting with the taxpayer's calculation of federal taxable income. It would be too costly for most states to enact their own income tax systems without being able to leverage the current system of W2s and 1099 filings.

To further reduce the likelihood of even some states imposing income taxes on their residents, if elected I would ask Congress to introduce legislation to update Public Law 86–272 to prohibit states from taxing the business activity of any person or enterprise engaging in interstate commerce, and define this broadly enough to include even the solicitation of customers in more than one state.

Our Founding Fathers understood the power of the purse as an instrument of tyranny. Today, because the U.S. government taxes its citizens and then kicks back a portion of the money to the states (as it sees fit), the federal government exercises enormous unconstitutional power against the states through various federal mandates, ranging from No Child Left Behind to Real ID. Today's regime of personal income taxation facilitates this mockery of our system of federalism. Thomas Jefferson is surely rolling over in his grave.

Our vision for dramatic change in U.S. tax policy is as simple as it is revolutionary in scope. With our plan there will be only 50 taxpayers in our country writing checks to the U.S. Treasury each year (the 50 states). With no other source of revenue to the U.S. government, the balance of power would be forever dramatically reversed back to the states (just as our Founding Fathers envisioned).

Moreover, because these 50 states (and their taxpayers) will have a bias toward keeping tax dollars at home instead of sending them to Washington, they will have great incentive to mount enormous political pressure against Congress to reduce the size of the federal government—thereby reducing the money these 50 states would be required to send to Washington, DC.

Some of the unnecessary and wasteful federal spending first on the chopping block for this president (a perfect metaphor for the son of a butcher) is welfare, entitlements of all kinds including corporate welfare, dramatic cuts in foreign aid, a dramatic reduction in military bases across the globe, and dramatic cuts in wasteful pentagon spending. It's high time to stop spending billions of our tax dollars to defend wealthy allies such as Japan, South Korea, and Western Europe. Let's politely but forcefully ask them to pay for their own national defense (just as we do) from this day forward. It's bad enough that our federal government gives welfare to individuals and corporations, why choose to give welfare to other countries?

It's time to defund and eliminate entire government departments and bureaucracies—starting with the Department of Education (as mentioned in the earlier chapter on impoundment). The first step toward improving our education system (and saving our tax dollars) is to keep the money at the state and local level, giving less power to the federal government and teachers unions, and more power, freedom, and choice to parents.

Under this plan, if Congress chooses not to reign in out-of-control federal spending, it runs the risk that states respond by withholding taxes from the federal government, which is the ultimate "check and balance." This plan reverses the balance of power—instead of the federal government threatening to withhold highway funds if states don't enforce federal mandates, suddenly it is the other way around. Guess who suddenly has all the power? The states.

Power is restored to the states, just as Thomas Jefferson envisioned when he authored the Declaration of Independence. Jefferson declared that the primary responsibility of the President of United States was "to render ineffective and invisible the very government he is elected to lead." Jefferson and the Founding Fathers intended for taxes to be minimal and up to each state to decide. Jefferson said of taxes, "Government shall not take from the mouth of labor the bread it has earned." Jefferson believed taxes were completely up to the discretion of individual states when he said, "The true theory of our constitution is that states are independent as to everything within themselves. . . . " and even went so far as to recognize the right of states to nullify federal laws within their own borders, describing federal intrusion into state matters as "interference by a foreign government."

Our Founding Father Thomas Jefferson would certainly approve of this plan to switch the power of taxation and spending decisions from the federal to the state level.

With this one sweeping change, devolving power from Washington to the states, tax and regulatory policy at the state level instantly takes on greater importance. In this environment, competition among the states for business and residents likely becomes fierce. States that choose to impose high taxes, or forms of taxation unpopular with their residents (income taxes) are punished with losses in population. States that create an environment of low taxation and fair forms of taxation are rewarded with population gains. The point of this plan is to create competition among the 50 states for the lowest taxes and lowest spending. This idea of competition is nothing more than taking the guiding principle of capitalism (competition among companies keeps prices low) and apply-ing it to government.

Taxpayers are better able to monitor how their money was being spent up close and personal at the state and local level. A major shift of all taxation (and most spending) from the distant and draconian federal level to the state level is positive for the U.S. taxpayer. I believe this arrangement is exactly what our Founding Fathers intended—more power at the state and local level, less power at the federal level, and taxation determined by each individual state. This plan respects our Constitution, expands your personal freedom, restores power to the people (and taxpayers), and increases the money you keep in your wal-let. The impoundment spending plan from the previous chapter com-bined with this tax plan is the centerpiece of my campaign to restore federalism, returning power from Washington back to the states and to the people. Thomas Jefferson would be proud.

Later in this book, just in case these ideas are too big a first step for the United States, you can find chapters with smaller, more doable ideas for cutting spending and taxes. You see I am a reasonable guy. I accept either big tax cuts, or (if I have to) smaller cuts to start (to prove to the people that my ideas work). I accept either big spending cuts, or (if I have to) smaller cuts to start (and prove to the people that my ideas work). The only things that I won't accept are spending increases and tax increases.

Chapter 17

Eradicating Capital Gains

Why Do Liberal Politicians Want to Keep Older Americans Working Forever?

A government which robs Peter to pay Paul can always depend on the support of Paul.

—GEORGE BERNARD SHAW

I n keeping with our proposal to cut spending and the size of government, and give savings back to the people, the next solution is to eliminate taxes on capital gains.

I am so fed up with the liberal lies and distortions about capital gains and "giveaways to the rich." Democratic presidential contenders in the 2008 election were jumping over each other to announce new tax increases for "the rich." They said it as if being "rich" was a dirty word. As if being rich is something U.S. citizens deserve to be *punished* for. We all know that certain words are off limits—curse words, ethnic slurs, derogatory stereotypes, and so on. Maybe it's time to declare the "R Word" a slur and declare it off-limits. Maybe we should replace that dirty, negative, demeaning word "rich" with more positive terms like successful, high-achiever, self-made risk-taker, or "All-American role model." Now you can clearly see how important wording is. The masses (who incidentally pay few if any federal taxes) support taxing the rich. But few people would rush to support "punishing successful high-achievers." No one wants to "punish All-American role models." It's all in the wording and presentation. You may hate and envy the rich, but we all aspire to become successful. Even if it's too late for us, we all aspire for our children or grandchildren to become successful. How many parents would support punishing their successful children and grandchildren for the crime of being successful? Not too many.

Liberals use negative wording to try to pit the classes against one another to stir up anger, jealousy, envy, resentment—and most of all *votes*. That's how Democrats get elected—by dividing U.S. citizens by income, class, or race. And what's their number one whipping boy? *Capital gains*. Every Democratic Nanny State politician you meet wants to raise taxes on capital gains. Why? Once again, it's all in the wording. Liberals position capital gains as "dirty" and negative. This is money that rich people use to get richer. Can you imagine? How evil! "We can't allow this" the liberals cry, whine, and protest. "These are people that aren't even working with their hands. There is no blood, sweat or tears when people 'invest' instead of work for a living," the liberals whine. "We must tax them *double* for the crime of investing in America."

Worse, they say, is the fact that capital gains are taxed at a lower rate than your income. *Gasp*. "We cannot allow this," liberals cry, whine, and protest. They position it this way so that poor people, blue-collar workers, union members, and lower middle-class citizens will all grow to hate rich people—but most of all, they'll grow to hate the *investments* of rich people. "How dare rich people invest in homes, stocks, and small businesses, while I barely have enough money for food and rent. It isn't fair. And worst of all, the rich get taxed lower on their passive million dollar investment returns, than I do on my $700 weekly paycheck for working 40 hours a week." What a powerful (and effective) sound bite. But it's also a complete distortion of the facts. I call it *the big liberal lie*.

■ ■ ■

Here are the facts. Anything invested in what's called "capital gains" has already *been* taxed. To tax it again is *double taxation*. When I buy a home, stocks, bonds, or invest in a new business, I'm taking gigantic risks with my savings. Obviously the great stock and real estate crashes of 2008 prove my point that any monies you invest are a risk. Those who invested $150,000 in stocks like Las Vegas Sands at $150 per share, will certainly agree with me (as I write this chapter Las Vegas Sands stock is trading at $2 per share). Your $150,000 is now worth about $2,000. Those who bought homes in Las Vegas just a few years ago for $600,000, now own $200,000 homes. These homeowners understand the idea of risk. Every time you invest, you are risking losing your hard-earned money. What is my motivation for risking my precious and hard-earned savings on homes, commercial properties, stocks, or bonds that could go down dramatically in value? Worse, as evidenced by the market plunge in the fall of 2008, they could actually go to zero. If my capital gains tax rate for investing in the United States isn't low, I'm better off putting my money in the bank, or hiding it in the mattress.

But here's the problem that our liberally run government doesn't understand—the United States needs your money and mine to grow. Publicly traded companies need us to invest in them in order to raise money, to expand their businesses, and to create more jobs. If we stop investing or risking, there are no new jobs for our children. And of course this Great Depression II that started in 2008 proves the importance of real estate to the U.S. economy. Homes are the lifeblood of the economy. When they fall in value, the U.S. economy falls too. So, in fact, we need to encourage people to invest in the United States. Lower capital gains tax rates are what motivate investors to risk their money.

Please keep in mind that I'm taking these risks with money I've *already* paid taxes on. We all pay income taxes. The rich—those terrible people who so many people seem to hate and envy—already pay 80 percent (or more) of U.S. income taxes. They are only able to invest in real estate, stocks, bonds, and businesses with the money they have left *after* paying high income tax rates. What's wrong with that?

What our liberal Democratic friends aren't telling us is that the only way out of poverty in the United States (or anywhere in the world) is through investment . . . is through risk . . . is through capital gains. You must invest (risk) your after-tax monies in something that will produce profit while you sleep. Why would you have to be punished for that? Why would government want to discourage people from investing in the United States? Why would liberal politicians want their voters to ignore the only opportunity they have for upward mobility? Could it be because keeping voters poor, hopeless, helpless, clueless, ignorant, and angry at the rich also keeps those same voters dependent on government (and Democratic politicians)? *Now when you think of it that way, perhaps it's not the rich capitalists that are the evil ones.*

Capital gains are the only ticket out of poverty. Capital gains are the only ticket to success and upward mobility. You must find a way to get your money to work for you while you sleep—to earn interest and appreciation 24 hours a day while you're working, playing, eating, shopping, and sleeping. There has been only one proven way out of poverty since the day that the United States was founded—investment into real estate, stocks, and small business. You must invest your after-tax money to succeed, to save, to build success and wealth, to beat inflation, to pay for your children's college education, to pay your taxes and have anything left for retirement. *Is that bad?*

Shouldn't we strive to encourage investment of after-tax savings to create generations of productive, upwardly mobile people? Why do we want to discourage that? Punish that? All this investment is good for the United States. Turn off the faucet and slow (or stop) investment by raising capital gains taxes (so the risk is no longer worth it) and stocks plunge, real estate collapses, business stagnates, and jobs are lost by the millions.

What do you get when you turn off that faucet? Cuba. Before Fidel Castro, Cuba was a prosperous country. A huge class of professionals and business owners lived a wonderful life. Then Castro decided that capitalism was bad and socialism was good for the people. Now the country is frozen in time. Homes, cars, roads, government buildings—they are all dilapidated and broken down, frozen in time because without motivation, no one has invested in anything since 1959 (the year of Castro's revolution). Without incentive (low taxes and even lower capital gains taxes) no one builds anything. Why risk your money if the return is limited by the socialist state? So now people deliver supplies in Cuba via donkey pulling a wagon. The rich drive automobiles from 1959. Cuba is the country that time forgot. Liberals whine all day about "fairness." Life is completely fair in communist or socialist countries. In liberal utopias like that, taxes are so high that *everyone* lives in poverty and misery.

Everyone lives in broken-down shacks, drives cars from 1959, buys groceries in ramshackle supermarkets with bare shelves, and rations health care. Isn't fairness grand? That's what happens when liberal economic ideas are taken seriously.

The United States is the richest nation in the world because we encourage risk, we reward investment, we honor wealth. Or at least we did until the latter stages of the Bush presidency and the start of the Obama presidency. Now all of that is in doubt as we move toward either pure socialism (at worst) or European social capitalism (at best). But I'm betting that four years under Obama and his high tax-and-spend philosophy will snap our country back to sanity. At that point, I'll be waiting.

In the meantime, allow me to remind you of why capitalism works. Thank God for low tax rates that motivate citizens to risk their savings by investing in IBM, Microsoft, Exxon, and McDonald's. That willingness to risk our life savings in real estate, stocks, and business is what has created the greatest economy in world history. That is why we have created more small businesses, more jobs, more home ownership, and more self-made millionaires than anywhere else in the world. That's why a negative, unappreciative, liberal slug like Michael Moore is able to make $100 million by creating films that attack, demean, and denigrate his own country (and capitalism).

Can you imagine? Michael Moore is the greatest example of our country's greatness. In Cuba you can support your government and your reward is a lifetime of rationing, sacrificing, misery, and poverty. In the United States you can demean and denigrate everything this great country stands for and yet you are rewarded with a fancy mansion in Beverly Hills, daily massages, and vacations at Four Seasons Resorts. And, of course, the bonus is the undying admiration of bleeding-heart, limousine-liberal, Hollywood hypocrites. What a great country! We should thank Michael Moore for proving why the United States and capitalism are great.

■ ■ ■

But I digress. Back to capital gains taxes. Liberal ideas are so foolish, ignorant, and naïve. The current administration wants to raise capital gains tax rates. They position it as punishing the rich. I see it very differently—they are punishing all older citizens. They are making life miserable for those 55 and older. They are making college unaffordable for the children and grandchildren of millions of overtaxed Americans. They are making retirement impossible, or at best, postponing it for an entire generation of 55 year olds. They are ruining the golden years for those older Americans already out of the rat race. Higher taxes on passive investments (capital gains, dividends, interest) are an unmitigated *disaster* for anyone nearing retirement or already retired. *In reality we should be eliminating capital gains taxes altogether.*

I propose the elimination of capital gains taxes for all U.S. citizens 55 and older. That would mean that Americans could retire with far lower taxes, far lower burdens, far lower stress, and a far lower "monthly nut." Why should we not reward older people for a lifetime of hard work and sacrifice? After working a lifetime—often working ourselves to death—why shouldn't the reward be lower taxes—which creates extra money for peace of mind, golf, vacations, restaurants, or paying for our grandkid's college educations. All of this spending (with the extra money you keep from lower tax rates) is what makes the economy go and grow. Let's stop punishing people for saving (and slaving) their whole lives. Let's reward them with lower taxes so they can retire early, or retire with peace of mind.

Elimination of taxes on capital gains, interest, and dividends for citizens 55 and older would encourage all of us to work hard, save, invest, and look forward to retirement. It would boost the entire U.S. economy. It would eventually trickle down to all of us—in the form of a robust stock market, thriving real estate market, more investment in small business, which translates to more jobs, more economic prosperity, and, of course, upon our death more money for our children, grandchildren, and charity. What an economic boom. What a win/win for everyone.

A little author's note here—aimed at those of you who would argue that I attacked government employee union members for retiring at 55 years old, yet now I'm encouraging people to retire earlier by lowering capital gains taxes. My argument with government employees is that they are retiring early on my dime (taxpayer money). But this is a free country. I encourage anyone who can afford to do it after a lifetime of hard work and building a career or business, to retire whenever their heart desires. We should all be free to retire at age 36 if we want—if we've earned enough money to do it *without* taxpayer help. In a free market society, everyone is free to retire whenever they want. You just have no right to ask government or the taxpayers to help you do it.

And my wanting to give people 55 and older tax-free income on investments is perfectly fair and logical—that's the money they have left over after a lifetime of hard work and paying taxes. Why not encourage them to invest it tax-free into the United States. That benefits all of us—young and old. It creates jobs and sells homes that otherwise might fall into foreclosure.

Instead of the biased liberal media always asking out loud if the rich are "greedy," perhaps they could ask some questions of the left-wing tax-and-spend crowd? Here are four important questions I'd like to see asked of Obama and the current liberal administration:

1. Are liberals *against* older people?
2. Do they think older Americans should pay higher taxes that force them into miserable golden years?
3. Or do liberals want to force older people to *never* retire?
4. Are liberals against older people enjoying life?

They must be. Why else would they support older U.S. citizens paying more taxes on dividends, interest, investments, and capital gains? Passive investments are what older people live on after retirement. Remember, they no longer have a job. Eliminate capital gains taxes and instantly, older Americans could retire on *half* the income. What a wonderful gift to the people who have worked and sacrificed and slaved to create a better life for themselves and their children.

Anyone 55 or older would have to be crazy to vote for any liberal Democratic politician. After all, these politicians want to punish you, tax you to death (literally), and force you to work until the day you die. They don't want you to play golf, or take a cruise, or eat out at a nice restaurant with your own hard-earned money. They think your money belongs to government. After you work, toil, and pay high taxes your whole life—liberals want to raise tax rates on the money you have left. They support *double taxation* on your capital gains. Then after you die, they support "death taxes" on whatever you've left behind. Is this the future that most older people embrace? Maybe the media should be asking these questions of liberal politicians.

It's time for a new way to think about taxes. High tax rates are about slavery. They make you work harder, work longer, work forever—all for the government. We need to change the conversation about money in this country. It's *your* money. It's *your* property. You deserve to enjoy the fruits of your labor. Liberals are lying, distorting, and scheming to steal more of your hard-earned money, to force you to work more hours to pay for their big government spending, to force you to postpone or eliminate retirement.

Why do liberals want to spend ever-higher amounts of your money? So they can buy the votes of people too ignorant to understand that the very policies they are voting for are keeping them poor, helpless, hopeless, aimless, and clueless. Let's work together to stop them.

Chapter 18

Destroying the Fed
Before the Fed
Destroys Us

*Little by little, business is enlarged with easy money. With the ex-
haustless reservoir of the government of the United States furnishing
easy money, the sales increase, the businesses enlarge, more new enter-
prises are started, the spirit of optimism pervades the community . . .
bankers are not free from it. They are human. The members of the
Federal Reserve board will not be free from it. They are human . . .
Everyone is making money. Everyone is growing rich. It goes up and
up . . . until finally someone whose judgment was bad, someone
whose capacity for business was small, breaks; and as he falls he hits
the next brick in the row, and then another, and then another, and
down comes the whole structure. That is no dream. That is the history
of every movement of inflation since the world's business began, and
it is the history of many a period in our own country. That is what
happened to a greater or less degree before the panic of 1837, of
1857, of 1873, of 1893 and of 1907 . . . when credit exceeds the
legitimate demands of the country, the currency becomes suspected and
gold leaves the country.*

—A POLITICIAN NAMED ROOT

Remember back in Chapter 1 when I attempted to prove through the words of my hero Barry Goldwater that nothing in politics ever really changes. His words back in 1959 could easily be used today to describe virtually all of our country's problems—and few would even notice that Goldwater's words were spoken a half century ago. If only we had listened back then.

Well, the quote above by a certain politician named Root certainly describes the economic crisis of 2008 to a T: the bailout, the bankers' mistakes, the stock market collapse, the credit freeze, and the reaction of the Federal Reserve. But they aren't my words. And they weren't spoken about the government banking crisis and bailout of 2008. Yes, they were the words of a politician named Root. Just not *this* Root. Those words were actually spoken in 1913 by Elihu Root, U.S. Senator from the state of New York. That distinguished politician named Root went on to become Secretary of War and Secretary of State under President Teddy Roosevelt. Despite being almost a century old, those words almost perfectly describe our current economic crisis. Once again, proving that nothing ever really changes. History repeats itself again and again—it's just a recycling of the same events and same mistakes. Only those who study history can hope to avoid making those same mistakes over and over again. As a former member of the 2008 Libertarian presidential ticket who speaks across the country about economic issues, I am constantly asked, "How would you solve our current economic crisis?" I've already explained how I'd dramatically cut spending and taxes. I've explained the greatest threats to our economic prosperity—big government, big unions, and big taxes. More specifically, the union threat comes from teachers unions, autoworkers unions, lawyer unions (known as the Bar Association), and perhaps the most damaging of all, government employee unions. Later in this book, I describe the threat to our economy from proponents of global warming. Now I present to you another important piece of the puzzle: The elimination of the Federal Reserve (the Fed).

■ ■ ■

I have come to understand that we must destroy this cancer on our economy before the Fed destroys us. And in concert with the elimination of the Fed, we must go back to the gold standard. Is this a new solution? No, my namesake Elihu Root had the same advice back in

1913 when arguing against the formation of a central bank. If only we had listened to a politician named Root back then, just as we should have listened to Barry Goldwater back in 1959.

"Eliminate the Fed? Are you crazy?" I can hear the naysayers now. But the Federal Reserve isn't the solution. Like big government (of which they are a tool), the Fed is the *problem*. Virtually every economic downturn since 1913, when the Fed was created, can be traced to Fed policies. Lest we forget, the Fed was around in 1929 when the stock market crashed. They were around for the Great Depression—actually they were right smack dab in the middle of the worst economic mess in U.S. history. Their policies helped to turn a deep recession into the Great Depression. Even if you're a Fed defender, and don't agree that they were a contributor to the Great Depression, you certainly have to admit that the Fed didn't prevent or solve the deepest economic crisis in U.S. history. Nor did they see it coming. But then they never saw the financial tsunami of 2008 coming either.

As recently as last April 2, 2008, the Fed didn't even know we were in a recession. Back then, Federal Reserve Chairman Ben Bernanke testified before a joint Congressional committee where he said, "A recession is *possible*." He described the economy back then as in "slight contraction." In response to those remarks, I wrote a political commentary. My shocked and angry response was to ask, "Are the Feds cooking the books?" That's how certain I was as a small business owner that we had already been in a deep recession for months. I believed Bernanke's statement to be so ignorant, naïve, and just plain dangerous, as to indicate he was either purposely lying to the U.S. public or hopelessly out of touch.

How is it possible that a small businessman like me clearly understood how bad things were in the U.S. economy way back in April 2008, while our Fed Chairman was completely in the dark (or in denial)? The answer is simple—While I live on Main Street, the Fed lives in an "Ivory Tower" and hasn't a clue what's happening in the real world, until *after* it happens.

The Fed doesn't run a business. The Fed simply *reads* about business. They study reams of economic statistics, thereby deducing we have a problem long after guys and gals like me with a dozen, or a few dozen employees, have already experienced it. Small businesspeople are the "canary in the coal mine." Little ol' me knew there was a huge economic crisis going on, when the big, bad, powerful Fed still didn't have a clue. *How scary is that?* These are the geniuses running the entire U.S. economy. Worse, Bernanke is widely considered one of the world's experts on the Great Depression. This is a man who once served on a panel of experts that determine when recessions begin and end. Yet it turns out he doesn't know his front from his end. It is obvious that if you want to know whether we're in a recession or not, you're better off asking the butcher, baker, or candlestick maker. Or in this case, the butcher's son.

■ ■ ■

By the way, in that same political commentary, I reported that the economy for small businesspeople like me was so bad that we were not only already in a recession, but facing the deepest recession since 1929—possibly a second great depression. It turns out that my prediction is far more accurate than anything that came from the lips of Ben Bernanke, or anyone in the Fed in the spring of 2008. Perhaps we need to put a small businessperson in charge of the Fed. Or better yet, eliminate it altogether.

■ ■ ■

The Fed's strategy is simple: The Fed floods the economy with "easy money" by either artificially lowering interest rates or printing more money. That creates an artificial economic boom to help politicians to get elected or reelected. Invariably this artificial economic boom is followed by a very real "economic bust." Recent examples of this artificial bubble bursting can be seen in the dot.com (technology and computer) world implosion in 2000, and again when the banking, credit, and real estate markets collapsed in 2008. Do you notice a pattern there?

If it's so easy to see the mistake, why does the Fed continue to pursue a failed strategy? Good question. The answer is simple: political pressure from fat cats (big contributors like banks, Wall Street, real estate firms), special interests (big contributors), and voters who demand prosperity, easy money, low interest rates, and entitlements from big government. Someone has to pay for all these giveaways, handouts, goodies, corporate welfare, bailouts, stimulus packages, and entitlement Ponzi schemes. The Fed makes it all possible by printing up new money to pay for it all. Without the Fed printing presses working overtime, politicians couldn't make promises to pay for every program under the stars. They certainly couldn't afford to pay for all those promises.

But nothing in the Constitution gives Congress the authority to give control of monetary policy to a central bank. *Nothing.* That same U.S. Constitution demands that our U.S. currency be backed by stable commodities—such as gold or silver. The gold standard is a very simple concept: paper notes (our currency) are simply set at a fixed value, by matching them to preset fixed quantities of gold.

The return to the gold standard is (excuse the pun) the gold standard for a stable, credible, reliable money supply, and a true free market economy. Why don't politicians want to set our currency to the gold standard? Simply because the gold standard stands in the way of the goals of big government proponents and their endless spending programs. The gold standard prevents politicians from inflating the money supply to hide the actual costs of the welfare state—from welfare itself, to corporate welfare, bailouts, handouts, entitlements, stimulus packages, and wars across the globe. A billion here, and a billion there, and eventually this stuff starts to add up to serious money! That's exactly what politicians fear.

I spend a lot of time attacking Democrats (because it's so easy to do), but in reality it seems it's always Republicans who abandon their principles and make the big mistakes (opening the door to liberalism and socialism). In 1971 it was Republican President Richard Nixon who totally removed the dollar's link to gold. This final death blow to "real" U.S. money created the fiat currency (paper notes) that we all use today. With this decision, the Fed could now print unlimited amounts of inherently worthless paper dollars, and, in their eyes, were immune from any (immediate) consequences. Why did Nixon do it? To hide his out-of-control government spending on the Vietnam War. Bombs, bombers, and tanks cost big money. Governments can't afford them, unless the Fed covers the actions (and tails) of big spending politicians by creating more money out of thin air.

Needless to say, since 1971 inflation and the CPI have *soared* and the savings of hardworking U.S. citizens have been subtly robbed to fund our welfare system that exists today. Unlike the deflationary early 1930s, when the United States was on a gold standard and hence couldn't print unlimited dollars, today the United States has no standards at all (excuse the pun). The Fed can and does print (or create via computer) as many dollars as it wants and the money supply growth has vastly outstripped underlying real economic growth since 1971. Wall Street fraudster Bernard Madoff has nothing on the U.S. government. Our government runs the biggest Ponzi scheme on earth.

■ ■ ■

What a great contrast between traditional politicians—Republicans and Democrats—and Libertarian politicians. Traditional politicians despise the gold standard because it threatens their agenda, and threatens their power grab. It threatens to limit their imaginations (and reelections). It ruins their party. It keeps their greed in check. With a gold standard in place there is no ability for a central bank to create money out of thin air to fund any and every pet project or earmark. The gold standard forces politicians to live within their means. It forces banks to lend only to those with the credit to afford it, because the federal government is prevented from printing unlimited new money to bail them out.

Libertarians like me (and the great Ron Paul) love the gold standard for those very reasons. We want not only the size of government, but also the imaginations of politicians *limited*. The gold standard is a Libertarian's dream precisely because:

- It prevents deficit spending.
- It prevents the unlimited hiring of government bureaucrats—and the unfunded pension liabilities that come with them.
- It hinders government's ability to dole out massive welfare and entitlement programs, and, consequently, stands in the way of government's ability to redistribute wealth and pursue economic reengineering.

With the gold standard in place, government automatically becomes more open, honest, and transparent—it either lives within its means or raises taxes, as opposed to simply printing more money (creating a *stealth* tax called inflation).

Instantly, with the gold standard in place, government is more responsible and accountable to the people and the taxpayers. Inflation caused by the wholesale printing of money by the Fed is theft—government-sanctioned white-collar crime. Because of the wholesale printing of money by the Fed, taxpayers and citizens lose the value in their savings accounts and assets without knowing how or why.

Under the gold standard, money regulates itself. The gold standard regulates government by keeping spending under control. The gold standard regulates the behavior of banks (limiting their lending to qualified borrowers). The gold standard regulates savings—citizens are automatically incentivized to save more if their money is actually worth something. Why save $1 today, if that same $1 is worth 30 percent less tomorrow due to the Fed printing enormous amounts of new money?

The gold standard regulates interest rates, which suddenly reflect real supply and demand for credit, not numbers artificially created out of thin air to reflect political needs. The gold standard regulates business, as CEOs must base their business decisions on sound policy (knowing government or the Fed won't be there to bail them out).

Elihu Root realized all this back in 1913. It's a shame we didn't listen. Please study history and explain to me where the elder Mr. Root was wrong? Explain to me what exactly the Fed has accomplished in the almost 100 years since then? How have those results been an improvement in performance over the economic results the U.S. economy achieved under the gold standard?

If you don't believe this Root, or that other politician named Root, just listen to the words of Thomas Jefferson, the Founding Father who wrote our Declaration of Independence:

> I believe that banking institutions are more dangerous to our liberties than standing armies. If the American people ever allow private banks to control the issue of their currency, first by inflation, then by deflation, the banks and corporations that will grow up around the banks will deprive the people of all property until their children wake-up homeless on the continent their fathers conquered.

Ask yourself the most important question of all: With record-setting budget deficits under former President Bush, trillion dollar bailout packages under former President Bush, even bigger trillion dollar bailout programs under President Obama, even bigger trillion dollar stimulus packages under President Obama, record-setting handouts, entitlements, and redistribution of wealth under President Obama (due to higher taxes), record-setting national debt under President Obama, and the Fed printing presses working overtime to create unlimited quantities of depreciating dollars (to cover up all this lavish spending), why would anyone want to own the dollar? Why indeed. We are in for a rough ride.

Once again, my intent is to show that I am not your typical politician. I do more than complain. I provide practical and commonsense solutions. The antidote to corrupt, selfish, and irresponsible politicians addicted to recklessly spending our taxpayer money is simple: Eliminate the Federal Reserve and restore the gold standard.

To put it bluntly, destroy the Fed before the Fed destroys us.

Chapter 19

Term Limits

Stopping the Insanity

The nine worst words in the English language are: "I'm from the government and I'm here to help."

—RONALD REAGAN

Another solution to the insanity, stupidity, and arrogance of politicians is so simple: term limits. We are governed by modern-day versions of kings and queens, otherwise known as career politicians. And it's not just kings and queens that rule U.S. citizens—but family dynasties handed down to princes and princesses. Our commander in chief was named either Clinton or Bush for 20 consecutive years. We almost extended that streak to 28 years with Hillary Clinton. Instead we elected Obama, and he immediately turned around and named Hillary Clinton Secretary of State.

But far worse than the arrogance and sense of entitlement by political dynasties with names like Kennedy, Cuomo, Bush, or Clinton, is the arrogance, greed, and alleged corruption of politicians like Illinois Governor Rod Blagojevich. The media has made Blago into a monster (and a household name). He has come to symbolize everything wrong with politics. But there are Blagos all across this country, at all levels of political office. They are career politicians with a talent for raising money, twisting arms, doing favors, and winning elections. We should not be naïve enough to believe that Blago was the first politician to allegedly try to sell a political office, or the last. We should not believe he was the first politician to allegedly expect a favor in return for a political appointment. It happens every day, although usually in more subtle fashion (and not on federal wiretap). Politicians like Blago prove the old adage that "Power corrupts, and absolute power corrupts absolutely."

But how does a politician become absolutely powerful, arrogant, and corrupted? By gaining power and then keeping it for years, in many cases decades. Doug Bandow of the Cato Institute pointed out in 1996 that there had been more turnover at the Soviet Communist Party Central Committee in previous years than in the U.S. Congress. It has only gotten *worse* since 1996. It is almost impossible for a reformer with fresh ideas to unseat an entrenched incumbent at any level of government. Having politicians like U.S. Senator Byrd in West Virginia or U.S. Senator Harry Reid in Nevada may be good for bringing home the bacon to West Virginia and Nevada, but it's absolutely terrible for the nation as a whole. Career politicians become special interest tyrants, demanding favors and federal dollars for their long list of friends and contributors—and with seniority and power gained over the years, rest assured they get whatever they want. The best example occurred as this book went to print. Senator Harry Reid made sure that billions of dollars were included in Obama's economic stimulus bill to build high-speed rail lines from Disneyland to Las Vegas. Was this good for Nevada? Only time will tell. But is it good for the United States? The answer to that question is a resounding *no!* What does it have to do with economic stimulus? Nothing. It can only be branded as waste and earmarks at the behest of the Senate Majority Leader. The goal isn't to help Nevada, as much as it is to help Senator Reid get reelected in 2010. Only term limits can bring an end to the absolute power and corruption of powerful career politicians like Harry Reid.

■ ■ ■

The current political system encourages spending and special interest favors, which in turn encourages career politicians. And, of course, having career politicians in office is exactly what encourages a bigger and more powerful federal government. It is a vicious cycle.

How does this cycle work? First, if a career politician faces a citizen politician in a race, who has the advantage? Of course, it's the lifelong DC incumbent who has all the fundraising connections, has done favors for powerful special interests, and knows all the political dirty tricks. So the small business owner turned citizen politician (like me) is at a huge disadvantage.

Second, politics as usual (without term limits) tends to attract people who want to be career politicians. It attracts people who actually admire government (and the power of government). That type of person also can't wait to use the power of government to rule the lives of others. That type of person loves to use the power of incumbency to stay in office for life. That type of person knows how to use the system to benefit special interests (so they will help him stay in office for life). That type of person expands the size of government, increases the power of his or her office, and hires more government employees—who are forced to vote for politicians who support bigger government (in order to keep their jobs and increase their compensation). Is this the kind of individual you want in control of our economic and personal decisions? Is this the kind of individual you want to have power over your life? Is this the kind of individual you want in charge of our government? Do you want this type of individual in power for *life?*

Term limits provide at least some form of reasonable check on this kind of abuse of power. They give a fighting chance to our odds of electing true reformers and citizen politicians. They give a fighting chance to achieving true reform and change. They give a fighting chance to those looking to break the power of incumbency. They give a fighting chance to the possibility of electing candidates with a diversity of backgrounds, as opposed to nothing but Kennedys, Clintons, Bushes, Cuomos, and in my adopted home state of Nevada ... Reids.

And then there are the Bloombergs of the world. Michael Bloomberg is the mayor of New York. Limited to two terms by term limit laws passed by the citizens of New York, Bloomberg had the gall to go around the people and get the New York City Council to overturn the law so he could run for a third term. Like Rudy Giuliani before him, this egomaniac actually believes he is the only man on earth capable of saving New York City from death and disaster. Giuliani (after 9/11) also flirted with the idea of overturning the term limit law to install himself as perpetual ruler of New York. But even Rudy held his ego in check and thought better of it. (Isn't it funny how New York has managed to survive just fine without Mayor Giuliani?)

But Bloomberg went a step further than Giuliani and actually overturned the law to try to get himself installed as king of New York for a third term. Even when ignored or overturned by arrogant politicians, term limits serve a purpose. Without term limits we could never understand the true heights of ego, arrogance, and ruthlessness possessed by our rulers.

■■■

Even politicians who appear to be reformers oftentimes show their true colors once elected into office. Please don't be fooled by public announcements from "reformer politicians" meant to create an image of honesty and integrity. The key word here is "image." The reality is far different. Nothing changes so long as we keep electing a political class whose entire career and life are tied to politics. As a prime example, President Obama set a "bold standard" to rid the White House of lobbyists and ties to special interests. Isn't it funny how career politicians who know their way around Washington also happen to find ways around the rules (and the truth)? Let's examine the reality of the Obama administration.

Let's start with Obama's first choice as Secretary of Health and Human Services (HHS), Tom Daschle (longtime Senate Majority Leader). No, Daschle wasn't officially registered as a lobbyist before his appointment. He was only a "special policy advisor" for the lobbying law firm of Alston & Bird. During Daschle's three years in that role advising this lobbying group, the firm earned more than $16 million representing (can you guess?) many of the most powerful interests in the health care industry. A perfect role to avoid charges of conflict of influence for a Secretary of Health and Human Services, don't you think? Lobbying disclosures list the firm that Daschle "advised" representing health care companies, hospitals, pharmaceutical companies, nursing homes, and pharmacy benefit managers. No potential for conflict of interest there. No violation of Obama's new anti-lobbyist pledge, right?

How much money is there in this lobbying business? Health South paid Alston & Bird nearly $1.5 million to lobby the Department of Health and Human Services (as well as Medicare and Medicaid) on its behalf. Note to U.S. consumers and patients: As Secretary of HHS, Daschle's job was to oversee a wide range of health regulations, decisions on which drugs can come to market, and Medicare and Medicaid reimbursement levels. Are you getting sick to your stomach right about now? Don't worry, I'm sure Daschle can recommend a drug for that. In any case, there is no need to lose any sleep over the Daschle appointment. He resigned before a Senate confirmation vote. Why? Not because of conflicts of interest. No one minded that. But poor Daschle couldn't survive the issue of cheating on his taxes. He just happened to forget to report more than $100,000 of taxable benefits from a fancy car and driver provided to him by special interests. And he forgot a huge monthly payment, too. And he forgot to mention that he made millions in consultant fees during his few years out of public office. And he forgot to mention that health care firms paid him huge money to give speeches in front of the very people he was going to regulate.

But wait—it gets better. Several of President Obama's top choices to run our government are *married* to lobbyists. Tom Daschle's wife Linda Hall Daschle (why is this not a surprise) is one of the most powerful aviation lobbyists in Washington. New Energy Czar Carol Browner is married to Tom Downey (a former Congressman), the founder of one of the most powerful lobbying firms in DC—which just happens to represent (can you guess?) energy companies. Exxon Mobil and Chevron are among its many powerful clients, as well as foreign governments. And let's not forget one of lobbyist Downey's biggest past clients—subprime lender Fannie Mae. Starting to feel a need for a shower right about now?

Hillary Clinton is our newest Secretary of State. Does anyone find it a conflict of interest that her husband, ex-President Bill Clinton, has accepted more than $100 million in donations for his Presidential

Library from foreign governments that Hillary might be dealing with? No conflicts there, huh?

Vice President Joe Biden's son Hunter has been a registered federal lobbyist since 2001. Obama, his wife Michelle, Biden, and virtually everyone they have appointed at every level of government are lawyers. You think they may be a bit biased toward trial lawyers?

■ ■ ■

The longer politicians stay in office, the more powerful they become, the more hooked on power and greed, the more deep their tentacles grow into the political establishment. John McCain was no "maverick." Obama couldn't spell "change." Those were merely campaign slogans their advertising agencies and political strategists desperately wanted you to believe. Obama and McCain are both career politicians. They are not Republicans or Democrats. Career politicians have only one party affiliation—*Beltway Insider*. None of this should surprise us. Smart, ambitious, tenacious, driven people using their power and connections to advance their career and enhance their power in Washington DC is not exactly a shocker.

But there is one simple way to cut short the careers of career politicians: *Term limit them out of office.* Change the ID of our politicians from lifelong careers in political office to the vision of our Founding Fathers, to that of citizen politicians. Our Founding Fathers were farmers, property owners, small business owners, and entrepreneurs who put down their pitchforks and muskets, and set aside their business careers, to serve their country as civil servants. They served for short periods of time, and then went back to their businesses and families. They could not even imagine a lifelong career in politics. That is precisely why our Founding Fathers created a Constitution to limit the power of government and politicians. Limiting their time in office is a simple way to limit the actual power of government.

Term limits quickly and efficiently create a new political "brand"—from career politicians to citizen politicians. Suddenly our government will rely on citizen politicians who earn their livelihood outside of politics. Term limits aren't perfect. They're certainly not the only answer.

But they make it harder for seasoned, connected, professional politicians to "game the system" in favor of their friends and special interests.

Want more proof of the importance of limiting the power of the wolves, frauds, and corrupt cons who run our political process? Look no farther than my home state of Nevada. Our state constitution limits our legislature to the role of part-time politicians—meeting only for four months every two years. Nevada has also enacted term limits on the state level. Are those limits on a politician's power perfect? Far from it. Our Nevada politicians manage to cause plenty of damage in only the few months they meet every two years. But keeping our politicians sidelined for most of the time has kept our state government in check for a half century now. Nevada is among the lowest tax states in the United States. And, of course, we have also been the fastest growing state in the country for most of the past quarter of a century. Nevada provides proof that limiting the power of government (and the politicians that run it) breeds success and more power to the people. Once again, look to my home state of Nevada as the model for the United States.

■ ■ ■

Let's end the political dynasties. No more kings or queens, no more princes or princesses. No more hoods (Blagojevich) who rule like Mafia dons handing out patronage. Let's end the political machines, end the sense of patronage, end the arrogance once and for all. Let's end the earmarks, graft, and waste created by some powerful career politicians.

No politician in the United States—at any level of office—should serve more than two to three terms. *Period.* That's enough to do what they pledge to do, then force them to retire from public service, and go back to their real careers. That reduces the opportunities for corruption, the pay for play, and the special interest domination. That keeps them in touch with the real world instead of spending their lives isolated in Washington, DC, or state capitals, around other politicians every second of every day. That eliminates the endless need for fundraising (because there is no reason to fundraise if you are not running for office again), and the conflicts of interest that are created by endless fundraising. That eliminates the need for politicians to vote for bills just to curry favor with special interests (in order to collect more money, so they can get reelected). That eliminates the power of incumbency, and encourages more diversity in our elected officials. Term limits restore some measure of balance of power back to the people—just as the Constitution intended.

It's time to restore the citizen politician to lead this great country—just as our Founding Fathers intended.

Chapter 20

The Magnificent Seven (Times Two)

Putting the Citizen Back in the "Citizen Legislature"

The issue today is the same as it has been throughout all history, whether man shall be allowed to govern himself or be ruled by a small elite.

—THOMAS JEFFERSON

W hen Congress was first created, the House of Representatives was populated with citizen legislators who were able to fairly represent their constituents' interests. Today, we instead have politicians who care more about representing special interests. Congresspeople have evolved into a power-seeking elite with personal fiefdoms.

So what went wrong? The answer is simple: The size of the congressional districts grew dramatically. In 1803 there were 142 members in the House of Representatives, with each one representing less than 40,000 citizens. Today, we have 435 members, a number that has remained fixed for nearly a century, and each member represents close to 700,000 citizens . . . and growing. In our lifetimes, we could easily see each member of the House representing one million people (or more). That is not, in my humble opinion, representative government. That does not represent the intent of our Founding Fathers, who wanted government for the people, by the people, and of the people.

Today it is government for the special interests, by the special interests, and of the special interests. The number one commandment each Congressperson follows is "Thou Shalt Get Reelected." Once someone acquires power, it's difficult for him (or her) to want to give it up, and since many politicians rely on their congressional salaries to make their mortgage payments, it's easy for them to rationalize why it is so important that they stay in office—at any cost.

Let's say that you are a member of Congress and you are required to campaign for your job every two years. To do that, you need to convince voters that you deserve to stay there. Is it possible to meet hundreds of thousands of people one at a time, or even in small groups? Of course not. You're going to have to communicate with them through television, radio, and direct mail. That's going to cost you money . . . a lot of money. And this need to raise large sums of money to keep your job is just an invitation to corruption. When you have to depend upon lobbyists and special interests for your campaign funds, you respond to them far more efficiently, and with far more interest, than to your average voter.

The consequence of this need for stockpiles of campaign cash is that Congresspersons (and all politicians) have every incentive to grow the size of government, as well as the amount of government spending, in order to obtain their campaign funding. And they have very little incentive to restrain government spending to protect their constituents. As a matter of fact, when you need to raise $5 million to $10 million (or more), no one constituent means very much to you.

Some well-meaning people believe they can control the corruption by limiting how much can be spent on campaigns. I oppose that idea. Leaving aside the First Amendment issues of limiting political speech, that's treating the symptom instead of the disease. The fact is that government has grown so large that the stakes are too high for the special interests to ignore. There is gold in the hills of Washington, DC, and the halls of Congress. One way or another, the money flows to influence the outcome of elections. If the money doesn't go directly into the candidates' coffers, it is instead spent directly by "independent committees" or special interest groups aimed right at the voters (through TV, radio, direct mail).

■ ■ ■

Below are seven interesting ideas for creating a Congress that is closer to the people it represents. I call them the "Magnificent Seven."

1. **Limit Congress representation:** Let's have each member of Congress represent no more than 100,000 citizens, and have state legislators represent an even smaller number of citizens (30,000 or less). Wouldn't that create even more politicians? Yes it would. As much as I can't stand politicians, or more bureaucrats in government, it is so important to have politicians represent a smaller (more manageable) population of constituents that I'm willing to actually add to the number of politicians in order to make government more responsive to the people.

2. **Make Congresspeople part-time employees:** Make Congress and legislatures *part time*, so as to reduce the amount of damage elected officials can do. It has worked in my home state of Nevada, where government is smaller, taxes are lower, and the state constitution limits the legislature to part time status. Nevada legislators are limited by law to meeting only four months, every other year. If they met twice as often, I'll bet our taxes would be twice as high. If they worked full-time, I'll bet our taxes would be tripled or quadrupled. These limits can and should be implemented on the federal level as well. We can limit Congress to two sessions of two months each year. That's still twice as much as the Nevada legislature meets. It's more than enough time to do the people's business. This part-time schedule would automatically limit the role of the federal government in all of our lives. It automatically limits the damage Congress can inflict on the lives of citizens and taxpayers. And it automatically strengthens States' Rights and the role of state legislatures across

the country. For those critics who argue that four months a year is not enough time to do the federal government's business, I answer, "That's exactly the point." The fact that Congress meets so often is the problem in the first place. The more time they have to meddle in our affairs, the worse it gets for the citizens.

3. Pay them! Pay Congresspeople well during their time serving, so they do not feel desperate to sell out their constituents in order to support their families. Many Libertarians and political reformers want to see lower pay, or perhaps no pay at all, for our public servants. I disagree. One of the problems in politics is that low pay tends to attract people with the talent levels commensurate with low pay. We need to attract CEO types used to making excellent compensation for their important executive positions. Being a Congressperson is certainly as important as being a CEO. Why not pay them like a CEO? Raise the pay, make Congress a part-time occupation, and you also raise the quality of the people who are attracted to public service. When I need heart surgery, I want a doctor who is highly skilled and highly paid. People in a capitalist society tend to get paid what they are worth. A guy who operates on your heart is worth $500,000 to $1,000,000 per year. Doesn't the same theory apply to politics? The people who make our laws are very important people. We should try to pay them enough to attract the very best and brightest.

4. Expand a Congressperson's terms: In the case of Congresspeople, expand their terms from two years to six years, so that they do not have to raise money 24/7/365 from the first moment they are elected. It works in the U.S. Senate, so why not extend this term to the House?

5. Limit a Congressperson's time in office: Limit their time in office to two terms (12 years) so that they will ultimately have to live under the laws they help create. These term limits also ensure that politicians can't stay on for life to enjoy such a cushy position and attractive compensation, at the expense of taxpayers.

Think of the advantages of a return to a true *citizen legislature*. Today a lobbyist needs to buy a majority of the 435-member House in order to get the appropriation they desire, or the special favor that they are seeking. That's downright *cheap*. It becomes almost 10 times as expensive for any corporation or lobbyist to accomplish this with a 3,000-member House. If each member of the House is a part-time citizen/politician instead of relying on just a Congressional paycheck to make a living, independence and integrity in government increases (as it's much more difficult to buy favors from such a person).

6. Modernize meetings: To those who would argue that a 3,000-person Congress meeting in one place would be unwieldy, I'd argue that it's time to bring our government into the twenty-first century by letting Congress meet from their home offices (in their districts) on video teleconference. With the help of technology, the entire Congress can be run from anywhere in the country. This allows Congresspeople to remain home in their districts, serving their constituents. This keeps Congress in touch with the U.S. citizens and away from the special interests in Washington, DC. And it saves millions of dollars in travel costs.

7. Maintain a lower constituency: A campaign chest to reach voters in a 100,000-citizen district is less than in a 1,000,000-citizen district. It now becomes possible for an incumbent to organize a low-budget campaign for reelection, while it becomes less expensive for a challenger to unseat a legislator who fails to represent the taxpayers. With a smaller number of constituents, each vote (and voter) becomes more important to each legislator. It becomes more meaningful for voters to interact with their legislators (and vice versa). When there are fewer people to represent, the need for large numbers of legislative staff disappears, so the cost of each legislator's staff funding is reduced.

Our Founding Fathers understood that serving in a legislature was never meant to be a full-time career. It was a sacrifice to serve. We need to return to the ideals of public service and this will only be possible again with part-time, small-district, term-limited legislative bodies.

■ ■ ■

Perhaps most importantly of all, we should reexamine the voting process itself. One of the more vexing situations voters face occurs when they arrive at the voting booth. The reason the Republicans and Democrats have a monopoly on the system is because of the "wasted vote syndrome." Often voters find one candidate they really believe in, another candidate they despise and are deathly afraid of, and a third candidate they dislike (but less than the one they despise). Let's say we have an election where candidate A (your favorite) gets 28 percent of the vote, candidate B (the one you despise) gets 37 percent of the vote, and candidate C (one you dislike but can live with as a compromise) gets 35 percent of the vote. Under our system of plurality voting, voters feel that they have "wasted their vote" and handed the election to a hated candidate (candidate B). It happens every November in our current political system.

This system ruins the chances of candidate A (your favorite) ever having a chance. He or she is labeled a "spoiler" and a wasted vote that helps elect the candidate you despise. It happened in November of 2008 when I ran as vice president on the Barr/Root ticket. Our 6 percent of the national vote (6 million to 7 million votes) reported in an August 2008 Zogby poll turned into 520,000 votes by Election Day because millions of conservative voters feared that a vote for Barr/Root would hand the election to Barack Obama. So because of our current system, they held their nose and voted for John McCain (the lesser of two evils) instead of the candidates (Bob Barr and Wayne Root) who actually stood for smaller government, reduced spending, lower taxes, economic and personal freedom.

This was no anomaly. It happens every year in races across the country. In this system known as plurality voting, voters can be so fearful of one candidate that they feel they have no choice but to vote for the lesser of two evils, rather than the one who best represents their values. The entire process is designed to discourage you from voting for independent candidates, or simply the candidate you really like best. The result is a loss for voters—the system that has failed us, never changes. That's the way the people in power like it.

There are better voting methods available. With "Ranked Choice Voting" for example, you get to decide which candidate you like best, which one you like second best, third, and so on. Assuming that no candidate receives a majority of the first place rankings, whichever candidate receives the fewest number of votes then gets dropped, and his voters get to have their number two pick included in the tally instead. This process repeats itself in successive rounds until one person emerges with a majority of the votes cast. So, in the above example, if those voting for candidate A (the one they actually like), select candidate C as their second choice (the lesser of two evils), candidate C will win instead of B (the candidate they despise and fear the most).

This method is practiced today in San Francisco and has proven successful.

Another suggested voting method is Score Voting, where voters get to imitate an Olympic judge, or a judge on *Dancing with the Stars*, and award each candidate a score from 0 to 10.

I believe that any one of the voting methods discussed above is a big improvement over our existing system of plurality voting. However, I'm inclined to support Ranked Choice Voting because of its successful track record in the United States. Smaller citizen legislatures selected via Ranked Choice Voting result in better representation and increase each representative's accountability to the voters. But there is more that can be done to increase accountability and transparency in our government.

■ ■ ■

Since it is unlikely that the voting system will be changed overnight, I want to at least assure that our present system is open, honest, and accountable. Below are seven interesting ideas for creating a more open, honest, and limited federal government. Let's call them the "Magnificent Seven II."

1. Promote accountability and transparency: No proposed bill should be enacted into law unless it has been read out loud in its amended form in the presence of a quorum in Congress, and then posted on the Internet at least one week prior to a scheduled vote. This gives citizens the time to discover a problem, lobby their citizen legislators, and prevent last-minute changes slipped in during the dead of night. Heck, it might even give legislators the time to actually *read* the bills they are passing. Perhaps the most notorious example of this problem of Congresspeople not reading the bills they vote on was the passage of the Patriot Act, which was many hundreds of pages, the copies of which weren't even made available to the members of Congress before they passed it. Require Congress to read the bills out loud and the result will be shorter and less

complex laws that ordinary citizens can read, understand, debate, and comment on to Congress. But don't think the Patriot bill was an anomaly. The same thing happened with the trillion dollar bailout and economic stimulus bills. Our elected representatives are not reading bills that give away trillions of dollars of our money. They are voting based on what they *think* is in the bill, without ever reading the fine print. How frightening is that?

Government spending must also be posted on the Internet for citizens and taxpayers to see in detail every second of every day. The Bailout is a great example. Trillions of dollars have been spent, yet our government refuses to disclose to whom much of the funds have been given. This can never again be permitted. If a bank refused to put your bank account online, would you continue to bank at that institution? I'd withdraw my money tomorrow. Well, every dollar spent by government is my money . . . and yours . . . it belongs to all of us. We the taxpayers have a right to see how every penny is spent online at any time we choose.

Also, any document that is currently available under the Freedom of Information Act must be posted on the Internet. With today's technology, citizens should be able to monitor the work of their government, without first having to make a special request to discover that the documents even exist (and paying for their copying charges).

2. Bring the referendum process to the *national* level: In the United States, the term "referendum" typically refers to a popular vote to overturn legislation already passed by the legislature. On the other hand, "initiatives" are newly drafted legislation submitted directly to a popular vote as an alternative to adoption by a legislature. I really like how citizens are able to limit taxes and the size of government in the various states through the initiative and referendum process. The most famous example is Proposition 13 passed in California. In Nevada we twice passed a referendum mandating that tax increases can only be passed with a two-thirds vote of the legislature. Twenty-four states allow for referendums or initiatives, but there is no equivalent at the national level. James Madison argued that direct democracy would devolve into a "tyranny of the majority," and he may very well be right. But I see it as a very positive move for

U.S. citizens if our Constitution is changed to institute a national referendum process, a process that can only be used to repeal existing laws. Of course, it's not likely to happen as long as most states do not grant to their citizens the ability to change laws through the ballot box.

3. Give citizens the right to petition the federal government: The First Amendment guarantees us "the right to petition the government for a redress of grievances," but there is no procedure where Congress is compelled to address such a petition. At the very least, Congress should institute a rule where they are required to reconsider any law when a petition signed by, say, one million people is requesting such.

4. End earmarks forever: Here's an easy one. If any Senator or Congressperson is afraid to put their name on a bill, or to put that bill up for a vote without secretly attaching it to another bill, it should be *killed*. No federal dollars should be spent if they are not open to public scrutiny and debate on the floor of Congress (and if no Congressperson is willing to publicly defend the bill). *Period*.

5. Give the president the line item veto: It is insanity that a President of the United States must vote yes or no on all bills in their entirety. All presidents should have the right to carve out or reject any and all wasteful spending attached to any bill. Billions of dollars (if not trillions) of waste would disappear forever from our budgets—cutting the deficit and national debt dramatically.

6. If it ain't constitutional, it doesn't pass muster: Thomas Jefferson put it best when he said, "Congress has *not* unlimited powers to provide for the general welfare but only those specifically enumerated." That news comes direct from the author of our Declaration of Independence. What that means in simple layperson's terms is that if a spending bill is not authorized (or enumerated) by our Constitution, the money should not be spent. That would eliminate billions (if not trillions) in wasteful spending overnight.

7. Offer more freedom to America's children (our future leaders): As long as most of our children are educated in government-run public schools, the government bureaucrats running them will instill the idea into the heads of their captive audience (our children) that *more* government is better. A federal appeals court judge in California laid

bare the government brainwashing plan last year for all the world to see. This judge, for all intents and purposes, banned home-schooling if not taught by "government-credentialed and licensed teachers." He actually stated the reason out loud—because children must be taught patriotism, manners, and "loyalty to the state." Really? Which state is that? Was he referring to the Soviet gulag? Should children stay loyal to the state if a Castro-like dictator takes over? Loyalty in this case means that free speech (dissent) would be banned. Isn't free speech protected by the First Amendment of our Constitution? Perhaps our federal judges need to go back to school to study the Constitution. My educated guess is that Jefferson, Madison, Adams, and George Washington are rolling over in their graves.

Government-run public schools teaching students that government is always right should not come as a surprise. Religious schools certainly promote religion, so it's perfectly understandable that the government schools are going to promote bigger government. If we are to build a citizen population that protects and values free speech and dissent, and allows critique and questions of government, than it's critical that more citizens be educated outside the government-run school system. I'm quite heartened by the increase in the number of children being home-schooled. We can accelerate this process by expanding educational choices to include more access to private school, charter school, parochial school, and home-schooling with vouchers at the state level.

This Magnificent Seven (times two) is just a start to help build a better nation, a more open, transparent, and accountable government, empower the people, limit the size and power of government, and create a more educated electorate. I urge you to send me ideas on more ways to downsize government and increase power to the American people. My contact information is at the end of this book.

Chapter 21

Government in Rehab

Outing Our Little Addiction Problem

I place economy among the first and most important of republic virtues, and public debt as the greatest of the dangers to be feared.
—THOMAS JEFFERSON

You've already read my impoundment strategy in a prior chapter. It's a great idea, but will the corrupt big-government, big-spending politicians ever allow it to happen? Probably not. This simple and detailed 14-step plan below is doable and realistic. This is my Plan B.

It was my hero Barry Goldwater who first pointed out that cutting spending was far more important than cutting taxes. As a matter of fact, cutting spending (first) automatically leads to lower taxes, and more importantly, ensures that those lower tax rates will be *permanent*. George W. Bush, although a fellow Republican and supposedly conservative like Goldwater, proved the polar opposite is true as well. Allowing government to grow and spending to increase dramatically results not only in the unraveling of tax cuts, but the destruction of the economy. Bush will go down in history as the man who destroyed the GOP brand

and betrayed the conservative movement with his poisonous brand of "compassionate conservatism."

Bush found it impossible to say *no* to any bill, any program, any politician, any proposal to spend. He called that "compassion." I call it weak-willed, self-destructive *stupidity*.

Some people imagine the president as the parent of our country. But as any good parent knows, you can't say *yes* to everything your child requests. Bush was the typical rich parent who spoiled his children (Congress) rotten and lived to regret his lack of strength and discipline. He said yes to his child's request for ice cream for breakfast every single morning. It sounds good in theory . . . it certainly tastes great going down . . . but it results in a 300-pound, grossly obese child, with a mouth full of cavities, and no friends (who gets tortured, bullied, and beaten up in school). Is it worth it to give your child everything he or she wants? Or is your child better off with a bit of discipline and a serving of spinach now and then? Under George W. Bush, Congress got all the ice cream it wanted 24 hours a day/365 days a year—and then some. And the American people got an economic Armageddon.

George W. Bush talked incessantly about how "sticking to his principles" (in standing tough regarding fighting the Iraq war) would help him in how he is portrayed by history. If only Bush had been that committed to conservative fiscal principles versus the war on debt, he wouldn't go down in history as the man who presided over the worst economic crisis since the Great Depression. And perhaps it's time for Bush to admit that spending a trillion dollars on the Iraq war was a contributing factor to our economic collapse.

But Bush isn't the only bad guy. There is plenty of blame to go around. W was only one in a long line of U.S. presidents to enable our national spending addiction. The addiction problem has been left untreated for far too many years. Federal government spending didn't hit the magic $100 billion spending level until 1962 (179 years after the founding of the United States of America). It took only 25 years to break the $1 *trillion* level in 1987. At that point the trickle turned into a flood. By 2002, spending outlays had breached the $2 trillion level. By Bush's last year in office (2008) the flood had turned into a tsunami—breaching the $3 trillion level. Since my hero Barry Goldwater started talking about our government's spending addiction in the 1950s, federal spending is up

7.5 percent per year, more than doubling every 10 years. That was before Obama's first budget—an almost $4 trillion disaster that includes levels of spending, borrowing, and taxing never seen in U.S. history.

None of these numbers reflect the infamous government bailout of 2008. By the time we're through, experts estimate we'll have given away well over $9 trillion more in bailout goodies to corporations, banks, mortgage companies, automakers, Wall Street, plus, of course, stimulus checks to virtually everyone in the United States (except those who pay most of the taxes and create most of the jobs). Think about those numbers for a minute: $9.7 trillion in bailout plus a trillion or so in stimulus money (so far) on top of almost $4 trillion in spending—now that's starting to add up to some *serious* money. And a deficit in Obama's first year of almost $2 trillion. It's almost unimaginable. Records are falling fast and hard because no one in either party knows how to just say *no* to anything. We're raising children who eat ice cream with sprinkles and chocolate syrup for breakfast, lunch and dinner. Think of the long-term consequences—obesity (deficit), diabetes (debt—a long term killer), and cancer for our economy.

We don't have a tax problem. Taxes aren't too low. Spending is simply too high. Government is dysfunctional. Government has a spending addiction problem. Government is also addicted to raising taxes to cover up their spending problem. Government raises taxes so that it is easier for them to sell debt, especially internationally. If taxes were lower, it would be impossible for government to float bonds backed by future taxes. To deal with this spending and taxing addiction, our government needs to enter *rehab*.

■ ■ ■

Under President George W. Bush federal tax revenues streamed in at all-time highs. Ditto for state tax revenues across the country. Yet federal, state, and local governments are broke and panicking. Why? *Because they spend too much.* No matter how high the tax revenue, government spends more. If federal or state governments had spent 80 cents of every dollar and saved 20 cents (remember, they get access to that *entire* dollar because they don't have to pay taxes, lucky for them), there would be no deficit, no debt, no sudden shortfall, no pending bankruptcy, and, most importantly, no need to panic.

Let's examine this spending addiction on the federal level: Between 2001 and 2009 (under Bush), inflation-adjusted spending increased by more than one-third, about 35 percent. But don't just blame defense spending and the war in Iraq. Real *nondefense* spending rose 27 percent over the same period.

Spending grew dramatically in nearly every category—health, education, energy, transportation, science, technology, social services, Social Security, Medicare. If it moved, Congress *dramatically* increased spending on it.

But that was just the budget. Off-budget spending (called earmarks) grew even more dramatically. Before I even get to the numbers, can I ask a question? What the heck is *off*-budget spending? If it's being spent, isn't it part of the budget? If we spend $1 billion on health care and $1 billion on something else, why on earth would they be put in different places? Why would $1 billion wind up in the "off-budget" category? If you eat 6,000 calories a day and the result is that you gain 25 pounds, can you claim that you gained nothing because you put the 25 pounds in an "off-body" category? I'd call that pretty misleading. Actually I'd call it fraud.

The money in our budget is all being spent, no matter what category we put it in. The reality is we can't afford any of it. Not the bloated budget, or the off-budget. Isn't this just another way of saying our Congress is committing *fraud?* If I played games like that on my company's books, I'd be thrown in prison. Just more proof that government needs to enter rehab. Perhaps we need to invite Congress to an intervention. Someone needs to honestly confront them, point out their signs of an addiction problem, and escort them straight to rehab. Quickly before a health crisis turns into tragedy (death and default).

Back to the numbers: In 1991 there were 546 earmark projects funded at a cost of $3.1 billion (under Bush's daddy, George H. W. Bush). By 2005, under W, earmarks had reached 13,997 projects funded at a cost of $27.3 billion. The son certainly one-upped his father in the wasteful spending category. Worse, George W. Bush never managed to veto any of these off-budget items. I guess it just didn't seem as important to him as spending a trillion dollars on controversial wars around the world.

But those numbers are based on a full year. Let's examine one single lard-filled bill. Back in 1987 Ronald Reagan vetoed a transportation bill because it contained 121 earmarks. Eighteen years later in 2005

Congress included 6,300 earmarks in a transportation bill that George W. Bush signed. If that's progress, I guess I'm a fan of the old days.

That $27 billion in earmarks in one year may not impress the "Beltway Insider" crowd, but it sure sounds like a lot of spending on pork to me. Then to deflect blame, big-spending politicians blame taxpayers, claiming taxes are too low. Do you realize that if taxes are doubled (thereby killing the economy and costing millions of jobs), earmarks would undoubtedly double, too (plus an extra billion here or there for good measure). No matter how high tax revenues go up, spending goes up higher.

Here's the Congressional formula for those of you who still don't understand. When taxes go up, spending goes up. When taxes go down, spending goes up. Death and taxes may be certain, but government spending is just as certain . . . plus 20 percent.

But state and city governments are just as addicted to spending the taxpayer's money as the federal government. California may be worse than Congress, if that's possible. The most dysfunctional state in the country was looking at a $40 *billion* budget deficit over the next two years (see the chapter on the California nightmare), until the federal government bailed them out with the economic stimulus package. Remember that California has the first or second highest income tax rates in the country (they struggle with New York every year to see who can outdo the other). Just like the federal government, no matter how high the taxes, California spends it all—and then some. I'd compare California to a drunken sailor, but that would be an unfair insult to drunken sailors everywhere. California is more like a drug-addicted hooker.

But New York City is not much better off. The Big Apple is in *big* trouble. Mayor Bloomberg, who calls himself a fiscal conservative, originally blamed the trouble on falling tax revenues from Wall Street. It is true that Wall Street is in historic trouble, with tens of thousands of layoffs and record-setting losses. Tax revenues are dramatically down. But what Mayor Bloomberg forgot to mention was that in the past year alone, New York City added more than 40,000 workers to the public payroll. That's *40,000* new government employees. *In one year.* What did we do the year before, without those 40,000 extra employees? How did we all survive?

Do you realize the cost of 40,000 government employees long term? First, taxpayers are stuck with the bloated salaries, pensions, and health care benefits of these 40,000 extra bodies for 25 to 30 years until they retire. Then, the taxpayers must pay their pensions for another 25 to 30-plus years (until they die). Then, all of those job openings must be refilled, because no job created by government is ever lost. So with one new government employee, plus the pension for the original government employee, we have *double* the expense *forever*. Please keep in mind that 40,000 is only the number of new government employees in the last year. The actual total is now 313,965 people working for New York City government. And you wonder why we're bankrupt? Now keep in mind I originally wrote this chapter back in December of 2008. On April 9, 2009 Mayor Bloomberg announced that sweeping layoffs of government employees would be needed to prevent the bankruptcy of New York City. Bloomberg said, "We cannot continue. Our pension costs and health care costs for our employees are going to bankrupt this city."

How destructive is the number of government employees? Am I exaggerating the threat? Is it really that big a deal to taxpayers? In my home state of Nevada, the Public Employees Retirement System has lost more than $4 billion (due to the stock market and economic downturn) this year alone. Add that to the $6 billion in unfunded liabilities for government employee pensions—that's $10 billion of debt in a small state. That's just the unfunded part—the amount we can't pay to government employees that has been promised. That number has nothing to do with the *actual* amount due. In all cases, guess who's stuck with the bill? Taxpayers.

Why is this happening? Because in the real world (private sector), employees must work longer (perhaps until age 70), to receive full pension and Social Security benefits. That's *if* they get a pension. In the fantasy world of government, Nevada government employees can retire at the ripe old age of 45 or 50 after only 20 to 25 years of service, and receive a huge pension for the rest of their lives. The average Nevada public employee retires after 25 years of work, then collects almost full pay for another 25 to 30 years. In many cases, government employees now collect close to full pay in retirement for *more* years than they actually worked. And the pay of government employees (that their pensions are based on) is bloated in the first place. The *Las Vegas Review-Journal* reported on a study by the Las Vegas Chamber of Commerce in February of 2009 that disclosed that the average firefighter in Nevada earns a salary of $95,000 per year. That's the "average." The same report disclosed that the average police officer in Nevada earns $75,000 per year.

I've always been a big fan of police officers and firefighters. They take huge risks, so I can see the value in paying them more for a dangerous job. How much more is up for debate. What age they can retire with full pensions should be up for debate. How much the public contributes to their pension plans should be up for debate. But their value to society is not up for debate. They deserve higher pay than other government employees for the risks they take and heroism they exhibit.

But unfortunately *all* government employees are paid far more than private sector employees. Take a government-employed janitor for example. Is a janitor's job dangerous or stressful? Should they be paid far more than a private sector janitor? That same Las Vegas Chamber of Commerce story reported that by age 78 a government janitor would be paid $600,000 more over his or her lifetime in pay and benefits than a private sector janitor. $600,000. No wonder we're going bankrupt! *This is insanity*.

If these are the numbers in low-tax, small-state Nevada, can you even imagine the numbers in New York City? Or Chicago? Or Los Angeles, San Francisco, and every big city in California? Now, add in the federal government and you can see what a disaster spending on government employees adds up to for taxpayers. Forget the Iraq war. This is the spending and debt war that truly affects our children's futures. Yet, no one is saying anything about it, let alone doing anything about it. Heck, Obama just announced he's adding millions of new federal government employees as part of his "stimulus package." And his stimulus plan will give a hundred billion or so to state and local governments so they can avoid laying off their government employees (and in many cases, give them *raises*). All that's going to stimulate is bankruptcy ... *sooner*. This is insanity squared.

As I write this chapter, private industry is announcing massive layoffs of hundreds of thousands of employees per month. My question—why isn't government laying off hundreds of thousands of its employees, just like the private sector? Why aren't they cancelling raises?

Under Governor Arnold Schwarzenegger, the California budget has grown by 40 percent over four years to $144.5 billion. To solve this spending addiction problem, Schwarzenegger now proposes dramatic hikes in taxes, but, of course, few spending cuts are proposed. There is no proposal to lay off any significant number of government employees, cut government employee pensions, or to cut government entitlement programs. The state now has the distinction of having the highest debt and the lowest credit rating among all 50 states. Is it now clear? The problem isn't a lack of taxes, it's always been a spending addiction problem. And don't forget, Schwarzenegger is a Republican. Those are supposed to be the fiscally conservative "good guys." With friends like Schwarzenegger and Mayor Bloomberg, who needs enemies?

Need more proof of this addiction? Let's look at education. Education is funded at the local level by property taxes. We hear again and again in the media how education funding is too low. Schools are forever claiming they don't have enough money. They always need more teachers, higher salaries, bigger pensions, more textbooks, more supplies, more tax revenues to build more schools. The list is endless. Yet property tax revenues go up every year like clockwork. Why isn't there enough money? Because they spend it all—just like state and federal government. It's the oldest trick in the book—spend every dime the government gives you, so no one can possibly demand a reduction next year. Actually, when you spend it all, you can claim that it wasn't enough, and next year demand more. We're at the point where we no longer argue over actual cuts in budgets. Education bureaucrats and teachers unions scream, complain, and predict disaster over cuts in their annual spending *increases*. No one ever dares touch the actual budget itself—it's a chore to even try to pare back a tiny portion of each year's dramatic spending increase.

How robust are the property tax revenues that fund education? *USA Today* recently reported "property taxes are rising across the USA despite the steepest drop in home values since the Great Depression." The U.S. Bureau of Economic Analysis (BEA) reported that while home values dropped 17 percent, property tax collections *rose* 3.1 percent. State and local governments will collect more than $400 billion in property taxes in the next year. Where do property taxes go? They are used almost exclusively for funding our failing public schools.

Here's the kicker: The BEA reports that property tax revenues haven't fallen since 1934. Yet it's still not enough for the education bureaucrats or teachers unions. Not a single decrease in tax revenues in 75 years . . . and it's still *not* enough. It's never enough when you're an addict. More signs that it's time to enter rehab.

What can you or I do with revenues that steadily increase without fail for 75 years? Government finds a way to spend it all and then some, create the worst public schools in the industrialized world, with 50 percent dropout rates among minority students in urban schools, produce failing grades in competency tests, and complain they need still more money. No other business in the world fails every single year and then complains they should be rewarded with more money. Then they fail some more. The problem is clear—we have a severe spending addiction in the education world, just as we have an addiction problem at all levels of government. Think about it. Capitalism had a bad year in 2008. Businesses across the world lost gobs of money. One bad year. The first one in my lifetime. The result: Obama and his friends complain about capitalism and want to throw it overboard for big government socialism or social capitalism (as they call it in Europe). But government has *never* had a good year. Not once in history has government ever made money. Government loses billions. Every department of government bleeds massive losses. If the deficit is $1.75 trillion in 2009 (at best) why don't we throw government overboard? Or at the very least, fire everyone associated with those massive losses. So let me get this straight—capitalism has one bad year and Obama wants radical changes, new regulations and oversight, as well as nationalization of banks and entire industries. But government has never had one good year in history, and he wants to keep it, expand it and make it more powerful.

■ ■ ■

Here is my simple straightforward approach to starving the Big Brother leviathan. It has never happened under either Republican or Democrat administrations (not even Ronald Reagan). So now it's time to try it the *Libertarian way*. It's time to cut the actual budget, not just the annual increase in the budget. It's time to treat government just like a serious business in the private sector. It's time to treat a trillion dollars like it's serious money.

Step 1: Institute a government-wide spending freeze on my first day in office. It's that simple. Stop growing the beast. Stop the spending addiction. Stop the insanity. In these tough economic times, families and businesses across the United States are tightening their belts, cutting spending (or certainly freezing it), putting off buying anything but the most essential items, and laying off employees (in the case of businesses). Why shouldn't government do the same? The Heritage Foundation estimates a spending freeze would save $176 billion. Not bad—a billion here and a billion there, and pretty soon we're talking about some real money! Keep in mind that only a few years ago, saving $176 billion would have eliminated the entire budget deficit. Now it barely gets us one *tenth* of the way there. But it's a good start.

Step 2: We must add a balanced budget amendment to our Constitution. This is the way to solve Congress's spending addiction—tie their hands so they have no choice in the matter. We can't accomplish a balanced budget any other way—not when the system encourages reckless, irresponsible, and unlimited spending. The reason why is simple: Each member of Congress increases his or her chances of being reelected by "bringing home the bacon" to their district or state. The more they spend, the more favors they do for special interest groups and contributors, the better their chances of reelection. So where is their incentive to *save* money? There is none. A balanced budget amendment would require a three-fifths majority of all members of Congress, on a roll-call vote (so no one can hide), to approve either deficit spending, or any increase in the national debt. Our lawmakers would be required by law to pass a balanced budget. Now there's one new law that I can live with.

Step 3: Eliminate earmarks. Period. If you want to spend the money, put it in the budget. Let it see the light of day. Make the author of that spending item claim ownership. If it isn't important enough to be included in the budget in the light of day, why add it secretly after the fact? If it isn't important enough to be included "on budget," why should we fund it "off budget?"

How "important" are earmarks? You decide—how important is it to spend billions on things like floriculture research, Philadelphia Father's Day Rally Committee, aquariums, the American Sailing Training Association, the Lobster Institute, the National Wild Turkey Federation. The list goes on and on. Should the federal government be involved in this kind of stuff? To be blunt, it's enough to make me sick. None of it is authorized by the Constitution. If people enjoy sailing or aquariums or floriculture or wild turkeys, let them raise the money privately to fund it themselves.

Step 4: No more bailouts. Period. In capitalism, corporations and businesses sink or swim on their own, without government interference. It's bad enough that individuals need government handouts, food stamps, welfare, and so on. Now we've graduated to giving those handouts to *corporations*? Why? So AIG can pay $440,000 for their executives to enjoy a corporate golf and spa vacation at the Ritz Carlton in Dana Point? So that the CEO of Merrill Lynch could pay $10-plus million year-end bonuses for 11 top executives, while the company was busy losing $28 billion for the year? The *Wall Street Journal* reported that 149 other Merrill employees received more than $3 million each in bonuses, all with the help of a $10 billion taxpayer's infusion. Are you kidding me? So our own Treasury Secretary could actually refuse to release the names of recipients of the taxpayers' bailout money? We need the opposite of secrecy, we need fiscal *transparency*. No more future bailouts is my mantra—but in the meantime to ensure our taxpayer money isn't wasted on this one, we must ask every company that receives bailout money to post their finances to the web daily. Taxpayers are now your partners—we have every right to see where every dollar goes. I'd ask the same of all branches of federal, state, and local government. Show us online where every dime is going. The U.S. taxpayers deserve online bank statements on a regular basis. Can you imagine putting your personal money in any bank that denies you the opportunity to see your account online?

Step 5: Vetoes, vetoes, and more vetoes. Remember the lieutenant colonel played by Robert Duvall in the movie *Apocalypse Now*? Remember his famous line standing on the beach as bombs fell all around him? He said, "I love the smell of napalm in the morning!" ***Well, I love the smell of vetoes in the morning!***

I'll be the *veto president*. If Congress wants to increase spending at all, they better pair the spending up with even bigger spending cuts elsewhere. I'll veto everything that raises spending irresponsibly, or raises taxes at all. U.S. citizens don't need any more taxes—we're already taxed too much. I'll veto everything that is not authorized by the U.S. Constitution. I'll need extra pens. I'll need daily hand massages. I'll set records for presidential vetoes—*daily!*

And as a sidebar to all this, I'll fight for a presidential line item veto, so any bill that I don't veto in full, I will carve up like a Thanksgiving Turkey. If the entire bill isn't waste, we all know that some parts of it are. The president must have the right to carve out the parts of a bill that he or she does not approve.

Then, of course, there's the impoundment option that I described in a previous chapter. If my vetoes are overridden, I'll impound the funds and hand them back to the taxpayers.

Step 6: Banish corporate welfare. I will end corporate welfare, as we know it. Why blame the welfare mother with five kids in Detroit for taking thousands of dollars in government handouts, if you're going to give a pass to giant corporations taking billions of dollars in handouts and bailouts? Seems a bit hypocritical, no? Seems a bit absurd, no? Experts estimate that our federal government gives away about $100 billion per year in corporate welfare. As bad as that sounds, we just gave away $80 billion just to one company AIG (in the bailout). And, of course, the giveaway to the Big 3 automakers will no doubt reach $50 billion (or higher) by the time we're done (or they're bankrupt). Overall, we gave away as much as $9.7 trillion to fat cat companies in the combined bailouts. That's *trillion* with a "t." This may be the biggest difference between my Libertarian philosophy and the supposedly fiscally conservative GOP. I'm pro free markets, *not* pro big business. I don't believe in giving handouts to friends, or friends of friends, or lobbyists of friends. Of course, that could be why Libertarians have a hard time getting elected on the national level. If you're not willing to sell out the U.S. taxpayer to corporations, you don't get fat corporate political contributions. No matter; I'll go straight to the people with my agenda.

The worst offenders in the federal government are the departments of Commerce, Agriculture, HUD (Housing and Urban Development), Defense, Energy and Transportation. Their main purpose seems to be to give away taxpayer money to their buddies in the companies and industries they oversee. Interesting conflict of interest? That's why these federal departments should all be eliminated (with the exception of Defense). In the case of a department like Defense that is necessary on the federal level, as you'll see below in my proposals regarding defense spending, we must dramatically reduce the spending, waste, and hiring.

But for the majority of these government agencies and departments, the only way to stop this insidious, corrupt culture of corporate welfare and bribery (pay for play) is to just eliminate these departments *permanently*. If their duties are truly important, they'll be replicated on the state level. My guess is they'll fade away and we'll never notice they're missing from our lives.

Step 7: Decrease foreign aid: I will rein in foreign aid, and military and defense spending. Do we really want to be the world's police officer anymore? Can we afford to be? The answer of course is a resounding *no*. The George W. Bush administration spent about $500 billion on normal Pentagon operations in its last year. That's more than at any time since World War II. That's half of all military spending in the world. That's four to five times as much as the next closest country, China. On top of that comes another $200 billion for the wars in Iraq and Afghanistan. Then there's foreign aid piled on top of that. The numbers are truly staggering.

How do we cut it? First, hire experts to study it and find waste. Do you have any idea how much money is wasted by government in that big a budget? We can't even account for billions of dollars in cash sent to Iraq to hand out to Iraqis. Obviously someone—probably quite a few someones—are retired, sitting at their beachfront villa, watching the sun go down (and counting their hundreds of millions looted from U.S. taxpayers). Obviously billions of dollars have gone to military contractors like Haliburton and Blackwater, and who knows how many more. I don't even fault that. Someone has to be hired to fulfill government contracts. But what I fault is who is overseeing the dollars spent. How do taxpayers know that they are getting their monies worth? I want every penny accounted for.

Just to give you an example of the waste in the defense budget, a GAO (Government Accountability Office) study was conducted of just 95 programs at the Pentagon. According to the *Washington Post* article headlined "GAO Blasts Weapons Budget" published on April 1, 2008, the GAO found that the cost overruns alone for these 95 programs were $295 billion. Yes, I said $295 billion. So if only 95 programs contain $295 billion in cost overruns, what is the price of cost overruns for the entire military budget? And why are unlimited cost overruns allowed? Here we can save $295 billion without cutting a single program, just by eliminating the cost *overruns*. If you added up the cost overruns of all the Pentagon programs, plus axed entire programs that are wasteful, plus wound down the Iraq and Afghanistan wars, what would the savings be? I'd certainly like to give it a try and find out.

I haven't even mentioned the savings possible from cutting military bases all over the world. Why are we paying for the national defense of wealthy countries like Japan, South Korea, and Germany? Let them pay for their own national defense. World War II has been over for half a century. The Cold War has been over for almost 20 years. It's time to ask our allies to take responsibility for defending their own nations. Do you realize that by paying for the defense of these wealthy allies we free up billions of dollars from their budgets, to be used to subsidize their economies, and prop up their automakers and electronics manufacturers, thereby competing against U.S. manufacturers? Now that makes a lot of sense, huh? We're wasting billions of dollars on other people's defense (who could afford it themselves) and defeating ourselves economically at the same time. This is a welfare program for our allies. So now in addition to wasting billions on welfare for individuals and corporations, it becomes clear the American taxpayer provides it for entire *countries*.

I believe that the United States should stop subsidizing prosperous and populous allies. And we must give up on the idea of "nation building" once and for all—who cares if Iraq is democratic or not? How does that change anything in the United States? How does that benefit a taxpayer in Nebraska or Wyoming? Why should our soldiers die for their democracy? Who cares if Afghan farmers grow poppies or not? Why should our soldiers die wiping out their poppy crops? In the end, we're blamed, demonized, hated, and murdered for our efforts. So I say it is time to stop worrying about other countries. I propose dramatically cutting foreign aid, military bases, and military spending all over the world. Bring our boys and girls of the military home to concentrate on one thing only: *defending the United States*.

Step 8: End illegal immigration: We must secure our borders and bring illegal immigration to a screeching halt. How? By protecting our borders with all those troops we will bring home from Germany, Japan, South Korea, and around the globe. It's time to stop talking and start acting. I'm not anti-immigrant. To the contrary, I'm unabashedly *pro* immigrant and immigration. Remember, I'm a second-generation U.S. citizen myself. My grandparents were fresh off the boat. Immigrants (like my grandparents) are the lifeblood of the United States. But they must come here legally, and they must *not* come here expecting government entitlements and handouts.

Illegal immigration is threatening to destroy our economy—from schools bursting at the seams, to hospital emergency rooms stressed to the breaking point, to Social Security being overwhelmed. How can we allow people to come to the United States to get free education, free breakfasts and lunches at school, special classes for English as a second language, welfare, food stamps, aid to dependent children, free health care, and eventually Social Security? And to make it worse, because they are illegal, these immigrants are being paid in cash—thereby paying little or no taxes into the same system they expect so much out of. We've allowed them to jump to the front of the line over immigrants here legally, and drain our government dry. At a time of bloated deficit and debt, we can no longer afford to look the other way while illegal immigrants use vast amounts of our resources. The situation is critical, if not fatal.

I believe immigration is a healthy and vibrant positive for our country. Political freedom and escape from tyranny demand that individuals not be unreasonably constrained by government. Economic freedom demands the unrestricted movement of human, as well as financial, capital across national borders. But economic freedom also demands that we not allow unfettered access of foreigners to our generous social services and entitlement system. Further, the immigration issue is also a terrorism and national security issue. We cannot allow the entry into our country of foreign nationals who pose a threat to security, health, or property. It is therefore in our national interests to secure the borders.

What then is the perfect solution to illegal immigration? What do we do with the millions of undocumented illegal immigrants already here? I believe those issues are up for national debate. But I know the current situation is unlivable. To stop the insanity of the current situation (unfettered access to our borders, massive government entitlement spending, shortages of workers in some industries) there are five things we can and should do immediately:

1. Secure our borders against those who might try to enter our country to do us harm.
2. Bar immigrants from receiving welfare, public assistance, or entitlements.

3. Scrap the existing quota system and allow anyone who wants to come into our country who will agree to the limitation above, and who is purchasing or opening a business that will employ him or herself and others. These immigrants are welcomed to our country with open arms.

4. Allow any immigrant into our country as long as they agree to buy a home of $250,000 or more. This solves our entire fore-closure problem. Millions of immigrants with money from all over the world will come to America to buy up our bargain homes now sitting in foreclosure. This will instantly turn around the entire real estate market and create appreciation in our real estate prices. Best of all, America gains an entire new generation of wealth-*producing* immigrants who will bring assets, businesses and jobs with them. These are educated, skilled, and prosperous immigrants from day one who will not stress our economic or entitlement system. They will not require any welfare or enti-tlements. To the contrary, they will work immediately—thereby adding to our tax base and helping to shore up Social Security. Think of it: A million, or perhaps *millions* of new Americans will flood into our country from all over the world—all bring-ing enough assets to buy homes, cars, consumer items (clothes, groceries, furniture), build businesses, create jobs, invest in the stock market. What a boon (and boom) for the U.S. economy. In this way, with my plan, immigrants are a benefit to the U.S. economy, instead of a drain. Instead of allowing millions of poor, needy, uneducated immigrants to cross into America (because of lax border security) and limiting the skilled, educated, prosper-ous ones, I propose the opposite. Protect the border, stop the flow of illegals, end the welfare system for non–Americans, and *welcome* millions of prosperous, educated, skilled new citizens who will buy a home, build a business and invest in America as their first step in this great country.

5. If we cannot convince Congress to eliminate the quota system and institute the rules and restrictions above, then we should dramatically raise present quotas for immigrants in industries and occupations that can prove a shortage of workers.

Step 9: Reposition the war on drugs. Let's admit that the war on drugs is a failure. If we can't stop the flow of drugs into our *prisons*, how can we stop it on our streets? We must find an alternative to the current war that fails to stem the flow of drugs, makes them more expensive (thereby encouraging crime), and results in the incarceration of more than 500,000 U.S. citizens for nonviolent marijuana possession violations. We have the highest prison population in the world and millions of citizens branded for life as drug felons, and for what? What have we accomplished? What have we spent to put pot smokers in prison? This is madness.

Let's start by legalizing medical marijuana across this great country, in order to save billions of dollars being currently wasted on police resources, prisons, and prison guards. Add in the wasted money spent on legal fees from all those attorneys for all those 1.8 million drug defendants, and the tens of millions of dollars in lost productivity (and welfare for their spouses) while 500,000 nonviolent marijuana users rot away in prison. Are you starting to get the picture?

Let me state *loudly* that I'm no fan of drugs or drug users. I've never used a drug in my life, not even marijuana. I'm as straight-laced as they come. I counsel my children every day to stay away from drugs (and anyone that uses drugs). Drugs are a plague upon society that ruins lives every second of every day. But I'm not discussing drug dealers or traffickers here. I'm discussing nonviolent possession of minor drugs like medical marijuana (with a doctor's prescription). I don't want my children's lives ruined because of one small mistake of trying marijuana. Do you want your children's lives ruined for a minor nonviolent possession charge? Do you want them branded as a "drug felon" for life, thereby preventing them from getting a student loan for college or a decent job? Do you accept that a person dying of a major illness like cancer, with a doctor's prescription for medical marijuana to relieve the pain, should be branded a criminal, or barred from access to a potentially lifesaving drug? It's time to consider major reform. What we're doing now is just *not* working.

But there are some industries that are flourishing because of the war on drugs—government, law enforcement, the court system, lawyers, and the prison industry—their budgets are exploding. For them, business has never been better. The question is, what is it costing in U.S. dollars wasted and young lives ruined? I guess in my mind the conclusion I've reached, after many years of study and reflection, is that while illegal drugs are a terrible problem for society, drug prohibition may be even worse. Let's start with a small step—let's legalize medical marijuana nationally, or barring that, on the state level. As a States' Rights issue, it is none of the federal government's authority in the first place. This one small step will save the taxpayers billions of dollars.

Step 10: Eliminate unnecessary government departments. We must eliminate entire departments of government that are bloated, wasteful, and do more harm than good. Will they be resurrected on the state level? Quite possibly, should they be deemed necessary. Although that's only *if* anyone even notices they are missing. And on the state level, I'm confident they'll be smaller, more efficient, and be held more accountable to the people. Some of the places I'd start are the departments of Education, Commerce, Energy, Agriculture, DEA, ATF, and FCC.

I'd also privatize many of the assets of the federal government, thereby freeing up trillions of dollars to clean up the financial mess that the politicians have made. This list of assets that could and should be sold off includes power companies, buildings, highways, oil and mineral rights, Amtrak, the U.S. Postal Service, and millions of acres of land (including many in my home state of Nevada). The government will net trillions of dollars to pay down our budget deficit by selling off these assets, save billions more by no longer having to run them, and they'll be run more efficiently by private industry.

Step 11: Institute the Nevada model—make gambling legal (and taxable). I'd use Nevada as a model for the nation. Our combination of lower taxes, smaller government, and legalized gambling works. In this high-tech world, online gaming is the entertainment of choice of tens of millions of U.S. citizens. That choice in a free society is none of government's darn business. As you know by now, I'm no fan of taxes. To the contrary, I despise taxes. But taxes on gaming in my state of Nevada dramatically *reduce* the tax burden on the citizens. A tax on online gaming is a way to dramatically reduce taxes on the American people. We must legalize it, regulate it, and tax it. A new study by

PriceWaterhouseCoopers projects that legalization would bring more than $50 billion in new tax revenue into the federal government's coffers over the next decade. That's a conservative estimate. I believe the number would reach closer to $75 billion to $100 billion. That doesn't include the taxes on profits paid by online gaming companies, or the payroll and income taxes paid by employees of this thriving new industry. Those billions of dollars in revenues flowing to the government are dollars no longer paid by taxpayers. Like Nevada, taxes can actually be reduced because of legal online gaming. How wonderful. That's less time working for the government, and more time for me and you to spend with our family. *That's the Nevada model!*

Step 12: Routinely review federal programs. I think we must establish a "Sunset Commission" to review all federal programs on a rotating basis and propose reforms, spending reductions, and elimination of entire departments and programs. And offer generous cash rewards to government employees who present ideas that result in budget cuts and savings.

Do you have any idea how much waste is in the federal budget? U.S. Senator Tom Coburn does. He estimates the number at $385 billion due to waste, fraud, and duplication by government. His "Worst Waste of 2008" report came out in December 2008. The items he lists are enough to make a grown man cry, like $2.4 million for a retractable shade canopy at a park in West Virginia, or $5 million for a bridge to a zoo parking lot in St. Louis, or $1 million for bike paths in Louisiana. I personally believe that with our country trillions of dollars in debt, we could have lived without any of those. How about Senator Coburn's revelation that Congress has already allocated $24.6 million to the National Park Service to commemorate the service's centennial . . . *in 2016*. Can you even imagine the multitude of ways that government bureaucrats find (and race) to waste our money? Well, here's a quick and easy way to save a cool $385 billion. With a budget deficit of $1.75 trillion nowadays, this may not sound like much—but every little bit helps.

Step 13: Run government just like a business. Few employees in the business world are guaranteed a job for life. Why are government employees? If they perform well, they should keep their job. If they fail, they should lose their job—just like anyone else.

I propose that we pay government employees just as employees are paid in the private sector. Bring in experts to compare the pay of government jobs to similar jobs in the private sector. All new hires should receive the same pay and benefits as private employees receive. That will save trillions of dollars going forward.

Why should government employees get automatic annual pay raises based on seniority? Raises should only be based on merit. Mediocre performance deserves no raise. Poor performance demands the loss of your job. No more free rides based on sitting in your chair for 25 years.

Most importantly, incentivize government employees to save money, instead of wasting it. Every time government employees complete a project and bring it in under budget, allow them to share in the savings. That's how it works in the private sector. Pay government employees less, but reward them with bonuses for a job well done.

Step 14: Reform Social Security, Medicare, and Medicaid. I've saved the toughest and worst problem for last. I could write an entire book on the topics of Social Security, Medicare, and Medicaid. The total unfunded liabilities for these programs are in the neighborhood of $100 trillion (depending on the time frame you calculate). Taking care of senior citizens (Social Security and Medicare) is the single largest expense in the federal budget. Suffice to say, I'll keep my solutions brief in this space. You can go to my web site www. ROOTforAmerica.com for more details.

When it comes to Social Security, major reforms are desperately needed. First things first. Let's tell the truth about Social Security. It is a giant Ponzi scheme. Every year of your working life the government takes about 15 percent of what you earn (up to about $100,000) and spends it. It is *not* set aside for your retirement. There is no actual "Social Security Lockbox." The money is gone. It's not in a bank account earning interest for you. It's spent or wasted on whatever politicians wanted to spend it on or waste it on—perhaps buying votes, or propping up some faraway regime we support (for the moment) with foreign aid, or building monuments to themselves. All the typical things politicians spend your money on.

When it comes time for you to be paid your IOU, our government will search for the wages of a younger generation to pay you. That new generation of victims includes your children and grandchildren. But as

U.S. citizens grow older, and fewer are working to support the rest of us, eventually the game is up. Eventually the government will run out of money (and new victims to pay the bill), and refuse to pay your IOU, or decrease the payment dramatically. It's all a giant Ponzi scheme run with your money. If you or I followed this business model, we'd be sent to prison for fraud. But for the U.S. government, it's simply "business as usual." These government bureaucrats make Bernard Madoff look like an amateur. The weakness in Madoff's plan was that he did not have the power to tax.

The entire system is designed to run—like all government programs—by taxing and spending. That's the only way politicians know how to play the game. Tax you and spend your money; then when the money runs out, raise your taxes. It's quite a game, if you can get away with it. It's not a Ponzi scheme if the minute the money runs out, the government raises taxes to make up the shortfall. That's the only thing keeping the government bureaucrats from being charged with fraud- the ability to raise taxes.

So what can we do to "save Social Security?" First, if we want to save it, the age for receiving benefits must be raised to 70 to reflect medical advances and a society living longer. This one step would safeguard Social Security for decades, without raising taxes. Just keep in mind that all we're actually saving is a program that taxes and spends your money, until your bill comes due, then looks around for someone new to tax and spend, so they can pay your bill. So we are extending the life of a Ponzi scheme run by the federal government.

Second, in order to "save Social Security" we must create private retirement accounts for at least a small portion of Social Security. Personally, I'd favor complete privatization (with the right to opt out of the current system), but we all know Congress doesn't have the stomach (or guts) to do what's right.

So let's compromise and settle for a moderate and reasonable solution. Every U.S. citizen should have the freedom to create their own private retirement accounts. To do this, they'll only need to set aside a small portion of their current FICA contributions. That small portion of your FICA taxes invested in a private account will reward each person with a far higher rate of return, thus saving the system. But it's a small enough amount that it will not endanger the stability of the current system.

To the critics of my plan, I say if it's good enough for the government employee unions of America, it's good enough for the rest of us. Are government employees better than the rest of us? Are they a "privileged class?" Some government employee unions pay into only a private retirement account system. Some pay into both Social Security and a private system. But in either case they are earning far higher rates of return than anyone in Social Security.

How is this possible? Few are aware that Congress established only one loophole for Social Security—certain public employees could opt out of the system the rest of us were trapped in. There are a multitude of examples of public employees paying into their unique private system at the same rate of social security, but enjoying double, triple, or even higher returns. One prime example is CalPERS (California Public Employees Retirement System), the largest public pension in the country. Congress also has their own private retirement system that invests in stocks, bonds, and real estate with a much higher long-term rate of return than Social Security. Yet these hypocritical politicians and government bureaucrats deny us the same opportunity. Why does this not surprise me?

Don't U.S. taxpayers deserve the same rights as government employees? Don't we deserve the opportunity to earn the same high rate of return on our retirement accounts as our Congresspeople? Shouldn't a private citizen have the same opportunity to grow their retirement account as an employee of the IRS or the Department of Agriculture? Why is this privileged class allowed to invest their money in a way that we are not?

The biggest benefit of private retirement accounts isn't even the higher rate of return. It is that we would all gain whole ownership of our private retirement accounts. It becomes our private property. It goes with us wherever we go. We can choose to leave it to our children and grandchildren. Currently if you die at age 64 (or 74, or 84, or 94), you lose the rest of your Social Security benefits. But under my plan, if you have $300,000 still due, you could leave it to your children or grandchildren. You could pay off your grandchildren's college education. Why don't liberal politicians want you to have this right? Isn't it our money?

So that's how we save the current "Social Security" system. But the best solution of all is to offer any U.S. citizen the right to opt out entirely and open a private retirement account with that full 15 percent or so that government grabs from your paycheck (with employer contribution). Government's current "contract" or IOU is a Ponzi scheme. It may never be paid according to current terms (or at all). But if you put 15 percent in your own private retirement account, you control your own future. You have a guaranteed contract with yourself. And you own it—you can use it for retirement, or leave it to your children. You can choose to use it to fund your grandchildren's college education. It's yours to do with, whatever you want. Since it has been invested in high-yield investments—just like government employee unions and your Congressperson—you'll have a much bigger retirement account to use as you see fit. With this option, we take Social Security out of the hands (and control) of government, and put it into the hands of the individual taxpayers. That's a good thing—with all due respect to Allstate Insurance—we the taxpayers are the "good hands people." The problem is that there is no Social Security fund or "lockbox."

The government desperately needs your Social Security taxes to pay its current bills. But isn't this a Ponzi scheme? Aren't taxpayers being defrauded? On Wall Street if you raised money based on using it to invest in real estate, but diverted part (let alone all) of it to a different investment, you are charged with fraud. Why isn't government held to these same standards?

As far as the growing problems of Medicare and Medicaid, there are obvious commonsense, doable solutions here, too. Medicare and Medicaid together will soon account for as much as one-fourth of all federal outlays. These two programs are the big leagues of financial disaster. They make Social Security look like a minor league problem. Cato Institute projects that by 2042 Medicare will eat up *half* of all federal income tax revenues.

Medicare pays for routine doctor care, lab tests, and prescription drugs—virtually every medical expense under the sun. What is the incentive for older people to try not to see the doctor on a weekly (or even daily) basis, to try not to have expensive surgery, to try not to have every exam and lab test imaginable? We all know from our experience with business expense accounts that if someone else is paying, it's no holds barred. Since Uncle Sam is paying for anything and every-thing, older people are buying whatever the doctor is selling. But the Medicare program is bankrupting our country. Changes must be made. It isn't as if anyone wants to cut back on spending for older people, it's just that based on demographics (the increase in older people and decrease in younger workers to pay for Medicare), there just isn't a choice. Medicare's obligations are literally *unsustainable*.

If the goal is saving the program, and avoiding bankrupting the entire U.S. economy, we need to morph it into a catastrophic health plan based on vouchers from the government, combined with a high deductible (based on income), and with a health savings account (that is fully tax deductible). Senior citizens could then take that voucher (with a set amount of money) and purchase health insurance, or choose to deposit the money in a health savings account. Any unused money at the end of the year, *they keep*. This gives senior citizens an ownership interest in the money they are spending. They are incentivized to save money, instead of spending like they have an unlimited expense account (courtesy of Uncle Sam). The taxpayers win. The problem may not be solved, but it sure is greatly improved.

Like Medicare, the Medicaid program is bleeding our nation dry. The problem with Medicaid (the medical program for the poor) is that the federal government matches every dollar spent by the states on medical care for the poor. It's obvious that no person with any business sense or business experience runs our government. Common sense tells me that if the feds will match every dollar my state spends with another dollar, I'm going to be incentivized to overspend. The more I spend, the more I'm rewarded. The states are not responsible or accountable with this system. How utterly idiotic. Who designed Medicaid? They should be shot immediately for treason.

The solution to this flaw in the system is the Cato Institute model. Freeze Medicaid immediately at current levels, then turn Medicaid into an unrestricted block grant distributed to the states. Then let the states figure out how to keep their spending under the block grant amount. Anything they save, the states can keep. Now that's incentive to spend less.

This is my 14-step plan to dramatically downsize the federal government. I want to extend thanks to two very special (and brilliant) organizations who inspired much of my creative thinking above—the Cato Institute and the Nevada Policy Research Institute (NPRI).

Once the federal government leviathan has been starved by the spending cuts above, then it is time to return the savings to the people in the form of dramatically lower taxes. That is the subject of my next chapter.

Chapter 22

The Greatest Economic Stimulus Plan Ever!

The government is like a baby's alimentary canal, with a happy appetite at one end and no responsibility at the other.
—RONALD REAGAN

J ust like the prior chapters on cutting government spending, I have a Plan A and Plan B for taxes, too. You already read my Tax Plan A in Chapter 16. It would be a wonderful thing to end federal income taxes and the IRS forever, but will the corrupt big-government, big-spending politicians ever allow it to happen? Probably not. This simple and detailed plan below is doable and realistic. This is my Plan B for cutting taxes and stimulating an economic recovery and so much more—an *economic renaissance*.

■■■

The great big fat lie of liberal tax-and-spend politicians has been debunked. Liberals scream that we cannot allow the Bush tax cuts to become permanent. Why? The federal government cannot afford it. The cost? About $400 billion per year. Until recently, that sounded like a lot of money. But not after the events of the last few months—now we all realize that $400 billion is *chump change.*

How is it possible that we can afford to spend $80 billion on a bailout for *one company* AIG, but $400 billion in tax cuts is unaffordable? How is it possible to spend tens of billions (and counting) on a bailout for the Big 3 automakers, but $400 billion in tax cuts is unaffordable? How is it possible that President Obama could give away almost $1 trillion (in the first round—undoubtedly there will be more) for an economic stimulus package without hesitation, but $400 billion in tax cuts is unaffordable? How is it possible that we could give away more than $9 trillion in total bailouts, but $400 billion in tax cuts is unaffordable and unimaginable?

Obama campaigned for president on the theme that extending Bush's tax cuts would be unaffordable; $400 billion per year was a figure Obama painted as irresponsible. Yet now it turns out that when Obama wants to spend a cool trillion dollars on his pet project, it's available, reasonable, and necessary. *Big fat liberal lie number one is debunked.*

But the second line of reasoning by liberal tax and spenders is even more of a whopper. They say that a tax cut is a "giveaway to the rich" and that it's "unfair" and "greedy." Really? How can it be a giveaway when it's *our* money in the first place? The very definition of a giveaway is when government is giving my money to other people who didn't earn it. Now *that's* a giveaway. The real giveaway is Obama offering a "tax cut" to the 40 percent of the people who paid no taxes last year. The real giveaway is the millions of people who are on welfare, Medicaid, food stamps, aid to dependent children, housing assistance, free school breakfasts and lunches, the list goes on and on. That's a giveaway. *Big fat liberal lie number two is debunked.*

Tax cuts are not a giveaway, nor can they be categorized as "spending" by government. Giving people (who earned it) a tax cut does not raise government spending. It isn't government's money (or property) in the first place, so all they're doing is taking less of our money. That's not "spending." The truth is they never had it in the first place, nor had the right to spend it.

If someone stole your car, then had a change of heart and gave you the four tires back, would that be a "giveaway" to you? Would you feel like a welfare recipient because someone gave you back part of what they took from you in the first place? Would you thank them for being so generous and "fair?" Would you say they increased the spending in their personal budget by giving you back four of your own tires that they just stole? I think not. That's how millions of our most productive citizens feel when government says it adds to the budget deficit to give us back some of our own money.

You mean when President Obama spends a trillion dollars on infrastructure building, that isn't called "government spending?" That doesn't add to the budget deficit? When Obama spends a trillion dollars giving money away to people who never paid taxes in the first place, that isn't called "government spending"? That doesn't add to the budget deficit? But letting us keep more of our own money—the one item that isn't spending at all—that is called budget-busting government spending? Wow, those liberal tax and spenders certainly have a way with words. *Big fat liberal lie number three is debunked.*

And as far as the "G word" greedy, well, that's the biggest, fattest lie of all. You mean it's greedy to want to keep more of your own money, but it's *not* greedy to ask government to give you someone else's money? *Big fat liberal lie number four is debunked.*

Now into this picture of big fat lies enters Barack Obama with his first big act as president—a just under trillion dollar stimulus plan. He wants to build infrastructure with a large portion of it: highways, bridges, schools. By the way, many of these projects that he calls "necessary" are a bunch of fat, lard, pork, and waste that until today used to be called *earmarks*. Now they will be packaged up in an economic stimulus package and called "necessary for the survival of the United States." With the rest of the stimulus package Obama will send government checks to millions of people—many of whom never paid taxes in the first place; many millions of others have steady government jobs and their income is no worse than last year. So why give them a check? Oh, and just for good measure, Obama will spend a bunch of leftover money to create millions of new government jobs. This action will bankrupt taxpayers not just today, but for many decades to come. I call this mess *Obama's Excellent Stimulus Adventure.*

But, I have a more effective and efficient plan. Why on earth would
you give away almost a trillion dollars to stimulate the economy, but
give not one dollar to the people who do all the business building,
job creating, and economic stimulating? Obama's plan rewards everyone *but* the actual stimulators of the economy. He punishes the group
that pumps the money into the economy, pays most of the taxes, and
therefore pays the freight for government. He punishes the group that
matters most if we are going to recover sooner (or at all)—small business owners, entrepreneurs, and the self-employed (the actual taxpayers,
producers and job creators).

■ ■ ■

Here's my version of an economic stimulus plan: *Let's give U.S. taxpayers
(i.e., those who actually do pay the taxes) a one-year tax vacation.* Yes, I want
to suspend all federal income taxes for a year. Obama and the tax and
spenders will howl that we can't afford it. Really? The entire amount
of income tax paid by individuals each year in the United States of
America is about $1.3 trillion. So as expensive as my idea sounds to sus-
pend federal income taxes for a year, it's actually about the same cost as
Obama's stimulus plan. It's a tiny fraction of the $9 trillion (and count-
ing) that the federal government has given away in bailout monies to
rich, fat-cat corporations and bankers. It's far less than the $2 trillion
or so (and counting) in cash that the Federal Reserve has simply printed
to put liquidity into the banking system.

But like all liberal tax and spenders, Obama doesn't want to simply
let us all keep our own tax money for one year. Government wouldn't
get enough credit for that. Obama wants government to meddle in our
lives. Obama wants to be able to give our money away in the form of
a government check—to make all of us dependent on government. He
wants to take it from us (in the form of taxes), and then give it back
(to some of us), so we're all impressed by the power and generosity of
government. He wants to choose winners and losers, by giving it back
to whomever he decides is worthy. He wants to give the money away to
people who did not pay taxes in the first place.

I, on the other hand, choose to give my trillion dollars or so away to
the people that paid all the taxes in the first place. I, on the other hand,
want to simply allow the taxpayers to keep their own money—without

ever getting government (or government checks) involved. For one year, you just get to keep *all* of your own money. How's that for simple? My plan has no middle person (government) grabbing your tax money first and taking his cut. You just keep it all for a year. Now isn't that simple?

But there are two problems. First, most of the savings would go to the top 20 percent of earners, simply because that's who pays most of the taxes. How terrible. How unfair. The people who actually pay the taxes would gain the benefit. And since they own virtually all the businesses in the United States, they'd pump the money back into their businesses, or create new ones, thereby creating millions of new jobs. That just makes too much sense for government.

Second, the administration's tax-and-spend crowd would be petrified that my Income Tax Vacation would set a precedent. They'd be petrified that maybe if we all paid no income taxes for a year, we'd start to actually *like* it. They'd be petrified that maybe we'd all start to notice that the federal government could actually survive without collecting our income taxes. They'd be petrified that we might all demand that income taxes never be reinstated. Wow, how that thought must really frighten big-government liberals. They must toss and turn all night long. They must wake up in the middle of the night sweating profusely. My version of the economic stimulus plan is *the Liberal Nightmare*.

Please keep in mind that my idea rewards and incentivizes the U.S. citizens who fund all the businesses in the United States, who create all the jobs, who buy the luxury goods, who invest in the things that make our economy go and grow—stocks, bonds, real estate, investment property, small business. If you let this group keep all of their income taxes for one year, do you realize what they'd do with it? They'd open a new business or expand their current business, pumping billions into the economy. They'd hire employees, giving jobs to people who need them. They'd pay off their mortgages, thereby giving a windfall to banks and energizing the credit markets. They'd buy stocks (now at their lowest point in years as I write this chapter) as a sign of faith in the United States. They'd go out and buy stuff: cars, vacations, furniture, eat out at restaurants, remodel their homes. The U.S. economy would start humming again. People would go back to work. Now that's an economic jolt. That's an economic stimulus. Put the money in the hands of those who create it in the first place. Put it in the hands of the same people who know what to do with it, in order to make *more* money. Now add in my plan (from Chapter 21) to welcome millions of new immigrants who are willing to spend at least $250,000 on a new home in America, and/or start a business. Add it all together and we can turn a depression into an unprecedented economic expansion in a matter of months.

Do you realize that Obama's plan gives away money to everyone *but* this very crowd that I'm talking about? Obama's plan takes the money from the taxpayers, and gives it back to everyone *but* the small business owners and job creators. I've never gotten a stimulus check. I always earn too much. Isn't that amazing? I'm the one who creates all the jobs, pays all the taxes that pay for all these big government programs and overpaid government employees. My taxes pay for the stimulus plan, but I'm the minority that's excluded. Seems like discrimination to me. When it comes to stimulating the economy, I'm the last guy they want to motivate. Well, there are millions of Wayne Roots. We're the ones who government ought to be helping—or rather, not hurting. You should always help the people who stand the best chance of helping and uplifting millions of others.

But that is only part one of my economic stimulus package. That's the first trillion dollars or so. We all know Obama's stimulus plan will be doubled or tripled or quadrupled. If not in 2009, certainly in 2010 he will give away more money, and more, and more. Because no matter how much he gives away, it will never be enough to fix the economy that he has broken with his irresponsible and unsustainable spending. So here are a few more ideas to motivate and stimulate the producers and earners and taxpayers and small business owners who make the country go and grow. These will be trillions of dollars of spending that actually *make* money for the government. This is my seven-point Economic Stimulus Plan:

1. We must institute a One Year Federal Income Tax Vacation. We already discussed this key idea in detail above. Now to the important corollaries.

2. We must institute a five-year Capital Gains Tax Phase Out. Anyone who invests in the United States (stocks, bonds, homes, commercial real estate, small businesses) deserves a reward for his or her risk. I suggest phasing out capital gains taxes over a five-year period.

Any gains earned after one year = 15 percent, after two years = 10 percent, after three years = 7.5 percent, after four years = 5 percent, after five years = *zero* capital gains taxes owed. This will unleash the greatest economic expansion and explosion in world history.

3. Elimination of all capital gains taxes on investments, dividends, and interest for people aged 55 and older. This was discussed in detail in Chapter 17. But the point of this idea is to reward older Americans who are entering their retirement years and allow them (after a lifetime of hard work) to retire on half the amount of savings (because they owe no taxes on their assets—the very things they'll live on for the rest of their lives). But it's the aftershocks of this idea that will help the U.S. economy recover. With this kind of a reward, think of the trillions of dollars older citizens (the very people with the most assets and disposable income) will spend on investing in the United States—knowing that the big payoff will come from what they are leaving their children and grandchildren.

4. Business income taxes (taxes on corporations) in the United States are the second highest in the industrialized world. We must cut corporate income taxes to 20 percent (or lower) to remain competitive and encourage big business to not move offshore, or ship jobs outside the country. While New Zealand (with a wonderful and enlightened fiscally conservative government led by John Key) is lowering corporate income taxes, and countries across the globe are considering doing the same, we are punishing business owners with more regressive taxes.

   But more importantly, to encourage the formation and success of small businesses—the economic engine of the United States—we must lower the income tax rate for small business even lower to 10 percent. This tax reduction, combined with the five-year capital gains tax phaseout discussed above, will encourage an incredible tsunami of investment into small business. That one-two punch alone unleashes billions (if not trillions) of dollars sitting on the sidelines into new business investments, creates millions of new jobs, and turns the deepest recession of our lifetimes into an economic renaissance!

5. To encourage the housing market and home sales, we must cut capital gains taxes on the profits from the sale of principal residences to *zero*. To liberal tax and spenders who scoff at that idea, it was your

hero Bill Clinton who cut the capital gains tax on the sale of principal residences to zero on the first $500,000 of profit. He passed this law back in the 1990s. But it wasn't indexed to inflation. If updated and indexed for inflation, Clinton's bill would today give home sellers a zero tax on up to about $750,000 of profit. If the idea was good enough for Clinton, it's good enough for me. But I'm adding a creative twist—I'm proposing *infinity* as the limit for your real estate investing success, profit, and prosperity. You invest and risk your money in a principal residence and hold for a minimum of two years, and you get to keep *everything* you make. Period.

Pass this law and watch the housing market explode. Watch people who wouldn't even think of risking their hard-earned money to buy a home yesterday, *rush* with both fists and both feet to buy a home tomorrow. The home industry is perhaps the most important business in the United States. As housing goes, so goes the U.S. economy. If people feel their home is appreciating they feel rich, and they spend (on anything and everything). If they don't, they don't. This idea is how you get the economy moving again.

And of course we've already discussed the corollary to this idea—welcoming immigrants to the United States who are willing to immediately buy a home worth a minimum of $250,000. This would instantly end the housing crisis, remove millions of foreclosed homes from the market, and create real estate appreciation for U.S. homeowners.

6. To encourage the creation of millions of new jobs and the hiring of millions of people currently out of work, I propose a $7,500 tax credit that goes directly to any employer who hires a new fulltime employee during the next three years, increasing to $10,000 if the person they hire was out of work at the time. You want new jobs? Give the business owners some incentive. You get far more in a capitalist system with a carrot than with a stick.

7. If and when income taxes are reinstated (and unfortunately you know they will be), I propose a national flat tax with only two rates: 15 percent and 10 percent. But here's the creative catch. I call it a *reverse flat tax* to encourage and motivate productivity and success. I propose a flat tax rate of 15 percent on any and all income

up to $500,000 per year; then a 10 percent flat tax on any and all income above $500,000. That's it.

Can you think of why U.S. business is successful? The biggest businesses in this country are successful because the more their employees make, *the more they let them keep.* Whether the industry is stocks, investment banking, real estate, insurance, mortgages, automobiles, retail sales, or even Hollywood talent agents, the best salespersons and producers (called "rainmakers") get to keep the most money for their efforts. Those who produce and earn the least, get to keep the least. That's the way all successful businesses are run. You reward the 10 percent of employees at the top who always create 80 percent of the revenues (and success). They build your business from the top down. It's always been that way, always will.

But the U.S. tax code is built *backward.* We punish success. We punish the job creators. We punish the daring innovators and risk-takers. Don't we want to encourage someone to take their million dollars out of the bank, or out from under the mattress, to invest in stocks or start a business? Under the present income tax system, the more you make, the more the federal government takes from you, *the less you keep.* Now, that makes no sense whatsoever.

Why would we want to discourage success and achievement? The federal government should want to motivate the country's best and brightest. It's certainly in their best interest to incentivize you and me to want to work 24/7, to want you and me to build more businesses, to want you and me to hire more employees, to want you and me to risk and invest more money, to want you and me to make more money. Greed, in fact, is good. Greed is what motivates us to serve others because when we make customers happy, they'll reward us greatly. Greed is good for the United States. Greed is good for the federal government. Greed is good for tax-and-spend liberals like Obama. The greedier I am, the more willing I'll be to risk my capital, and, as a result, the more tax money will eventually flow to the government.

My Reverse Flat Tax finally solves that problem. Our tax system has operated backward since inception. It does not motivate or reward success. To the contrary, it punishes success, creativity, ingenuity, and productivity. Once again, by restructuring the income tax system to emulate the most successful business models in the United States, we are treating government like a business, a business with common sense.

Because the proposed tax rate up to $500,000 is a flat 15 percent, my plan is "fair." It treats virtually every person who earns anything from zero to $500,000 in the exact same way. All taxpayers, including lower income earners, get a low rate of taxation. No one can complain. Almost every citizen is in the same boat, except those who strive or risk to do even better. You can only win with my plan. There are no losers. There are winners, and even *bigger* winners. That's as fair as any tax system can get. Everyone does well, and there's an opportunity to do even better.

For those who argue that not enough tax revenues will flow to the government from my Reverse Flat Tax, *that's the whole point.* We have to first cut government spending dramatically (see the previous chapter), and then we won't need the same high level of taxation. Then we can afford to let the people keep more of their own money in the first place.

Failing the adoption of a simple national flat tax, I would recommend a national sales tax (called the FairTax) to replace the income tax altogether. This tax would eliminate income taxes, Social Security taxes, business taxes and the I.R.S. in one shot. That's what I call a grand slam home run.

The point is that it doesn't matter which tax we choose (Fair or Flat) to replace the current system—let's start the debate. We can begin by instituting a one-year Income Tax Vacation, and during that year debate and pass a new tax system.

■ ■ ■

This is my Economic Stimulus Plan to get the United States going and growing again. Does it cost trillions of dollars? Sure it does. So do all of Obama's plans. So do all of Congress's plans. But my plan puts the money directly in the hands of the taxpayers, instead of diverting it through a middle person (called government). And it keeps money out of the hands of a middle person (government) that is inefficient and wasteful. Mine is based on business models that are proven successful over centuries. Mine is based on incentivizing all citizens to risk and invest and build. Mine is based on running the federal government (for the first time) like a business. Mine is based on allowing taxpayers to keep more of their own money, without relying on government to pick winners and losers. Mine chooses only one winner—the U.S. taxpayer. Mine is *the greatest economic stimulus plan ever*—at least if your goal is actually to stimulate the economy and strengthen capitalism.

Part Four

PROTECTING AND PRESERVING OUR INALIENABLE CIVIL LIBERTIES

Chapter 23

Welcome to the Nanny States of America!

"The more corrupt the state, the more numerous the laws."
—Tacitus, Roman Senator and Historian

We all know Libertarians don't win major national office (at least not until now—I plan to change all that). The two-party system is rigged to elect only Democrats and Republicans. My life has always been about winning. I'm what you'd call a *realist*, as opposed to an idealist. I understand that in the end, all that really matters is winning. All the principles in the world gain you nothing, if you're not in power to institute them. So winning really is everything (as the saying goes). Yet, this realist chose to leave the Republican Party and devote my life to the Libertarian Party simply because the corruption, hypocrisy, waste and inefficiency of our two-party system is so outrageous. It is really *that* bad.

The political system is in fact so bad that I could not be part of it anymore—even if the struggle to change the system is a Quixote-like uphill battle. Even if it takes 8 years, 12 years, 16 years, or even 20 years to achieve victory. Even if it takes *forever*. I just cannot stand by and watch the control freaks that populate our government at all levels continue to screw the people. I'm sure not too many presidential contenders would choose to use the word "screw" but it's the perfect word to describe what is happening to our country. We are being screwed. Badly.

■ ■ ■

To understand how badly we are being screwed, first you have to understand something very important about the two-party system. As mentioned previously, it is about only one thing: politicians acquiring and retaining power. That is their only motivation. The people don't matter anymore (to the politicians). The Constitution doesn't matter anymore (to the politicians). Both Republicans and Democrats want only one thing: *the power to control your life*. The more laws they can pass to control your life, the more powerful they become. And for each new law the politicians pass, it means some group or company or industry now has to pay them (they call it "contribute") to change the law, create a loophole, or rescind the law. Each new law created by the politicians comes with a sound: *cha ching*. It's music to their ears. The more laws, the more opportunity to collect legal bribes (campaign contributions) from the groups or corporations upset or thrilled with the bill.

My goal is very different—I don't want the power. I don't want more laws. I want to reduce the laws. I want to simplify the laws. I want to simplify the tax code (or better yet, scrap it). I want to make government smaller and less intrusive. I want to be elected as President of the United States to return the power back to you: the American people. This will not make me a popular person in Washington, DC.

It is important for you to know and understand the motivations of the political establishment—the politicians, the political power brokers, the union leaders, the lobbyists, the government bureaucrats. To know them is to hate them. These arrogant, hypocritical tyrants—from the left and right side of the aisle—actually believe they know what's best for the rest of us—*the little people*. They actually believe that they know better than you and I how to behave, how to live, what to do with our own money. They think they have a right to ban certain activities, even though they continue to secretly enjoy the same activities. They think they have a right to imprison people for victimless crimes between consenting adults. This is all part of the power trip. They just want to control our lives. Nothing matters to the privileged government class except acquiring and retaining power. Hence the term "Nanny State." Politicians want to control the people like a nanny controls the life of a small, helpless child.

But you need to know that these Nanny State politicians are hypocrites. They think the laws apply only to you. They think they have a right to confiscate our hard-earned money (by raising taxes), even though their money is in Cayman or Swiss or Costa Rican offshore bank accounts. Like the infamous ice queen Leona Helmsley, they believe that "only the little people pay taxes." They are willing to do anything, say anything, bribe anyone, condemn and prosecute anyone for anything—even innocent people for minor victimless crimes—to enjoy their power trip. They often enter political office with nothing, no assets. Yet on a $100,000 per year income (or less) they manage to retire 20 years later with millions of dollars in assets. How is that possible? In so many cases, this privileged government class is in fact a *criminal class*.

The best commonsense story that I ever heard to describe how we should feel about the people in power came from my lifelong best friend Doug Miller. Doug grew up in Nebraska. No one in the history of his small town ever locked their doors. One day a newcomer was hired as the new town sheriff. This newcomer acted shocked about the naïveté of these simple honest country folks. He demanded that from this day forward they all lock their doors. My friend's 80-year-old father was immediately suspicious of the newcomer. He said of the new sheriff, "Why should we suddenly lock our doors? We had better watch that guy. He's up to no good." I agree wholeheartedly. The next time a politician, government official, or political leader rails about new laws needed to legislate morality, *watch them*. It's always the closet creeps and perverts who try to control our lives, tell us how to behave, and how to live our lives. The people who claim to be worried about you locking your doors are the ones thinking of new ways to rob you. It works on the economic side, too. Show me a politician who accuses others of greed and selfishness for wanting to keep more of their own money, and I'll show you a greedy, power-hungry hypocrite looking to fleece one class of taxpayers on behalf of his supporters.

■■■

Let me give you just a few examples that prove that those who crave the power to tell the rest of us how to live our lives are often themselves the biggest offenders in our society. The best example of this in recent times has to be New York Governor Eliot Spitzer. Spitzer was one of those power-hungry, moral-crusading, hypocritical politicians willing to prosecute anyone, humiliate anyone, and destroy anyone to garner headlines, boost his ego, and fulfill his grand ambitions. Like most politicians, he relished and idolized power and used any opportunity to prove that he had it—*and the rest of us don't.* And because he had that power, he thought that he could play by a different set of rules than the rest of us.

Before becoming governor (as Attorney General of New York), Spitzer made a habit of garnering headlines by busting "dangerous criminals" such as Wall Street executives accused of minor misconduct or conflicts of interest, credit card companies, and payment processors that accepted money on behalf of online poker enthusiasts, and prostitution rings. Spitzer railed against the evils of prostitution in press conferences as he vowed to throw the book at madams, prostitutes, and anyone despicable enough to be involved in such an immoral business. So guess who was forced to resign after getting caught in a criminal scandal involving prostitution? None other than the esteemed Governor of New York. Yes, *that* Eliot Spitzer.

The same guy who went after minor misconduct on Wall Street with such gusto and glee that he treated Wall Street executives like murderers (before they were even proven guilty of minor misconduct). The same guy who went after financial companies for being involved in the sin of processing money for consenting adults who chose to make a wager on poker or a football game. But these weren't bookmakers, or mobsters. Spitzer went after credit card processors who merely handled the transactions. Big, brave Eliot Spitzer used the power of the state of New York to demand millions of dollars from those financial companies as "legal extortion" to stop further prosecution. He ruined people's lives over *poker!* Perfectly understandable. After all, New York doesn't have enough serious crimes for the police to investigate, do they? Unsolved murders and rapes be damned, we have more important things to do—there are bankers and CEOs of public companies actually allowing people to use their credit cards to play poker on the Internet. Quick, call the SWAT teams in!

But small-minded hypocrites like Spitzer always get their comeuppance. That same overzealous bully was forced to resign in disgrace as governor because of his involvement with illegal prostitutes. Wait, it gets better. He was caught on tape by a federal wiretap. Federal authorities went to the good governor's bank and studied his bank records. Eventually they found suspicious cash transactions. The rest is history—as was the governor's career. Ironically, it's my educated guess that Spitzer is one of those power-hungry politicians that enthusiastically supported warrantless wiretaps. I'm sure he authorized government and law enforcement agents to listen to many conversations, and look through many a citizen's private bank records over the years. It never bothered Spitzer when it was someone else whose privacy was being invaded by government.

Perhaps some prosecutor should have forced the governor to take the infamous "perp walk" in handcuffs in front of TV cameras—just as he never hesitated to do to so many others. Ruining a man's life, career, and reputation before proving him guilty never bothers crusading government bureaucrats like Spitzer. Actually it's what they live for: ruining the lives of others makes them feel important (for a moment or two). My educated guess is that Spitzer probably used the information he obtained in wiretaps to ruin the lives of many a big shot executive, or political rival, over a private decision involving a victimless crime.

Libertarians like me can only laugh and shake our heads at the hypocrisy. After all, here we have a "holier than thou" ethics crusader—a man named by *Time* magazine as "Crusader of the Year." Yet he resigned over the same type of criminal activity, involving the *same* victimless crimes he has blown out of proportion to garner headlines again and again. But, of course, powerful politicians like Eliot Spitzer think they're above the law. They think they can get away with making the same private choices for which they'd throw the book (and the entire justice system) at us for doing.

What is the moral of this moral-less story? *Never* trust government. *Never* trust politicians or government bureaucrats. *Never* trust moral crusaders. *Never* let others define morality for you. Because the people doing the crusading and defining and prosecuting often have an agenda, an out-of-control ego, and an outsized sense of entitlement. They certainly do not have your best interests in mind. Ambitious and vicious politicians like Eliot Spitzer only have Eliot Spitzer on their minds.

■ ■ ■

But Eliot Spitzer is just the tip of the iceberg. Illinois Governor Rod Blagojevich is another prime example. He fancied himself a man of the people, while he was allegedly trying to sell a U.S. Senate seat to the highest bidder. But on a scale of doing the worst damage to taxpayers, that's probably the *least* offensive crime committed by Chicago machine politicians. Remember that Chicago is the city where politicians voted to ban serving foie gras in restaurants. It's still served at restaurants all over Chicago, but when politicians or prosecutors want to make a statement about their power over the people, they use this ridiculous Nanny State law to justify arresting some poor hardworking restaurant owner to set an example. Of course, it will no doubt be a restaurant owner who contributes to an *opposing* political party. It happens every day across the country—politicians, police, and prosecutors use laws rarely enforced to harass or embarrass someone they don't like (always someone who doesn't support or contribute to their political campaigns).

Governor Blagojevich is now the poster boy for corrupt politicians, but trust me there are many more politicians out there who are just like him. There are Spitzers and Blagojevichs lurking in most every town hall, city council chamber, state legislature, and governor's mansion in the country. And that goes double for Congress.

Democratic Congressman Charles Rangel is another prime example of the hypocritical tyrants who rule our lives. It turns out that this powerful Congressman, who is *Chairman* of the Ways and Means Committee of the U.S. Congress (the group that determines tax policy for all of us), doesn't like to pay taxes himself. It turns out that he's owned a fancy home in a fancy Dominican Republic resort for years, allegedly *without* disclosing his rental income to either the IRS, or to Congress (on required Congressional disclosure forms). If you or I did that it would be called "tax evasion" and we'd be sent straight to prison. But Charlie Rangel appears to be different than your typical taxpayer. He simply confessed (after being caught red-handed by the *New York*

Post), agreed to pay a small fine, and now refuses to give up his powerful committee chairmanship deciding tax policy for the rest of the country. Can you imagine? He allegedly cheats on his taxes and now he thinks that he deserves to keep his job deciding our tax laws.

Then there are the politicians who tell you and me that we are greedy if we don't want to pay "our fair share" of taxes. The biggest tax raisers in Congress are people like Ted Kennedy and Charles Rangel, who doesn't report his income in the first place. Then there are Obama's cabinet picks. As reported by the *New York Times* and CNN, so far five of them have had tax issues." Could you or I choose to hide income off our taxes and avoid prison? Unfortunately this privileged class of politicians that we've created and empowered is filled with criminals and hypocrites. Rangel want to rule our lives, but they believe those same rules don't apply to themselves. Don't you just love and admire the people who run the Nanny State?

■ ■ ■

One of my favorite journalists, John Stossel, wrote about another outrageous example of the danger of allowing Nanny State politicians to rule our lives. In 2006 John Stossel interviewed Mayor Alfred Muller of Friendship Heights, Maryland. Muller is your typical anti-smoking zealot, who led the battle to pass the most onerous anti-smoking law in the nation. It didn't just ban smoking indoors, or in public buildings, it banned smoking outdoors, too. Yes I said *outdoors*. It banned smoking on any public property—even sidewalks, streets, or parks. Stossel scolded the mayor for being a busybody. The mayor told Stossel this ban was part of his job "to protect the general welfare of the citizens." Stossel reported that soon thereafter, Mayor Muller had to register as a *sex offender* as punishment for touching a 14-year-old boy's genitals in a public restroom. Needless to say, ex-Mayor Muller's smoking law was soon repealed by an embarrassed city council. As I've said many times before, the citizens of this country need to closely watch the moral crusaders who are trying so hard to tell us how to live our lives. When they don't want you smoking in public bathrooms, maybe it's because they want to reserve the bathrooms for their own enjoyment.

Please keep in mind that I'm not a smoker. I personally hate cigarette smoke. As a matter of fact, I'm severely allergic to it. But I'm also a defender of individual rights. Smokers have rights, too. They should certainly be allowed to smoke outdoors, or in the privacy of their own homes, or cars, or sidewalks.

■ ■ ■

Then there's my favorite Nanny State tyrant story of all. Debra Markham is an Oregon district attorney who in 2007 prosecuted two young boys for slapping girls on the butt at school. You heard me. This moral-crusader district attorney decided to arrest two seventh grade boys, stick them in jail for five days, and charge them with multiple counts of felony *sex abuse*. All for having fun at school. It turns out that the boys *and* girls were slapping each other on the butts. Both sides were having fun. But the girls say they were pressured by investigators into giving false statements. In other words, prosecutors and law enforcement might have been trying to build a solid case versus two seventh grade boys horsing around at school—like all 12-year-old boys do—in order (I assume) to get two more conviction notches on their belts.

Guess what penalty these poor scared little boys faced for horsing around at school? They faced 10 years in juvenile detention prison and a *lifetime* on the sex offender registry list. Their lives could have been ruined for slapping butts in the seventh grade? Is this really the United States? Because it sounds more like something that would happen in the Soviet gulag. Public outcry led to people from across the country donating $60,000 to the boys' defense. The case was eventually dismissed. But after spending five days in jail and facing 10 years of prison, don't you think these boys are psychologically scarred for life?

But there is good news to report: Guess what happened to the prosecutor? In December of 2008 Debra Markham was arrested for punching her husband in the face. She was terminated nine days later by the Yamhill County district attorney's office. These are the people in authority judging you and me. These are the people defining "morality." These are the people we're allowing or electing to make our laws. They're even willing to pick on little boys to gain more power and publicity. It is truly revolting.

■ ■ ■

Next, we come to the vaccine scandal of Texas Governor Rick Perry. From what I've read of him, Perry is nothing like Spitzer or Blagojevich. I'm a fan of any politician who tries to keep taxes low. But Perry is symbolic of the problem with Republicans. While Democrats support the Nanny State to rule our financial lives like tyrants, Republicans use the Nanny State to rule our private lives like tyrants. Governor Perry tried to mandate through executive order (bypassing his legislature) that all sixth grade girls in the state of Texas were required to get a cervical cancer vaccine in order to attend public school. What? Why should every sixth grade girl . . . 99 percent of whom have never had sex . . . be forced to endure a costly HPV vaccination with unknown long-term side effects? Who does this mandate benefit? That's the first question we should be asking about *every* new law—who stands to benefit? From my perspective it was clearly the pharmaceutical company that benefited.

This mandate was a clear-cut violation of the rights of parents. I believe that many childhood vaccinations pose a health risk themselves. I believe that our national epidemic of autism and ADHD has a definite connection to the large-scale vaccinations required of our young children—vaccinations that just happen to benefit pharmaceutical companies to the tune of billions of dollars a year. In 1983 the CDC (Centers for Disease Control and Prevention) recommended 10 vaccines for children. Now the CDC recommends 36 vaccines—that's a 260 percent increase in 15 years. Why? I have spoken to many holistic health professionals who believe it is the *quantity* of vaccines forced upon babies and toddlers in such a short period that is overwhelming their young immune systems with toxic overload and causing neurological problems (like autism and ADHD).

(Note: For more information on the connection between childhood vaccines and neurological diseases like ADHD and autism, go to Jenny McCarthy's wonderful and informative web site: www.GenerationRescue. com or read her book *Mother Warriors* (Dutton Adult, 2008). Incidentally the survey of 17,674 children across the United States commissioned by her foundation, and conducted by a professional national research firm, found that boys are 155 percent more likely to have a neurological disease if they've been vaccinated.)

Therefore, there could very well be a link between vaccines and a national epidemic of neurological diseases, yet here we have the Texas public health system mandating (forcing) unnecessary and untested vaccines on every 11-year-old girl in the state, without regard to the immediate side effects, yet alone the long-term effects. What's the rush? Why not make the vaccine available and let parents choose? Then let's study the results for 10 years (or longer) before a rush to judgment. I would personally pull my daughter out of school before I allowed any of my children to be guinea pigs for a new, untested vaccine whose long-term effects have not been studied.

It's also interesting to note that just a small number of women have contracted cervical cancer, yet pharmaceutical companies are trying to turn this into a national emergency—an emergency for which they stand to make billions of dollars. The true national emergency is the epidemic of autism and ADHD, and yet Governor Perry and the pharmaceutical companies felt no need to do something about that crisis. But, of course, pharmaceutical companies can't make billions of dollars by stopping or slowing the amount of vaccines we give our children; they can only make money by giving *more* vaccines.

I'm proud of the immediate two gut instinct judgments that I made when I first heard of this Texas public health controversy. The first thing that went through my mind was, "What drug company made a large contribution to the Texas governor to get him to issue this executive order?" It was only days later that it was disclosed that Merck, a major pharmaceutical company that happens to make the cervical cancer vaccine called Gardasil, just happened to make a contribution to the Governor Perry's campaign—as well as to eight other influential Texas lawmakers. And it was further disclosed that key members of Governor Perry's staff met with Merck lobbyists at about the same time the contributions were made. Soon thereafter came the Executive Order. "It was just a coincidence," announced the governor's office.

Did Merck expect something in return for a contribution? Who knows? But I'm sure, at the very least, that contribution opened the doors to a meeting at the Texas governor's office where Merck lobbyists had the opportunity to "educate" Governor Perry and his staff on the immediate need for 11-year-old girls in the state of Texas to get vaccinated. Perhaps the governor felt he was doing the right thing and the contribution had nothing to do with his decision. But his decision sure doesn't pass my smell test. As a matter of fact, I think the whole situation stinks to high heaven. Many Texas parents obviously agreed with me. The public outcry was so loud that the executive order was rescinded by the state legislature in a stinging rebuke to the governor.

My second immediate gut instinct was about something far worse than bribery or corruption. It was about life and death. I thought, "What makes anyone think this vaccination is safe for 11-year-old girls? How do we know little girls won't get sick or suffer long-term complications?" Later that month I took a business trip to London. There in the British newspapers I read that two U.S. girls had *died* from complications of this cervical cancer vaccine. Funny, I never read a story on those deaths in any U.S. paper. Perhaps our U.S. media is too hungry for advertising revenues from pharmaceutical companies to report the deaths of little girls from an untested vaccine.

But I can promise you that my children will *never* have any untested vaccine forced upon them by politicians possibly looking out for the interests of big corporate contributors instead of the interests of innocent children. In December British newspapers reported on the paralysis of a little girl within 30 minutes of receiving the cervical cancer vaccine. The death toll from Gardacil now stands at 30 little girls.*

Not all politicians are corrupt or criminals, but I'll wager an educated guess that many of their decisions (if not most) are somehow influenced by conflicts of interest. Here's a bit of common sense and compromise that does not involve any conflict of interest. Perhaps parents who know their young daughters are sexually active (at the age of 11) should consider giving the cervical cancer vaccine to their children and the rest of us should wait and see the long-term side effects. I know that I have zero interest in playing Russian Roulette with my teenage daughter's life after 30 young precious girls have already died. *Thirty.*

Down the road, if the vaccine is proven safe, and if the number of cancer cases goes down among the girls getting the vaccine compared to those who don't, then the medical profession will undoubtedly recommend that parents get their kids vaccinated. Only parents should be empowered to make the final decision. After all, who cares more about your children, you or the government?

Ask Governor Perry or any other politician a simple commonsense question: Why on earth would government mandate a dangerous and

---

*www.timesonline.co.uk/tol/life_and_style/health/article5337885.ece

untested drug on sixth grade girls, thereby creating a massive public health experiment and turning these innocent 11 year olds into guinea pigs? What right has government got to mandate any vaccine, on anyone, for *any* reason? Don't we have freedom any longer in this country? Don't we have the right to exercise free will over our own bodies? I'll decide what goes in my body, or my children's bodies—*not* government.

■ ■ ■

The list of idiotic, hypocritical, and dangerous actions taken by Nanny State politicians and government bureaucrats is long. My good friend Steve Kubby serves as a reminder of what can happen when you anger public officials. Steve has one of the deadliest forms of cancer there is, cancer of the adrenal gland. If the cancer doesn't kill you first, you'll die from a heart attack or stroke, caused by the tumor suddenly releasing extreme amounts of adrenaline. Steve is the only human in the annals of medical science to have lived more than a few years with his form of cancer and is currently celebrating his 35th year of surviving this cancer. Steve is literally a *walking miracle*. He credits his remission to one thing and one thing only: medical marijuana. Now I'm no fan of drugs. As a matter of fact, I've never smoked marijuana (or any other drug) in my entire life. It's just not my thing. But you can bet if someone I loved had a painful or deadly disease, and medical marijuana offered hope, I'd explore everything and try anything offered by medical science to save my loved one. *So would you.*

When someone has a deadly disease like cancer and medical doctors report possible progress, miracle breakthroughs, or just the easing of pain with the use of medical marijuana, should government remove that option for the sick and dying? Do you want government banning the only thing that might keep your father, or mother, or grandparents, or children alive? Do you want government banning the only medicine that doctors agree might ease your dying mother's excruciating pain? Does government even have the right to limit your medical choices or decisions? Perhaps that is why, despite the United States being a strongly anti-drug nation, medical marijuana has passed in nearly every state where it has been on the ballot—usually by huge margins of victory.

Steve Kubby has never hurt another soul on this earth by smoking marijuana. He's simply trying to stay *alive*. This brave man's life is on the line every day. He's lived like that for 35 years. Yet prosecutors in

California put him in jail and took away his medical marijuana, even though it was legal based on California law at the time. It was legal because Steve led the fight to pass Prop. 215.

The reason that Steve led the fight for legalization is because for years, politicians, police, and prosecutors told him "If you don't like the law, *change it*." So Steve and his friends did just that. They did exactly what government asked them to do. They ran a statewide political campaign—and they *won*. Steve Kubby and his friends convinced the voters of California to legalize medical marijuana. Little did they know that victory over the vicious and vindictive political establishment would come back to haunt them. The government came after all the leaders of the medical marijuana movement, and nearly every one of them ended up facing felony prosecutions. Steve faced 19 felony counts and 40 years in prison. But worst of all, they threatened to take his children away from him. They threatened his loving wife Michele that if she allowed their daughters near Steve, Child Protective Services (CPS) might have the children removed from her care and put in foster homes. *For what?* For the crime of having a deadly form of cancer and using a medicinal herb proven to work (but which pharmaceutical companies can't sell or make profits)? According to our government, that's a crime worthy of 40 years in prison and losing your children?

But 40 years in prison was only the stated term of punishment. In reality, by withholding the only known treatment that had kept him alive for over three decades, prosecutors tried to impose a *death sentence* on Steve Kubby. They made Steve lie shivering in a freezing jail cell, without a blanket, without the only medicine known to keep his cancer in remission. Soon Steve was blind in one eye, urinating blood in his cell, and suffering from horrendous blood pressure attacks of 260/220. Doctors testified that if he were not released from jail soon, Steve would surely die. This sounds more like the way we'd treat a terrorist who just blew up the World Trade Center and murdered 3,000 people, than a cancer patient trying to prolong his life by smoking medical marijuana. *Is this my United States of America?*

What were these California prosecutors protecting us from? Why were they willing to *kill* Steve in order to prevent him from taking an herb that was keeping him alive? How did Steve's decision to take medical marijuana affect anyone else's life? Who was Steve hurting in any way? How exactly is our society damaged by a cancer patient using an alternative therapy? This reminds me of the old story about the Holocaust. None of this matters—*until it happens to you.* Then it's too late—you've allowed the government to take away your rights, to grow too powerful.

Eventually Steve was released, and his record expunged by a judge. So the government was willing to let a man die (or put him away for 40 years) for a crime so minor that a judge eventually ordered Steve's record to be completely cleared?

I consider Steve a hero, not a criminal. Medical science should be studying Steve Kubby. His story and experiences offer hope for millions of present and future cancer victims. Remember, I lost my mom and dad to cancer.

But Steve's story proves once again the limitations of allowing government officials, politicians, or prosecutors to define "morality" on behalf of citizens. Should drugs that offer hope for seriously ill cancer patients be *banned* by close-minded politicians and government bureaucrats who have no medical background? Tens of thousands of patients die each year from *legal* prescriptions, written by doctors. Yet those drugs are allowed to continue to be sold by pharmaceutical companies unabated. Why? Because billions of dollars are on the line and lobbyists make sure they stay legal and available for sale. Yet no one has *ever* died from medical marijuana.

So why is there such a desperate need to ban it? Could it be because there are no lobbyists writing huge checks to politicians? Could it be because pharmaceutical companies don't make any money off its sale? These prosecutors must be the descendents of the Nanny State politicians of the early twentieth century who banned alcohol during Prohibition. We all know how well *that* experiment worked out. The results were that U.S. citizens kept right on drinking, the government lost millions in tax revenues on alcohol, ordinary people lost respect for the law, and organized crime was born. (Prohibition was the best thing to ever happen to Meyer Lansky, Lucky Luciano, Al Capone, and Bugsy Siegal.) Government proves every day that those who fail to study history are destined to make the same mistakes over and over again. The history of the United States is that government screws up virtually everything it touches.

■ ■ ■

Now I know that some of you reading this are going to say that Steve Kubby, whether he is right or wrong, was involved in marijuana. And marijuana is a controversial issue. Some of you, like me, are strongly anti-drug. So you just don't believe government will ever violate your freedom or intrude on your life the way it did to Steve Kubby. You think "this was just about drugs." Well, I'm sorry to burst your bubble. But government is violating our rights and threatening our lives somewhere in our country every minute of the day. And they don't even need drugs as an excuse to inflict damage on your life. Or do you consider *eggs* an illegal drug? Do you consider eggs a lethal weapon? Is selling eggs a serious crime in your mind? If so, you've found your heroes in the Ohio Department of Agriculture. These bureaucrats have made it their sworn duty to stop the illegal sale of . . . *gasp* . . . organic eggs.

Here's the remarkable and frightening story. An Ohio couple, John and Jacqueline Stowers, have run a food co-op for several years, trading organic foods among members of the co-op (primarily neighbors). A state agent from the fearless Ohio Department of Agriculture decided to "investigate." My first thought is, "Don't these bureaucrats have anything better to do than investigate family farmers for the crime of selling eggs?" But I digress. It turns out that "investigate" is another way of saying "entrap." The agent showed up unannounced, pretending to be a customer looking to buy organic eggs for his sick wife. The Stowers family explained to the agent (masquerading as a customer) that they do not sell food, but instead only trade among members. The agent refused to leave without his eggs. The family (I assume worried for their safety at this point about a suspicious, belligerent stranger demanding food) gave him the eggs to make him leave. The agent, allegedly against the family's wishes, left money on the counter for the eggs. Soon thereafter the harassment began. The government agency sent a letter to the family requiring they pay for a retail food license. Are you starting to feel nauseous yet? This is called a *shakedown* in the language of the Mafia. Government would put you and me in prison for fraud if we played this game (and rightfully so).

The family sent a reply to the bureaucrats denying any need for a license simply because they did not sell the agent food (nor had they ever sold food). The health inspector did not like the tone of the letter and soon thereafter planned and orchestrated a sheriff's department SWAT-style raid on the family's home. The Stowers and their 10 children were ordered into a room and detained for six hours. The raid was described by the Stowers family as "violent and belligerent." Officers allegedly rifled through the entire home searching and seizing most every possession in the home, many of which were not listed on the search warrant. More than $10,000 worth of food—their entire stock for the next year—was seized, along with the family's computers and cell phones. During those harrowing six hours, the family was not allowed a phone call.

The story should send chills down all of our spines, unless, of course, your role model for the United States is once again the Soviet gulag. Whether the issue is medical marijuana for dying cancer patients, or the sale of organic eggs without a license, it is clear our government is out of control. Simply questioning a government bureaucrat, or certainly choosing to stand up to one, is enough to attract prosecutions, SWAT raids, and even the death penalty. What if Steve Kubby had died in prison, simply because the only "medicine" (a *legal* herb according to California law) that kept his cancer in check was withheld by government? What if a child had been killed in that SWAT raid over the sale of organic eggs? Is this the kind of government we want in our country? Most importantly, are these the kind of people you want controlling our lives?

■ ■ ■

The lesson we should all learn from the examples of the Nanny State politicians listed in this chapter, is that it's time to take our country back from the dominating, intimidating, manipulating Republican and Democratic politicians who have forgotten that they work at the behest of the taxpayers. Actually it's *past* time. It's time to support a third party candidate—a Libertarian—who isn't beholden to special interests. Who isn't interested in prosecuting a quarter of this country's citizens to increase his power and importance. Remember the next person they choose to prosecute for a minor victimless choice could be your son or daughter. The next life they ruin in order to gain one more notch in their belt could be you. The next person to die in a SWAT raid over the sale of eggs without a license could be your child. The next person to die because some government bureaucrat mandated unnecessary, unproven, and untested vaccines could be your 11-year-old daughter.

It's time to put candidates in office whose goal is to give the power back to *the people*. Whose goal is limit the size, power, and scope of government. Our wise Founding Fathers wrote about power of the people, by the people, for the people. They did not write about putting power in the hands of morally corrupt, power-hungry, ego-driven, hypocritical politicians and government bureaucrats. They certainly did not intend for government to intimidate, arrest, and prosecute our citizens for "crimes" such as trying to defeat cancer with herbs not approved by pharmaceutical companies, or slapping butts on the school playground, or the failure to pay for government food licenses.

It's time to vote for political leaders who vow to stop the hypocrisy, the double standards, and the overzealous prosecutions that have nothing to do with morality, but everything to do with publicity. Eliot Spitzer should not have been forced to resign for his own personal choice of pleasure, but he most certainly *should* have been forced to resign for his hypocrisy, arrogance, power-hungry sense of entitlement, and most importantly, for the damage he's done to the lives of others by prosecuting victimless crimes—the same ones he allegedly enjoyed in his personal life. It's time to turn the tables. It's time for the citizens to take the power back from the power hungry, ego-maniacal politicians and government bureaucrats, just as our Founding Fathers envisioned.

Chapter 24

Education

The Civil Rights (and Economic) Issue
of the Twenty-First Century

The only time my education was interrupted was when I was in school.

—GEORGE BERNARD SHAW

T his book is primarily about economic policy and improving the country's financial future by limiting the size, power, scope, and intervention of government. But education is in fact an economic issue. Education is perhaps the most important economic issue of our time. It is the key to our economic future—as an individual, family, society, and country. Plain and simple—our children are the future. And like virtually every political, economic, or social issue in this country, freedom is the answer to creating a better future. The freedom to live the American Dream is all about getting a good education. And getting a good education is all about parents having the freedom to choose the best education for their children. Once again, the Libertarian solution is freedom, choice, and competition.

I believe this makes school choice the civil rights issue of the twenty-first century. But unlike the 2008 Republican presidential candidate, John McCain, who borrowed that line and gave lip service to the issue once or twice on the campaign trail, I *live* this issue as a home-school father. Unlike our new hypocritical President Barack Obama who sends his two little girls to the best and most expensive private school that money can buy (the Sidwell Friends School in Washington, DC), but opposes school choice or vouchers for the rest of us, I believe the availability of school choice for *all* parents is the number one economic fairness issue in this country today. It is not government's job (or right) to limit the best educational choices or opportunities for our children. It is not the government's right to take our property tax monies and then limit our abilities to use it for whatever educational choice a parent deems best for their child. That is the very definition of taxation without representation. The choice of the best education for any child belongs solely with that child's parents. **Here's the message that politicians need to hear loudly and clearly—it doesn't take a village or a government to raise a child—it takes a mother and father.**

■ ■ ■

It takes a mother and father who care. It takes a mother and father who are involved in a child's education every step of the way. Just as in the case of so many economic issues that plague our country today, when it comes to education, government isn't the solution, *it is the problem.* The answer to our education crisis is school choice, parental freedom, and more competition for the public school system. School choice and parental freedom are the civil rights issue of the twenty-first century because without the ability to exercise that right, our children are condemned to an inferior education, which limits their economic future.

We can only solve our educational crisis by reducing the role of the federal government in education. The same bloated federal government that mismanaged the Iraq postwar planning, Hurricane Katrina, Walter Reed Hospital, and even brothels in Nevada, cannot be trusted to manage the U.S. educational system without screwing it up. Remember Barry Goldwater's words back in 1959:

> . . . education is one of the great problems of our day . . . (lobbyists) tend to see the problem in quantitative terms—not enough schools, not enough teachers, not enough equipment. I think it has to do with quality: How good are the schools we have? Their solution is to spend more money. Mine is to raise standards. Their resource is the federal government. Mine is to the local school board, the private school, the individual citizen—as far away from the federal government as one can possibly go. And I suspect that if we knew which of these two views on education will eventually prevail, we would know also whether Western civilization is due to survive, or will pass away.

Well, now we've had 50 years—half a century—to see the results of more spending, more involvement by the federal government, and more meddling by the teachers unions.

And the results are clear. A recent *New York Times* article reported on the education level of typical U.S. teenagers. They found that fewer than 50 percent of U.S. teenagers know when the Civil War was fought, 25 percent are unaware that Adolph Hitler was Germany's leader in World War II, and 25 percent believe that Columbus sailed the ocean blue around 1750. These are the students taught by "state-certified" teachers.

We can clearly see the results—education has gotten worse, the system is failing, U.S. student test scores are among the lowest in the industrialized world, state-certified teachers don't guarantee positive results, and the future of the United States and Western civilization is certainly in doubt. The experiment is over. The facts are in. It's time to remove education from the federal government's authority. The Founding Fathers always considered education to be a States' Rights issue—handled entirely on the state and local level. They could not have imagined the distant federal government in Washington DC handling (and mandating) education for every child in America. The reward of moving education to the local level is to improve the lives and economic futures of our children. The bonus will be dramatically reduced government spending and a lower national debt.

■ ■ ■

Big government has run wild in many (if not most) areas of American life. Now Big Brother is trampling the rights of the U.S. parent. If the following story doesn't scare you, you deserve Big Brother as your master. These government bureaucrats actually believe they know better than you or me about how to live our lives, educate and raise our children, and let's not forget the biggest one of all—how to indoctrinate our children (a nice way of saying *brainwash*) to support bigger government.

There have been numerous Nanny State intrusions on the lives of U.S. parents of late. One of the most ominous government intrusions yet occurred in Prince George County, Maryland, where school officials playing Big Brother have ordered parents to vaccinate their school-aged children or the parents will be imprisoned. Yes, I said *imprisoned*.

Let's pause for a second, take a deep breath, and reflect on the quagmire called the public school system. First of all, our public schools are failing miserably compared to any other industrialized country in the world. Children are dropping out of high school in record numbers. A study by the Education Trust, released in the fall of 2008, reports on the dismal figures. The study shows that one in four children in the United States drop out of high school. Worse, among minorities the dropout rate is higher than one out of three. Worst of all, the United States is the only industrialized country in the world where young people are less likely to receive a diploma than their parents. Want further proof? Check out the following web site: www.ajc.com/opinion/content/printedition/2008/10/24/graduation.html.

But wait—the numbers get worse. In the 50 largest U.S. cities, the dropout rate is almost 50 percent according to Colin Powell's group America's Promise Alliance. Minority student dropout rates are as much as 25 percentage points higher than white students. Where do they get their statistics? Direct from the Department of Education. (If you want more information on this issue, log onto www.wsws.org/articles/2008/apr2008/scho-a03.shtml).

How important is the dropout rate? Researchers report that people who have not graduated from high school are eight times more likely to wind up in prison. How shocking and sad. These are the inferior results of the public school system of the richest nation in the world. And the worse the statistics get, the more teachers unions demand more money as a reward for failure, the more they demand all other options be removed, the more they demand that teachers pay not be based on performance, merit, or accountability. Well now we can all understand why. If pay were based on performance, our public school teachers would be fired in record numbers.

Even those who pass high school are often promoted only due to grade inflation. Look no further than my home state of Nevada for proof of the inferior education of high school graduates. In Nevada, many students entering our state colleges like UNLV or Nevada-Reno require remedial math and reading. *Remedial?* What are they doing in college if they need remedial classes on subjects they should have learned in high school? Why were they allowed to graduate high school? Why were they accepted into any college? These students are proof of the failure of our public school system.

Even worse, drugs, violence, bullying, and gangs are rampant within our public schools. Cases of teachers molesting and sexually assaulting underage children seem to be in the headlines on a daily basis. Our children are far behind in math and science versus high school graduates from other countries. Yet, public school teacher unions demand raises and increased spending as a reward for this horrible performance, and refuse any form of accountability or pay based on merit. And worst of all, powerful teachers unions hold our children hostage by refusing to allow competition. They will not allow a level playing field—by refusing to allow vouchers or any form of parental choice (so that parents in even the *worst* schools in the country are denied the opportunity to choose private school, religious school, or home-schooling with their own property tax money).

It's amazing! These facts make you want to either laugh or cry at how ridiculous (and sad) it all is. No matter how bad our public schools get, there are three things that teachers and teachers unions demand—higher pay, more (wasted) funding, and no parental choice. The more schools fail, the more obstinate unions get about denying access to competition. "Things are so bad we can't possibly allow competition" they whine in mock horror.

Name another industry in the United States with this kind of loser's mentality? The worst record in modern U.S. business history has to be the auto industry—and even *they* have accountability (top executives get fired all the time) and allow competition (Japanese automakers have been chipping away at our market share for decades). Can you imagine if we gave auto union members automatic jobs for life with unaffordable pensions and health benefits? Oh, right, *we did.* That's why our auto industry is bankrupt and fewer and fewer of us choose to buy U.S.-made cars anymore.

But even in the extreme case of auto unions, we didn't shield them from competition, give rewards for bad performance, or try to force the poorest among us to buy only American. Last I checked, there was nothing stopping me from spending my own money on my own choice of a foreign car. If I want to buy from Toyota, Nissan, Honda, BMW or Mercedes, I can. Wouldn't banning my choice of cars be un-American? Yet that's exactly what we've been doing for more than a century with our U.S. public school system.

We've been guaranteeing jobs for life to teachers who have failing grades, suspending kids for bringing aspirin or nail clippers to school (yet somehow some kids have no problem sneaking drugs and guns into schools), banning dodge ball because someone's feelings might be hurt, banning kids from school for the crime of touching or hugging others (thereby violating a no-touch policy), and throwing billions of tax-payer dollars down the rat hole of failing public schools—with worse results each year for every extra dollar spent. That's what happens when you award a public school *monopoly.* That's what happens when you allow teachers unions to legally bribe politicians (with massive union campaign contributions, and union employees masquerading as campaign workers). That's what happens when you give power to people who have never had a job in the private sector (where competition is a way of life).

Now we've gone a step further: We have empowered these power-hungry bureaucrats with the right to imprison parents who don't force their children to do as they say. No wonder so many of the kids who do somehow manage to graduate public schools are prepared only for a life as an order-taker at McDonald's. How can you ever become an executive, business owner, boss, or leader of any kind (even a union boss), if all you've ever experienced in school is 13 years of baby-sitting and learning to obey authority without question, reason or debate (now imposed with the threat of prison for your parents).

My wife Debra and I have found a better way to educate our children. My four children are home-schooled. They are bright, creative, passionate, motivated to learn, and full of life and love. They have not been exposed to government-run schooling (i.e., brainwashing), eight hours a day for their entire lives. They love their country. They value our Constitution. They actually admire our Founding Fathers. They believe in the power of capitalism. They respect their parents. They don't do drugs. They are not drugged with ADHD drugs like Ritalin (that happen to enrich the bank accounts of public schools with federal government funding for each "disabled" child). My children have never been in trouble in their lives. They are able to pray to God without worrying about who that might offend. And they will only get the vaccines that their mom and dad (in consultation with our private physician, not doctors chosen by the government) have studied and deem necessary, proven, safe, and effective.

No one from the government has the right to tell me, or my wife, how to raise or educate our children. That's the job of caring, involved, passionate, loving parents. No one has to provide meals for my children—they are fed healthy meals by their loving mother every day of the year. That's the job of good parents. Isn't it interesting that my kids are motivated, ambitious, bright, score at the top in nationwide exams . . . and how about this one—love learning, love to read, and look forward to school each day. How many public school parents can say that?

We have a problem in this country—too little personal (and parental) responsibility, and far too much government intervention. Schools will never improve because we spend more money. They will only improve when we give more rights, freedom, responsibility, and *choice* to parents. Producing smart, motivated kids (who stay out of trouble) has little to do with teachers, administrators, or unions. It has everything to do with good parents. The answer to our public school crisis isn't bigger government, stronger unions, higher paid teachers, more mandatory childhood vaccines, or prison sentences for parents who disobey government bureaucrats. It's old-fashioned parental involvement, parental choice, more freedom, and, most importantly, more competition. If public schools are failing, the answer isn't forcing parents to send their children to those failing schools. *The answer is giving parents the freedom to find a better alternative.* And, I think I have found one.

■ ■ ■

My proposal, or alternative, is simple and inexpensive: Let's give power back to the people and the parents. I'd start by dismantling the Department of Education. Our Constitution does not even mention education, simply because the Founding Fathers never intended education to be the responsibility of the federal government. The budget of the Department of Education doubled under President George W. Bush from $33 billion to just less than $70 billion. Anyone think that education improved by double? Anyone think our kids are twice as smart? Are we getting our money's worth? Education is failing precisely because the federal government is involved. I propose getting government out of the education business—effective immediately. Now Obama has super-sized education spending with an extra $100 billion or so from the economic stimulus bill. Want to bet on the outcome? I'll take your bet. Education will continue to plummet to new lows, despite an extra $100 billion. Money has never been the solution, it never will never be the solution. How do I know? In Washington DC we spend the most money in the country—$14,000 per student. The results have been the worst in the country for decades. Without parents who give a darn, even a trillion dollars wouldn't help. It's all throwing money down a sewer. But vouchers (providing choice) and charter schools have helped in low-income cities like DC and Milwaukee. Why have they worked? Because parents that take advantage of these programs care about their kids. Those are the parents willing to fight for their children's future.

I also propose taking the power away from teachers unions, who have destroyed our education system, just as auto unions have destroyed the Big 3 automakers, as well as bankrupted the city of Detroit and the state of Michigan. If unions have failed the auto industry, why would anyone assume the results would be any better in the education industry? Well, they haven't worked out any better. The results of teachers unions on our public education system can only be described as dismal. The only reason education isn't bankrupt just like the Big 3 automakers is that the education system is owned by government. You can't go bankrupt if no matter how much you spend, no matter how badly you fail, you just raise taxes and confiscate more money from taxpayers. But the sad reality is that our government-run public education system is bankrupt and failing just like the automakers.

I propose moving all education spending to the state and local level—where it is closer to the voices and concerns of parents and children. And in concert with this move, I support issuing vouchers (on the state level) to parents so they can choose where to spend their own tax dollars. Give parents and taxpayers the choice of public, private, charter, parochial, or home-schooling. How do I know that choice works? Because public school teachers send their own children to private schools at a rate far higher than the average U.S. parent. Shouldn't *all* parents have the same choice as teachers?

I propose accountability: Take away tenure and guaranteed jobs for life, fire bad teachers, and reward the best teachers for good performance. This is the model for any successful business. Why should education be any different? Oh, I forgot—the unions don't want accountability. It lowers their union dues. It breaks their monopoly on power. Whose side are the unions on? My home state of Nevada recently provided the proof. In the midst of a budget crisis, Nevada teachers unions refused to give up a pay raise. They solved the crisis (temporarily) by *quickly* agreeing to eliminate $50 million of state spending on new textbooks for the children of Nevada. That allowed the public school teachers to keep their raise. Interesting choice. Books? Who needs new textbooks?

And lastly, just as in the business world, I see competition as the savior of education in this country. My desire for school choice and parental freedom will not destroy public schools. To the contrary, it will *save* them. Public schools will either improve or perish. To improve, the unions will have to open their minds to dramatic reforms like merit pay, the firing of bad teachers, drastic reductions in the number of administrators (otherwise known as bureaucrats), giving principals more autonomy to hire and fire within their schools (like any CEO), and providing vouchers to parents.

We all need to ignore the cries of teachers unions that "more money is needed." If money was the answer, we'd already have the best public schools in the world, not the *worst*. And the places that spend the most—Washington DC and California would be the best of the best. Instead they are the worst of the worst. Throwing money at a problem rarely solves it. Catholic and private schools already produce far superior results to public schools, yet they spend far less per pupil, and pay their teachers far lower salaries and benefit packages. We need to cut education spending and reduce our national debt, not increase it. The model for turning around our public schools is private and parochial schools, which do so much more, with so much less. They are the "small business model" for the education world.

Small business produces more than 50 percent of all jobs in the United States and 75 percent of new jobs, yet they must do it all while living on a lean budget. Small business owners rarely (if ever) receive help from government. Small business owners receive no bailouts. Small business simply does more, with less. Small business is more successful than any bureaucracy. Private and parochial schools follow the small business model—and they are (not surprisingly) far more successful than public schools. They achieve all this success on smaller budgets, less spending per pupil, and they can even afford new textbooks for their students. Somehow they accomplish all this without unions. *Coincidence?*

■ ■ ■

My wife Debra and I have chosen home-schooling as the best choice of education for our children. That doesn't mean that I want to force home-schooling down everyone's throat, nor anyone's throat for that matter. Home-schooling is simply one educational choice that every parent should consider. Choice is an integral part of any free society. The United States is (supposedly) a free society. At least that's the rumor I've heard. A recent ruling by an arrogant California Appeals Court Judge *criminalizing* home-schooling certainly puts that theory to the test. This abhorrent ruling certainly competes with the threat of imprisonment for not vaccinating your child, for the worst example of government gone wild. This ruling makes criminals of caring parents who simply want the best educational choices for their children. And it makes outlaws of their children. What a travesty of justice.

Justice H. Walter Croskey of the California Appeals Court ruled in 2008 that parents do not have a constitutional right to home-school their own children. He said that the proper education of our children is reserved only for teachers certified by the state. Yet national test scores for home-schooled children have proven again and again to be 30-plus points higher than for public school children (taught by state-certified teachers). So exactly whose "best interests" is Justice Croskey looking out for? It sure isn't in the best interests of the children of California. They'd obviously (based on test scores) be better off being taught at home, rather than forced by the threat of imprisonment to learn in substandard, dangerous, drug-infested, gang-infested, government-run schools with the highest dropout rates in the industrialized world (and among the lowest test scores).

My educated guess is that it is only teachers *unions* that Justice Croskey is looking out for. The children don't even enter into the picture. Unless, of course, it's brainwashing and propaganda we're discussing. Croskey's quote as to why students need to be taught in government-run public schools by government certified teachers is a frightening mixture of Joseph Stalin, Fidel Castro, and George Orwell. Here is the quote direct from the mouth of Justice Croskey (or is it Trotsky?):

> A primary purpose of the educational system is to train [doesn't he mean *brainwash*] school children in good citizenship, patriotism and loyalty to the state and nation as a means of protecting the public welfare.

So government actually now admits publicly that its goal is to brainwash our children with their version of the truth, their version of fairness, their version of right and wrong, their version of citizenship, their version of patriotism, and their version of loyalty. Loyalty to *what*? To anything that the government blindly teaches them to be loyal to? Does Justice Croskey believe that if any of our children's thoughts are deemed to be "out of the mainstream" they should be punished, banished, banned, intimidated, or imprisoned? Should children that Croskey finds "disloyal" be sent to government reeducation camps? Is this the definition of freedom or free will? Is this the kind of education envisioned by our Founding Fathers? Obviously not because our Founding Fathers were . . . (gasp) . . . *home-schooled*. Doesn't Croskey's ruling sound more like the Soviet gulag system being resurrected than a democratic society? Shocking. Frightening. Orwellian.

Ironically, Justice Croskey's ignorant and offensive ruling comes at a time when parents are demanding more parental choice, freedom, and competition for public schools. A recent poll in my home state of Nevada proves that parents are crying out for education reform. Nevada parents were asked if they could afford it, where would they choose to send their children to be educated—public, private, parochial, charter or home-school? Eighty-nine percent of Nevada parents said that if they could afford it, they'd choose alternative forms of education such as private school, parochial school, charter schools, or home-schooling. Yes, I said *89 percent*. Liberal government bureaucrats and teachers union leaders must have been worried sick about those poll results. Perhaps worried enough to send Justice Croskey out to damage the competition?

No wonder public school advocates are worried sick: *home-schooling works*. To illustrate the remarkable talent, creativity, and intelligence of home-school children, I offer exhibit A: my 17-year-old daughter Dakota Root. She is beautiful, well mannered, disciplined, articulate, poised beyond her years, treats adults with respect, maintains a straight A+ average in her studies, scores in the 99th percentile of every national test she takes, devours as many as a dozen books a month (because she wants to, not because she has to), has achieved a black belt in martial arts, and is a world-class fencer who has participated in Junior Olympics, Fencing Nationals, and World Cup events internationally. And at the ripe old age of 16, she gave my nomination speech for President of the United States in front of a packed convention hall of Libertarian Party delegates from across the country, and broadcast live on national television on C-Span. I invite you to watch her speech. Google "Dakota Root" and it is the first item that pops up.

As I write this chapter, Dakota just received her S.A.T. (college entrance exam) scores. She not only scored at the top percentile of students across the country, but scored a *perfect* 800 in reading. *Yes, a perfect score.*

I will admit that when my wife first suggested home-schooling for Dakota, I, too, was skeptical. Skeptical, but unlike government bureaucrats, I was not willing to limit freedom and choice. I kept an open mind and told my wife to give it a try. After all these years, I can now report that it has been the smartest choice we've ever made. At the age of 17, Dakota can out-talk, out-think, and out-debate most every college student and adult that I know. The result is a young lady mature far beyond her years. Home-schooling had made the difference. Home-schooling and the personal attention it offers has brought out the best in Dakota. Her life is not about the silly things typical teenagers devote their lives to—shopping, gossiping, sleeping, drinking, smoking, drugs, watching *American Idol*, and so on. She is a disciplined, mature young woman whose life is dedicated to achievement, success, and the acquisition of knowledge—not the kind defined by state-certified teachers, but rather the kind defined by her free-thinking mind.

Dakota has narrowed her college choices to the Ivy Leagues, Stanford, Duke, and Northwestern. She is quite an exceptional and hopeful example of the future of our great country. She makes her old man very proud. And I'll bet she can run rings around close-minded bigots like Justice Croskey, who managed to criminalize home-schooling without ever meeting a diverse cross section of home-schooled students. I suggest unleashing Dakota Root on the U.S. Supreme Court (if that's where the home-schooling debate winds up). I guarantee soon thereafter that home-schooling will be the law of the land!

So now we come to the most important part of the story. Why are home-school success stories like Dakota's not covered by the mainstream media? The media doesn't just ignore positive stories about home-schooling. They go out of their way to feature *negative* stories. The biased liberal national media almost always portrays home-schooling as a form of inferior education practiced by ignorant trailer-park trash, or back-woods religious extremists. To the contrary, I'm here to educate readers that home-schooling is becoming mainstream—and in many cases such as mine, is actually preferred by parents who could afford to pay for elite private schools. My family is quite the symbol of the change in image and acceptance of home-schooling.

So why does the media bend over backward to try to smear home-schooling? Is it possible that the success of homeschooling threatens the liberal establishment? Is it possible that a positive story like Dakota Root threatens the funding of teachers unions? Is it possible that teachers unions believe that if more U.S. citizens are exposed to the success of home-schooling, parents might be emboldened to take their children out of failing public schools? Are they afraid that the success of home-schooling might lead to lower funding for failing public education, a weaker teachers union, and perhaps worst of all to these bureaucrats—lead to a national push for school choice?

Many adults who have had the pleasure of meeting Dakota have made the comment "Is your daughter home-schooled?" I always answer, "Yes, but how did you know?" The reply is always the same. "In my experience, only home-schooled kids are this focused, disciplined, well-mannered, and respectful of adults." After hearing those almost identical remarks on at least a dozen different occasions, I've started to appreciate the success and unique nature of the education we have given Dakota. And those kind of comments heard again and again lead me to wonder why the liberal news media never manages to find anyone willing to point out the many positives of home-schooling on camera? Perhaps they aren't looking very hard for proof that home-schooling works. Perhaps they're afraid to state the truth. Perhaps they're going out of their way to distort the picture.

So why has home-schooling been so successful in the Root household? Simple: Dakota has had the advantage of being taught one on one literally since birth, by people that love her . . . praise her . . . motivate her . . . and expect the very best of her. Her teachers have included her mother (my wife Debra) and grandmother Martha Parks, and even her tutors over the years have all become precious members of our family. Her first tutor, Sandy, is a like a second grandmother to Dakota and the other Root children. Please note that Sandy is a retired public school teacher. She is proof that there are many wonderful, brilliant, caring, dedicated public school teachers. The teachers are not the problem. The problem is the system, the union, and the bureaucrats (who never pick up a book or erase a blackboard).

Home-schooling is a success because Dakota has had precious few distractions that other students must deal with in a classroom setting. Perhaps Dakota has been successful because she wasn't slowed down by 20 to 30 other classmates moving at a slower pace. Perhaps it's because as a home-school student, Dakota has had the freedom to study what she enjoys, what she is passionate about, when she wants, at her own pace—instead of what a teacher or school district decides to force down her throat.

Perhaps home-schooling has been a success for Dakota because she is free to travel the world with her family at any time (no set "school hours" or schedule constraints). She gets to see and learn things other school-challenged kids could only dream of. Perhaps it's because she has been taught by her parents to watch History Channel, Learning Channel, Biography Channel, Noggin, FOX News, and CNBC, instead of MTV (and has no classmates to talk her out of these positive habits).

Perhaps it's because she eats a healthy, holistic, organic diet at home—prepared fresh by her loving mother for 17 years now—instead of eating junk food in a school cafeteria. Perhaps it's because she is free from the negative influences of jealous or dysfunctional classmates—envious of her high level of achievement, or looking to destroy her self-esteem. Perhaps it's because she has been able to devote her mind only to education, without the fear of bullies, truants, drug dealers, or disruptive, violent classmates. Perhaps it's because she has been able to educate and expand her mind without worrying about the distraction of boys. Perhaps it's because she doesn't have to rise at the un-Godly hour of 5 A.M. to get ready for school, catch a school bus in the dark, and start classes at 7 A.M., an hour when studies prove that children are unprepared to learn. Dakota gets up at the reasonable hour of 8 A.M. to get ready for her teacher to arrive at our home at 9 A.M. What a wonderful way (and time) to learn.

Or perhaps it's because Dakota has spent so much time talking and debating politics and business with her father, rather than discussing clothes and gossip with teenage friends. It's been a unique experience—*for both of us*. She speaks, thinks, and acts like an adult far beyond her years, because as a home-school student that's exactly who she's been exposed to her whole life.

In a nutshell, all the negatives that society, the liberal news media, and the jealous teachers' unions have spread about home-schooling are misleading, ignorant, and just plain wrong.

This story is not an attack on teachers. After all, my daughter Dakota's tutors are retired public school teachers. The world is full of good, honest, caring, bright, passionate educators. The problem is the public school system they are forced to teach inside, plain and simple, is a failure. I hope that telling Dakota's story might do some good for other thoughtful, caring parents considering educational alternatives to public school.

I think many educators and cynical media types would be shocked to meet Dakota, and hear her discuss business, politics, fashion, and life with opinions and observations that most adults would be hard-pressed to match. And to read of the story of a successful and educated couple with unlimited options, choosing to home-school their children. Just more proof that home-schooling is no longer an isolated fringe idea, but rather a popular mainstream trend. In the end the answer to why home-schooling works is pretty simple: a vast, faceless bureaucracy can never teach a child more effectively than his or her own parents. Therefore, the solution to the educational crisis must be increasing parental freedom, expanding educational choices, and encouraging competition to the current system. In the end, it's clear that a village doesn't raise a child. But, worst of all, a teachers union does *damage* to the education of a child.

I believe this vast audience of parents looking for freedom and school choice are a big part of the citizen army needed to empower the coming Citizen Revolution. That army is not limited to the small percentage of parents who home-school. It is not limited to the small percentage of parents with the resources to send their children to private school or parochial school. The real foundation of my citizen army is the 89 percent of parents (proven in the Nevada poll quoted earlier in this chapter) who simply want the choice of something other than public education, but can't presently afford it. That is a citizen army of tens of millions to empower the coming Citizen Revolution.

Chapter 25

The Answer to the Health Care Crisis

Less Government, More Freedom!

If you think health care is expensive now, wait until you see what it costs when it's free!

—P.J. O'ROURKE

I read a remarkable story in the news a while back that summed up the success of government-run health care. A left-leaning Canadian MP (Member of Parliament, our version of Congress) Belinda Stronach recently traveled to the United States for her breast cancer treatment. *What?* Now there's a grand endorsement for government-run health care, huh? Stronach is the daughter of Canadian billionaire business mogul Frank Stronach. Yet one of the richest members of Canadian society chose to leave her own country to get the best care that money could buy—in the United States of America. Does that surprise you? It shouldn't. Rich liberals have always been hypocrites—in any country, in any language. When I was a kid, I remember liberals fighting for school busing. They claimed to be fighting for equality for black children. They called anyone who opposed school busing a "racist." Yet as soon as busing became the law, they sent their kids to exclusive lily-white private schools. We called them "limousine liberals." Today you can find hypocrites just like that all over bastions of liberalism like Hollywood, Malibu, Beverly Hills, Scarsdale, Manhattan, and San Francisco. Rich liberals support equality, equal opportunity, and affirmative action—except at their homes, their businesses, and their own kids' schools. Rich liberals never think the rules apply to them. They think integrated public schools are great for *your* kids, but not for their precious spoiled brats.

Obviously that liberal hypocrisy translates to health care, too. The government-run health care system of Canada (a nice term for "Socialized Medicine") is good enough for you and your family, but not for the wealthy billionaire politicians like Belinda Stronach. Now please don't get me wrong. I support freedom of choice. I think what Stronach did was the right thing (for her). It's her body and her life and she has every right to choose any treatment, anywhere she likes. If I was sick with cancer, I'd choose to go wherever I could get the best health care. It just so happens that Belinda obviously agrees that the place for the best health care is found in the United States. Many Canadians understand that the "expensive" U.S. health care system is the best, and those who can afford it choose to cross the border (by the thousands) for quality (or speed of) medical care they can't find at home.

So now our U.S. health care system has been endorsed by a prominent liberal member of Canadian Parliament. You know, the same health care system that liberal Democrats here in the United States complain about day and night. The same health care system they want to tear down to force government-run health care (otherwise known as Socialized Medicine) down our throats. Of course, a free-market Libertarian conservative like me supports Belinda Stronach seeking (and paying for) health care wherever she chooses. But why isn't that free market available to the rest of her citizens? Why isn't the system that is forced down the throat of all Canadian citizens good enough for a billionaire member of parliament? You mean freedom of choice is something reserved only for the exclusive and privileged few when Big Brother runs health care?

As a son who lost both his parents to cancer 28 days apart, I feel Belinda's pain. My mom died of breast cancer, the same disease affecting Belinda. I will always have a special place in my heart for cancer victims. Not a day goes by when I don't think about my mom or dad. I want to defeat and eradicate cancer more than anyone on earth. I hope and pray that Belinda Stronach will make a full recovery. But I also hope this experience changes her political point of view, too. Doesn't *everyone* deserve freedom of choice? Doesn't *everyone* deserve to choose the medical care and physician that's right for them? Doesn't *everyone* deserve the best doctor that money can buy? Doesn't *everyone* deserve quick and competent care?

■ ■ ■

The thing that drives liberals absolutely crazy is that not everyone gets the best medical care in the United States. *But at least some of us get it.*

Perhaps even a majority of us get it. We have to pay through the nose for it, but we get it. But that's not good enough for bleeding heart liberals. They're not happy unless there's complete equality for everyone. In a government-run system there is in fact equality—it's miserable care for *everyone!* It's rationing for everyone. Unless, of course, you're a rich, limousine-liberal hypocrite. People like that (anywhere in the world) can opt out of the system and pay for their own private care at world-class medical centers, usually located in the United States of America, of course.

Don't believe me? A recent article by John Stossel (a hero of mine) in the *Wall Street Journal* reported that breast cancer survival rates are far higher in the United States. Among females diagnosed with breast cancer, one quarter die in the United States, while one third die in France, and almost half die in the United Kingdom. How's that for equality? How sad is that? How powerful are those facts? Where exactly do *you* want to be treated? The fact is that the smartest doctors in the world are found in the United States, not in spite of, but precisely because we have the most expensive health care system in the world.

Next time you need an eye operation, or a breast cancer operation, do you want the K-Mart "blue plate special?" Do you want your eye surgery done at a cut-rate medical clinic in the back of a strip mall? Do you want some foreign doctor who barely speaks English, who finished next-to-last in his class in Barbados Medical School? Or do you want the guy who finished first in his class at Harvard (who has written six books on his medical specialty)? That Harvard doctor is expensive. There is nothing cheap about good medicine. There are no "50 percent off sales" when you're talking about your eye, or your kidney, or your heart. Although for big government liberals, I think brain surgery should be cheap.

If you want the best medical care in the world, you'd better be willing to pay for it. We get it (most of the time) in the United States. They don't get it most of the time in Canada, United Kingdom, or France. Worse, when you do get medical care in countries with government-run health care, is it really free? A recent article in the *New York Times* about the Romanian health care system told the story of a mother-to-be who refused to pay cash bribes to the doctors (who make substandard wages in a government run system). She was not treated in a timely fashion and lost her baby. I called my friend who is a well-known CEO in Romania to ask if this was a normal situation or an anomaly. He confirmed that doctors in Romania are paid so little by the government that they routinely demand cash bribes or they withhold treatment. Romanian citizens die if they can't pay cash bribes for treatment. Is this the medical system that we want in America?

On the rare occasions that patients in government-run health systems receive first-rate medical care, they certainly don't get it in a *timely* fashion. Next time you need a hip replaced, why not wait 18 months in beautiful Paris or London or Toronto. Eighteen months of agony is no big deal, right? At this very moment, experts report that almost one million Canadians are on a waiting list for medical care (in a country of less than 20 million people). These long waits aren't just for cancer operations—this is for *basic* care. In the United Kingdom the wait for a dentist is so long, news reports say that patients are choosing to pull out their own decaying teeth. In Scotland, rationing is so severe that the government will not provide treatments that would keep the elderly from going blind. Do you still crave government-run health care?

Do you think that our government will be better at managing health care than Canada or the United Kingdom? How about letting the people who managed the response to Hurricane Katrina, or managed the medical care of returning veterans at Walter Reed hospital, run the whole country's medical care? How about putting in charge the government bureaucrats who oversaw the banking system and never noticed a problem in the months before the total collapse of the credit system, mortgage markets, or investment banking on Wall Street? Why don't we assign *those* fellows to oversee government-run health care? I can't wait for that. Oh I forget, those gentlemen aren't free to run health care—they are still in charge of the economy. Isn't government grand?

Government wants accountability and responsibility for CEOs, but never fires the people in government that fail. Government demands that banks break private contracts and not foreclose on homeowners who can't or won't pay their mortgages. Yet my wife paid our property tax bill five days late, while I was writing this chapter. Guess what happened? The state of Nevada fined us $250. I got a *penalty* for paying my property taxes in full, but five days late in the worst economic crisis since the Great Depression. Instead of a penalty, they should have given me a medal! But government doesn't live by the same rules as it asks private industry to live by.

Let me get this straight? If a homeowner can't pay one dollar of a $4,000 per month mortgage to a private bank (thereby breaking a private contract), government thinks the bank is being cruel and evil and greedy if it demands payment. But if a taxpayer pays his or her property taxes in full, but five days late, government thinks you must be punished with a penalty. And you want government in charge of every doctor in America? You want these same hypocrites in charge of deciding whether you get treatment, when you get treatment, what treatment you get, and whether you live or die?

How about competent treatment? Is that what you want? I know I do. When it comes to my eyes, lungs, heart, and brain—I think competence is a pretty darn important thing. Liberals don't understand why capitalism works. The answer is pretty simple: It attracts the best and brightest to U.S. medicine only because medicine *pays* huge dollars here in a private enterprise system. If we socialize medicine and cut the dollars dramatically, you'll attract mediocre doctors. Not the best of the best, but the worst of the best. Sometimes maybe even the worst of the worst.

The smartest kids will decide to go into law or business or investment banking. Or they'll leave the country. But I'll tell you what they won't do—they won't give up a decade of the best years of their lives (for medical school and internships) for a lifetime of mediocre pay and long hours as a doctor in a government-run medical system. Do we want a health care system that attracts incompetent doctors for mediocre pay? Are you really mad because your doctor can afford to belong to a fancy golf club? Is that a bad thing in your opinion? *If my doctor can't afford to play golf, I don't want him anywhere near my heart!* Next time I'm in a life-and-death medical emergency, I want the doctor leaning over my lifeless body to be very rich. *Filthy rich.* And to be American. *Harvard* American.

■ ■ ■

In the end, our U.S. health care system isn't perfect—far from it. In many instances, it is a disappointment. But there's nothing better out there. It turns out health care is like marriage. It's the worst institution on earth, except for all the others! I hear divorced friends constantly bad-mouthing marriage, yet two years later they're all married again. If it's so bad, why get remarried? Of course, the answer is that they experienced the alternative (being single and lonely) and couldn't find anything better. The truth is that humans like to complain. It gives them something to do. Complaining about marriage and health care are a national sport in the United States. That's fine. Just come get me when you find something better.

Now it's one thing to complain about the idea of government-run health care. It's more important to provide an alternative. Here are my five solutions to make the present system better. The answers, of course, are all built around the Libertarian free market solutions to most (if not all problems): Provide more freedom, choice, and competition.

1. Let's get the federal government out of the way. As usual, the government isn't the solution; *it's the problem.* The federal government has tied the hands of the states. I'm a firm believer in States' Rights. The answers to most problems can be found at the state and local level. The federal government (just like in the energy business) forces

byzantine rules and regulations upon health insurance providers. That means if I live in Nevada, I am forced to buy only a Nevada policy. If I live in California, I am forced to buy only a California policy. If I live in New York, I am forced to buy only a New York policy. You get the picture. Consumers have no freedom or choice. But why? Why shouldn't a Nevada citizen be able to buy the best and least expensive policy that fits their needs no matter where it is available anywhere in this country? If Nevada health insurance costs $1,000 per month, and the same policy is only $400 in New Hampshire, why shouldn't I have a right to protect my family with the best policy for my personal situation? What if forcing me to buy the most expensive health insurance policy in my state means I won't be able to afford *any* policy? Well, now you understand why there's a health insurance crisis. It's caused in many cases by the federal government.

My plan is to leave the issue to the states. Get the feds out of it. Let each state come up with its own rules and regulations. States are the "petri dish" of politics; 50 minds are always better (and more creative) than one. States from coast to coast will experiment with their own ideas, and one of them (or perhaps 50 of them) will come up with a health insurance plan that really works. If it's successful, that successful model will spread across the country. All U.S. citizens will benefit. So, first and foremost, deregulate and get the federal government out of health care.

2. Allow any person to shop for health insurance *anywhere* in the country. But it's not just the where, it's the what. Why should government mandate what is covered in the policy? Allow any consumer to buy any policy they want—thereby allowing the consumer to decide what should be covered, not the government. That will bring rates down everywhere. When Californians find out that health insurance is 40 percent cheaper in another state, that will cause a mass exodus by California residents to buy health insurance elsewhere. That will instantly bring down the cost of health insurance in California. That's how capitalism works. Any health insurance company that doesn't immediately drop its prices in response to cheaper prices elsewhere, and a mass exodus of customers, will go out of business. Competition is good for consumers. That's precisely why capitalism works.

In the old Soviet Union there was no competition. The government made, sold, and controlled virtually everything. They were the only game in town. That's why the lives of Soviet citizens were so miserable. Without competition, prices were high, quality was poor, service was horrible, and the system suffered shortages of goods (including food and medicine). With no competition, there is no quality or quantity. When government runs it, you can bet it will be a disaster for all citizens. Obviously, the United States can't be compared to the old days of the communist Soviet Union. But our health insurance system shares some aspects with the old Soviet system. Our federal government does not allow true freedom, choice, or competition. Our federal government mandates "one size fits all." That means insurers have to provide everything—we as consumers can't choose to opt out of certain coverage. That makes prices artificially high. This is bad for consumers. I believe we should allow any U.S. consumer to buy any policy anywhere that fits their needs. Institute my idea, and watch prices drop. What a novel idea—*freedom!*

3. We must unlink the connection between employer and employee health insurance. Offer the deduction for health insurance for individuals, not for companies. Allow a dollar for dollar deduction from taxes. That way your health insurance is "owned" by you. You can take it with you wherever you go. No employee will ever again have to worry again about losing his or her job, and automatically losing their health insurance. What if your child has cancer, or asthma, or diabetes? Should you be trapped for life with your employer? What if it's a bad employer who abuses you? Should you have to stay just for the health insurance? My plan ends this problem forever. As a bonus, when you unlink the connection between employer and health insurance, sick employees stand a better chance of getting hired for a new job. As it stands now, a cancer survivor might have a hard time getting hired for fear of a huge increase in monthly health insurance premiums for all the other employees in the "insurance pool" at a small business.

4. We must expand Health Savings Accounts. This encourages those consumers who can afford it to self-insure. Say I'm able to put away $10,000 per year in a Health Savings Account, with every

dollar deductible from my federal income taxes. Now I'm free to shop for a high deductible, catastrophic health insurance policy that starts covering my family when medical bills reach $10,000. Up until $10,000, the bills are on me—paid for by my fully deductible Health Savings Account. A catastrophic health insurance policy is far cheaper for the consumer. If I'm willing to pick up the first $10,000 per year of medical bills, my insurance rate could drop from $800 per month to only $250. Everyone wins: consumers, insurance companies, doctors, government. It's a win/win all around. Why isn't this happening? Politics. Special interests like the system just the way it is—they make millions, or tens of millions, or hundreds of millions, or billions off the status quo. So they legally bribe your Congressperson with campaign contributions to ensure that things stay exactly the way they are.

5. Finally, we must attempt to get the lawyers out of the process (as much as is possible in a free society). I support passing tort reform that limits frivolous lawsuits, limits (or "caps") damage awards, and requires the losing side to pay legal and court costs. This last idea is often called "the loser pays rule." In virtually every democracy in the world, except the United States, the loser of a lawsuit must pay the winner's legal fees (and often court costs as well). The fact that we are the lone holdout indicates why the United States has the highest rates of litigation in the world. Critics argue that this rule would stop legitimate plaintiffs with small incomes or few assets from filing lawsuits. Not true. The solution to that problem is legal expenses insurance, which is offered around the world. This insurance pays the bill if you lose a lawsuit. Problem solved. This rule prevents frivolous or nuisance lawsuits from ever making it to trial.

Limiting frivolous lawsuits would save almost $1 trillion for U.S. consumers. That is the cost that experts estimate of frivolous lawsuits annually in this country. But worse are the hidden costs of lawsuits because physicians practice "defensive medicine." *USA Today* recently reported that studies in Massachusetts and Pennsylvania found that 83 percent and 93 percent respectively of the doctors in those states practice defensive medicine. The Massachusetts Medical Society estimated that this costs consumers in their state alone at least $1.4 billion annually. Federal government statistics (provided by the Health and Human Services Department) put the losses at more than $60 billion per year nationally.

Frivolous lawsuits drive up the cost of virtually everything we touch as consumers. Is your health insurance way too high? That's because health insurance companies have to spend hundreds of millions of dollars on expensive teams of lawyers and settlements for frivolous cases. Are the costs of your doctor visits too high? That's because your doctor has to pay outrageous sums for medical malpractice insurance. Is your hospital bill high? Same reason—but add in the fact that every machine, tool, and device in the entire hospital costs substantially more because of the high costs of liability insurance (caused by frivolous lawsuits). Your personal cost for any medical problem goes up because your doctor must order extra (and often unnecessary) tests, procedures, or prescriptions to protect him- or herself from future lawsuits (that's defensive medicine). Every product you buy at the store (even those with no medical connection whatsoever) costs more because the liability costs for the product and the health insurance costs for the employees of the company that makes or sells that product is so high. The list is endless.

So if the solution is so simple, why don't we act to limit frivolous lawsuits and cap damages? The answer is simple, too. It's because most politicians are lawyers, or receive major contributions (legal bribery) from trial lawyer associations. Think of the presidential candidates who claimed they had the answers for the medical crisis—Hillary Clinton (lawyer), John Edwards (lawyer), and our new President Barack Obama (lawyer). They don't have the solution—*they are the problem.* Their goal is to make sure this problem *never* goes away.

My goal is not to put lawyers out of business, or to deny the possibility of lawsuits. Remember, I'm the guy who passionately supports freedom and free speech. Consumers have every right to sue, and lawyers have every right to represent them. I'd never change that. Besides, plenty of lawyers are on the side of the "good guys." My personal attorney, Lee Sacks, is one of my best friends. Lee has represented me as my personal attorney for 20 years now. He is one of the finest individuals you'll ever meet (and one heck of a lawyer to have on your side). My wonderful sister, Lori Brown, is a lawyer. One of our closest family friends, Geraldine Weiss, is a remarkable woman and successful attorney. Many of my trusted business associates are lawyers (like Rick Williams, Alan Anjozian, and Bobby Consentino). There are many great lawyers in this country. Lawsuits and lawyers are a necessary part of life. Without relying on the lawyers that I trust (like those above), I could not conduct business.

So there is nothing extreme about what I'm suggesting. My plan relies on common sense. My only goal here is to drastically reduce frivolous lawsuits that run up the costs of doing business and receiving medical care for all of us. I'm trying to eliminate "the lawsuit lottery" where people expect to get rich off one unlucky event in their lives (which raises the costs of virtually *everything* in life for the rest of us). I'm trying to weed the bad lawsuits out of the legal system.

If you want to seriously attempt to cut medical and health insurance costs, and end the medical care crisis in this country, frivolous lawsuits are the obvious first place to start. The answer is to cap damage awards, and to punish those who bring frivolous lawsuits by requiring the losing side to pay legal and court costs to innocent defendants. If our lawyers-turned-politicians won't accept that commonsense compromise, then we all know whose side they are on. And it isn't ours.

■ ■ ■

The solutions to our health care crisis are quite simple and achievable: Give consumers more choice. Get the federal government out of our medical system. Get the tyrants and Nanny State bureaucrats who think they know best out of the system. Get the lawyers out of the system. But then I'm repeating myself.

Chapter 26

The Audacity of Affirmative Action

Government is not reason. It is not eloquence. It is force.
—George Washington

I t's time to open up a dialogue and debate with the American people (and between citizens of different races) about a controversial,
but important issue. This issue is affirmative action. My book is
centered on economic issues. Well, what is more important than an issue
like affirmative action, which potentially determines an individual's
earning power for the rest of his or her life? Affirmative action changes
lives, determines jobs, and decides who is awarded contracts by government. It is the ultimate economic issue.

Since the issue of affirmative action is centered on race, most white
politicians are afraid to discuss it for fear of being labeled a racist. I am
not most politicians. Fear is not a word that affects my life.

As a person of color, Barack Obama has discussed this issue, largely unchallenged. I will challenge it. There is a second side to affirmative action—the white male perspective—that everyone is afraid to discuss for fear of being crucified by the bleeding-heart, guilt-ridden, liberal media types. It's a natural debate to have, so let's have it right now.

■ ■ ■

As discussed throughout this book, Barack and I are on opposite ends of the political spectrum, yet we graduated from the same college (Columbia University Class of '83) on the same day, with the same major. Every step of the way, whether it's spoken or not, race has played a part in our lives, our experiences, and the way that we have formed our political opinions on issues of importance to U.S. citizens.

To me, affirmative action is a civil rights issue. But, I'm sure, not in the way Barack thinks of "civil rights." You see the pendulum has swung past the midpoint where today my civil rights—as a white American—are being violated daily. I know, some of you are saying "Oh, poor, poor you."

But, let's look at the facts. Many of the most important economic opportunities are affected by decisions based on race—who gets into colleges, law schools, business schools, medical schools, who is hired at the biggest corporations in the United States, who is hired for state and federal government civil service jobs (that come with incredible pensions and benefits), who is promoted at the workplace, and who is awarded multimillion dollar government contracts in the name of quotas, affirmative action, or that famous buzzword "diversity." And in each case, if the decision or access to opportunity is based on reverse racism, it's wrong and a violation of our civil rights.

Reverse racism—no matter if the intent is to remedy some past wrong—is still racism. In each case it is a violation of everything for which the United States stands. To choose to exclude applicants who might be more talented, smarter, harder working, more worthy, but just happen to be white, in favor of those who happen to be black, is quite simply a travesty. It creates, not promotes, racial disharmony. Ironically, affirmative action encourages this idea of "two Americas" that liberals talk about nonstop. It divides U.S. citizens and creates anger, bitterness, and jealousy.

My parents taught me that two wrongs do not make a right. I was also taught that race should not and does not matter. Yet, the government says that it does and violates my civil rights by calling it "just." I call it what it is, reverse racism. How can you call it anything else when having a certain skin color gets you a job, salary, or college admission? How can you call it anything else when the color of your skin gives you advantages *mandated* by government? How can you call it anything else when decisions that affect the rest of our lives (for better or worse) are determined by race? In the 1950s and 1960s when this debate began, and it was people of color being discriminated against, it was called what it is: racism. Today, when it is a different color of people being discriminated against, how can it be called anything else? In my opinion, any form of discrimination is just plain wrong—whether the person on the receiving end is white, brown, black, red, or yellow.

Talent, and a willingness to work, should determine every person's level of success. Achievement should be based on what's in our heads, the decisions we make, how hard we are willing to work—never on the color of our skin. No one deserves to be hired, fired, qualified, or disqualified based on their skin color. The only color that matters should be *gray*—the gray matter in our brains.

The biased liberal media will tell you that racism, as I've just outlined it, doesn't exist, or that it is somehow just.

Barack supports affirmative action. I do not. Why? Simply because affirmative action has dramatically altered both our lives. What could be a more ideal forum for discussion and debate than comparing how it affected the lives of two high-profile college classmates—one the President of the United States. And one who wants to be.

People of color will tell you they are angry about being denied opportunities based solely upon the color of their skin. If so, don't I have a right to be just as angry if I was denied an opportunity because of the color of my skin? What if a poor white butcher's son applies to Harvard versus a wealthy black investment banker's son? Do you think the black kid who lives in a mansion in Beverly Hills should get into Harvard ahead of the white butcher's son who lives in a small apartment in the Bronx? I think it's a topic the citizens of the United States should want to confront with Obama in the White House.

In exploring this topic, we need to determine who is now being a victim of bias and prejudice. What if it turns out that I was the one treated badly by an educational system that bases decisions on the color of a person's skin? Is our country comfortable with this double stand-ard? After all, my family owes no debt to people of color. My family arrived in the United States at the turn of the 20th century. We were not here when blacks were sold into slavery. To the contrary, my rela-tives (of Jewish ancestry) were enslaved and murdered in many different countries because of their religion and race. Yet I've never complained once, never asked for reparations, never used past transgressions as an excuse to demand superior treatment today.

Isn't this an issue that Barack demanded we all talk about? Shouldn't a white U.S. citizen be able to discuss this topic openly and honestly— just like a person of color?

Well, here it is . . . and here I am. I'm putting it on the table once and for all. The time has come . . . the discussion is now open. I am not a racist. To the contrary, I've never judged anyone in my life because of the color of his or her skin. That's my point. Race should *not* matter. But it certainly cannot matter to only one group—while everyone else is forced to accept a discriminatory violation of their civil rights in the name of equality and walk on eggshells about the topic for fear of being called a racist. It is time for good people to speak up. Obama's election as president makes this the perfect time to discuss race and end affirma-tive action. No one in the United States ever has to feel guilty again. We have proven once and for all that race does not matter in the United States. We have proven that anyone can achieve anything in this great country. Ironically, Obama is the test case that proves the time has come to end discrimination supported by government. Obama's election proves that minorities no longer require government's help (or force).

■ ■ ■

The NBA serves as the perfect example of the folly and fallacy of affirmative action. If affirmative action is truly good for the goose, then it must be good for the gander, too. Therefore, it must be applied fairly—to *every* area of inequality—including the NBA. Would any of us want government to mandate that the NBA be more representative of race in our society? Should NBA draft choices be based on affirma-tive action? Should the NBA mandate that teams reflect the race of their geographic area? Should the Utah Jazz be mandated to field an all-white team to represent their all-white state? Should every NBA team feature a Jew, Asian, Hispanic, and Native American?

It would be offensive and unfair to fans who pay top dollar to watch the best talent available in the world, to be forced in the name of political correctness to watch mediocre players who were simply on the team because of the color of their skin. I would never want to mandate affirmative action in the NBA. The NBA should not be mandated 80 percent white. Nor should it be mandated 80 percent black. The color of the skin of the players should not matter. I simply want the best talent on the court—whatever the color of their skin. The same applies to boxing, football, hockey, golf, tennis, football, lacrosse, and so on. Let only those with the most talent reap the rewards (and the $50 million contracts). Race should never be a factor.

Well, if you agree, why should lawyers, doctors, corporate executives, or government contractors be treated any differently? Why should college admissions be treated any differently? Why should the office of the President of the United States be treated any differently? The man or woman who occupies the oval office should get the job because of their talent, not the color of their skin.

That is why I think this is a perfect time, place, and opportunity for an open and honest national discussion and debate about the need for affirmative action.

One of my heroes, Ronald Reagan, once changed the world by forcefully demanding, "Mr. Gorbachev, tear down this wall." I now throw down the gauntlet to my college classmate.

"President Barack Obama, take up my challenge."

Let's now choose to talk about racism from the perspective of all races. After all, at some point of our lives or our ancestors' lives, we have all been a victim of bias, discrimination, unjust business practices, misrepresentation, or unwarranted favoritism. Quite frankly, I believe Barack and I have the same goal—the elimination of racism. Who better than two college classmates to face the topic head-on?

Chapter 27

Stop the Global Warming Insanity

Facing the Real Global Threat

The urge to save humanity is almost always a false front for the urge to rule.

—H.L. MENCKEN

As a CEO, businessman, entrepreneur, and head of a large family (I guess you can also call me the CEO of the household), I am keenly aware that no individual, business, organization, or government can continue to operate at a perpetual deficit. It is literally *economic suicide.* And in the case of government, it imperils and impacts (and threatens to destroy) the lives of citizens, taxpayers, and worse—our children and grandchildren. Yet the federal government spends more money than it takes in *every single day* with no plans to reverse course. It is literally a big Ponzi scheme. The U.S. government makes Bernard Madoff look like a piker. The U.S. government is literally the *Titanic* headed for the world's biggest iceberg. And like Bernie Madoff, it all worked as long as the economy kept growing at a fast pace. But the moment things slowed down, there wasn't enough money coming in for Madoff to keep the charade going. The same economic tsunami that destroyed Madoff's scam will now destroy the scam of the U.S. government. The game is over—we are bankrupt. Actually we are bankrupt squared (to the tenth level).

We cannot possibly continue to spend at the same levels as when things were going good, now that things are going bad. There just isn't enough tax revenue coming in to keep spending at the same baseline. We can't keep spending far more than we take in, while at the same time the national debt from decades past keeps piling up unpaid. We are so broke, we can't pay last year's bills, let alone the new bills for this year. Yet Obama has decided to spend more in response to this crisis—*far* more. By a decade or so from now, just the interest on the national debt (according to Obama's own projections) will be $800 billion per year. How big is $800 billion? If you spent $1,000,000 per day from the day that Jesus was born until today, it still wouldn't equal $800 billion! And that's just the interest payment owed by the American people. This is insanity. It is financial madness. *This* issue is the biggest threat to our existence. This same threat, government overspending, massive entitlements, and mounds of debt reaching to the moon, is what destroyed the Greek and Roman empires. We are headed for the same fate. The U.S. empire is crumbling because of one issue: overspending by government.

Yet left-wing politicians, the biased liberal media, and biased liberal educators (many of whom are closet socialists) try their best *every second of every day* to brainwash the people (and an entire generation of U.S. children) that the greatest threat to our planet is global warming. Global warming is the *American Idol* of politics. It's all about the hype, hysteria, and sex appeal.

It certainly is exciting and sexy to tell children that global warming threatens to melt ice caps, raise ocean levels, cover major coastal cities with 10 feet of water, spur weather disasters across the globe, and wreak havoc with our world—killing or starving billions of humans in the process.

That makes for great news headlines. That makes for some very memorable talking points for politicians. And that would also make one heck of a script for a Hollywood blockbuster! Oh, I forgot it already did—Al Gore's *An Inconvenient Truth*.

On the other hand, it is not exciting, or sexy, or simple, in a fast-food, sound-bite, one-night-stand world to explain the dangers of overspending and debt to the *American Idol/Dancing with the Stars* generation. The idea that our federal government is growing far too big and far too fast, is spending much more than it takes in, and that this will eventually bankrupt our country and destroy our way of life, is exciting only to a mathematician, policy wonk, or economist. Throw in the fact that in many cases, the money that government is overspending is on *us* (in the form of entitlements, welfare, free school lunches, aid to dependent children, public school education) and you can see why it's much easier to "sell" global warming. No one wants to be told that the money being spent on *them* is going to bankrupt our nation. Most people are not long-term thinkers, so what might happen a year from now, let alone a decade from now, is unimportant to them. But worse, if the only way to prevent the disaster 10 years from now is to personally sacrifice today, the answer from most people in our selfish society is a deafening *no!*

Children certainly can understand the doom and gloom of global warming. It sounds like an action or horror movie they've watched recently. Physical disasters are easily understood, but losing a job or going broke are not threats easily explained or understood by young people. Losing a job or a home just doesn't put the fear of God into a young person who hasn't even had a job or owned a home yet.

Global warming is also easy for Hollywood entertainers and celebrities to understand—their lives are based on dysfunction, overacting, and being "drama queens." Entertainers are the *sensitive* personality type—they go into crying, shaking, and hysterical fits of rage backstage at their concerts, or on the set of their latest movie, if their order of caviar and Perrier is not perfectly executed. Can you imagine how stirred up you can get a Hollywood celebrity over the image of billions of humans suffering, starving, and dying due to the pollution caused by greedy capitalists? But as for the idea of a country going broke from overspending? That doesn't engender quite the same level of drama.

The image of debt just doesn't sell in Hollywood. In Hollywood, sex sells. Global warming has sex appeal, government debt doesn't.

The mainstream media certainly appreciates the pizzazz and sex appeal of global warming headlines—the global warming boogeyman sells newspapers and magazines, sells books, sells box office tickets, and raises TV news ratings. People flock to movies about Armageddon, environmental death and destruction, or liberal causes (ask Michael Moore or Al Gore). But who would flock to a movie about . . . *debt?* Who would be the star? What would they call it? *Two Economists and a Mathematician.*

Based on glamour, glitz, fear factor, hysteria, sex appeal, pizzazz, and propaganda potential, global warming is the victor—*hands down.* Based on facts it is not. Global warming is the perfect boogeyman for the left-wing agenda. Global warming is to liberals what the War on Terror is to the right-wing neoconservatives. They are both excuses to build hysteria, create fear on a massive scale, gain power, get elected, and grow government. What makes them so effective and believable is that neither is based on fraud or lies. Both terrorism and pollution exist. They are both *legitimate* threats. But only by exaggerating the threat to epic proportions can the political propaganda experts get your attention and convince you to willingly expand government to epic proportions.

Global warming is a dream come true for the type of person who wants to control the lives of others: liberal politicians and bureaucrats. In the face of death, destruction, and disaster on an epic scale, well-meaning citizens are helpless to say no to the big government Nanny State. After all, what kind of a greedy, heartless, capitalist pig can possibly say *no* to saving the planet?

The effectiveness of any boogeyman exaggeration is increased if it's based on some kind of reality. There is a threat of terror and there most certainly is a threat from pollution. The more we all fear terrorist attacks, the more likely we are to spend trillions of dollars more on bigger government—more defense contractors, more soldiers, more foreign aid, more military bases all over the world, more billion dollar weapon systems, more employees and executives hired by Homeland Security. This fear is used by politicians to increase defense budgets forever. A simple little 5 percent reduction in the *increase* in annual defense spending results in hysterical rantings and warnings of Armageddon.

And the same holds true for global warming—the more frightened we all are of global warming, the more likely we'll be to easily and quickly agree to allow government to tax business to death, hire millions of new government bureaucrats to enforce draconian new rules and regulations, and to spend trillions of dollars to protect us from the environmental boogeymen. The more likely we are to never allow a 5 percent cut in the global warming budget . . . or even a 5 percent cut in the annual increase in spending.

Both the left- and right-wing power structures use their own versions of boogeymen to spread fear and gain power. This is what elects politicians—*the fear factor*. This is what grows government and spending and bureaucracy—without a howl of protest from citizens and taxpayers. But most importantly, this is what fuels the U.S. economy. Republicans scare us into making government bigger. Democrats scare us into making government bigger. Government creates millions of jobs from these "fear factor" storylines. They just happen to employ a different group—*their* supporters and contributors.

Just as Bush gave billions of dollars in government contracts to Blackwater, Haliburton, and other defense contractors across the country in response to the threat of terrorism, now Obama will hand over billions of dollars in government contracts to environmental groups and their cronies in response to global warming. The idea of a modern-day New Deal announced by Obama to "stimulate the economy" is simply Obama's brilliant plan to dole out jobs, contracts, and entitlements to his group of supporters and contributors. After eight years of Bush making Republican contributors fat, rich, and happy, now it's time for Obama to make Democratic contributors fat, rich, and happy. They had to think of *something* to scare the people into accepting billions of dollars in new spending. Global warming is a great story to tell. You can turn down a billion in new welfare spending, but no one wants to turn down a billion (or trillion) in spending on green technologies to save the planet (and our children) from global warming. The democrats have invented the perfect boogeyman. Global warming isn't about saving the planet; it's about saving the Democrats.

As such, global warming is the newest gleaming prize for those who want to grow government and bloat the bureaucracy. It is the gift that keeps on giving. It is easy to explain in sound bites, easy to use to promote hysteria, easy to push on children at school, easy for the news media to hype during ratings week, and easy to blame as the cause of every new global weather disaster. It will be used for many years to come to justify every new increase in government spending and hiring.

But what is missing from the public discourse, are the *facts*. So, let's talk about the facts.

■ ■ ■

We don't know if global warming really exists. If it exists, it may in fact be part and parcel of a cyclical warming and cooling of the environment that has gone on unabated for millions of years. It may just be a part of the natural long-term cycle of nature. It may exist, but we don't know if it's here to stay or temporary. We don't know whether the damage it might be doing to the environment is temporary or permanent. We don't know if the damage it might be doing to the environment actually threatens our very existence. And if it does indeed threaten our very existence, we don't actually know if any drastic changes that we institute can actually affect global warming (or cooling). In other words, even if global warming exists, is it man-made global warming, or just a natural cycle of nature?

Case and point. As I write this chapter, my home in Las Vegas is covered by 10 inches of snow—the biggest blizzard to hit Vegas in 30 years. My sons and I were sledding today on the snow-covered golf course in front of my home. Yes, I said *sledding!* On the rare occasions that it snows in Vegas, it usually melts within hours. This snowstorm has blanketed the golf course in front of my home for six *days!* This is the third major snowstorm at my home in Vegas in the past six years. I may not be a professional weatherman, but it sure seems obvious to me that temperatures are not getting warmer, when we're getting hit with historic blizzards in Sin City.

But for the purpose of this chapter, let's assume that this was a freak occurrence and global warming is real, despite the fact that the cooling of the last few years would more likely indicate the start of a period of global *cooling*. If global warming is real, how do we know that anything mankind does would have an effect on it? The fact is that our effect on global warming is miniscule compared to the natural effect of Mother Nature. There is little evidence that man-made carbon dioxide is causing a spike in temperatures worldwide. The biggest factors that may be affecting temperature change are actually solar spots, solar winds, solar irradiation, and even big weather events like El Niño (the warming of the ocean). In other words, if we are warmer, blame the sun, the wind, and the oceans.

It is true that many of the warmest years in measured history have occurred recently. But there are a few other facts the biased liberal media have left out. The mean global temperature is now the same as it was in 1980. Yes, sea levels *were* rising, but now they have stopped rising. Hurricane activity *was* at all-time highs. But now hurricane and cyclone activity is at a quarter-of-a-century *low*. And here's the most important fact of all—while ice caps are melting in west Antarctica, the ice caps are expanding in East Antarctica. The hysterical, biased-liberal media only reports the ice melt. But finally as I did final edits on this book in late April 2009, scientists reported that ice is expanding in much of Antarctica. It just so happens that East Antarctica (where the ice caps are growing) is four times larger than West Antarctica (where the ice cap is melting). Overall, not only is the earth not losing ice caps, we are *expanding*. Do you see a pattern here?

And what if the "cure" for this unproven disease is worse than the disease itself? What if all of our valiant efforts to end global warming (which may not exist) don't add up to a hill of beans? What if our hopeless efforts result in widespread damage to our economy? What if implementing higher taxes, to combat a threat that may not exist, puts thousands of businesses out of business and costs us tens of millions of jobs? What if all our efforts are for naught, simply because India, China, and many other third world nations refuse to cut back alongside us? What if our efforts to combat global warming cripples the U.S. economy, but the net result is that pollution *increases* globally?

What if the steps recommended by big government proponents, liberal politicians, and environmental radicals just happen to expand government, put them in power, keep them in power, strengthen their unions, keep them employed, fund their grants, win the Nobel Peace Prizes, and enrich their bank accounts? Isn't there a conflict of interest there? Is global warming a threat or an *industry?* Why does the liberal national media report only on the melting of ice caps in West Antarctica, but not the expanding of ice caps in East Antarctica? Are you starting to see a joint effort to distort the picture you're getting?

Perhaps all this hullabaloo is one big attempt for the radical left to gain wealth and power at our expense. After all, they failed dramatically at making money in the game of capitalism. So now their plan is to change the rules of the game. Or perhaps to change the whole game— from capitalism to socialism.

What if these radical new laws to protect the environment lead to a doubling of the price of your gasoline bill, a tripling of your electric and utilities bills, the loss of millions of jobs, the closing of entire industries, and the wrecking of the entire U.S. economy? Would it be worth it to find out?

What if we are now reversing course and entering a global cooling period. What if the laws we put into place to deal with global warming cause *more* damage in a global cooling age? Once government puts laws into place, they are slow to change and almost impossible to repeal.

Do you trust that government has the right answers? Do you believe that government knows better than you? Do you think this is the first time this idea has been tried by government? As Yogi Berra would say, "It's déjà vu all over again." Jimmy Carter unleashed a "green revolution" on the United States way back in the late '70s. Carter wanted to do the same thing as Obama—create millions of politically correct "green jobs" by saving the environment. It was called the Synthetic Fuels Corp. and the only thing it produced was an economic disaster. Taxpayers lost $3 billion. That's chicken feed compared to the cost of Obama's ambitious green agenda. Can you even imagine what we could lose this time?

But Carter wasn't the last politician to fail promoting the latest and greatest green solution. More recently, the federal government chose ethanol as the latest and greatest new thing to save our world—again with lousy results. Politicians picked ethanol as the big winner to reduce our dependence on foreign oil and lower gas prices. Ethanol could never make money without massive government intervention, so politicians awarded the ethanol industry billions of dollars in tax credits, subsidies, and tariffs. The result? Ethanol caused a worldwide food shortage, resulting in food shortages and protests around the globe. But it gets worse. Ethanol not only failed to lower our dependence on foreign oil, it *raised* gas prices. It turns out you need more than one gallon of gas to create one gallon of ethanol. So our need for foreign oil went up, not down. So did grocery prices (because of shortages of corn feed for livestock). And here's the bonus—pollution went up, too! It turns out that ethanol pollutes even more than gasoline. That's one heck of a great combo, don't you think? Those politicians really make great decisions. What makes you think that their guesses on global warming will be any more accurate than their guesses on ethanol?

Or take the federal government's brilliant solution for energy conservation—Congress passed a law in 1992 called the Energy Policy Act to require federal agencies to buy alternative-fuel vehicles. The goal was to encourage Detroit automakers to produce more fuel-efficient cars. But the *Washington Post* recently reported that the government paid billions to purchase thousands of flex-fuel vehicles and located them in places with no access to alternative fuel. Result: More than 92 percent of the fuel used in those "flex fuel cars" is good old-fashioned *gasoline*. So we wasted billions of dollars on nothing—the government bureaucrats could have just kept driving their old cars. Worse, the Postal Service estimates their fleet consumed 1.5 million *more* gallons of gasoline than if this Energy Policy Act had never been instituted, simply because the "green vehicles" mandated by government only came in 6 or 8-cylinder models. The old "polluting" vehicles driven by postal employees were 4-cylinder models, thereby using less standard gasoline. Isn't government great? These guys are the Keystone Cops. Can you see now the folly of government mandating us to do anything? It all sounds nice, but it never works out according to the plans of lame-brained civil servants.

Just remember that the same people who convinced us that ethanol was the solution to our dependence on foreign oil, and that "flex fuel cars" were the solution to energy conservation, are now trying to convince you that they have the solution to global warming. Be scared. Be *very* scared.

■ ■ ■

One other "little thing" we might want to consider before turning the entire U.S. economy over to the green movement: Virtually every government program in history has cost more than originally projected. Usually *far* more. Rarely do environmentalists, or politicians like Al Gore or Barack Obama, even mention the possible costs of fighting the global-warming boogeyman. That's because it's too big to even fathom—just mentioning these gigantic numbers would frighten citizens and put doubt into the entire project. But whatever billions or trillions the global warming crusade will cost, we might want to use past government projections as a measuring stick and therefore triple or quadruple the estimated costs. Although I'm not sure if you can quadruple "bankruptcy." What is four times more than the cost of bankruptcy? Let's just call it "Bankruptcy Squared." It's a term I originally coined to describe California's economy. If we allow politically correct, power-hungry liberal politicians to change our national economy in the name of global warming, we can now apply this term to the entire U.S. economy.

So what is Obama's politically correct plan to combat global warming? He'll do for wind farms and bio fuels what politicians have already done for ethanol, by spending billions of your tax dollars on tax credits and subsidies for products that are proven less efficient and cost-effective than coal and oil. We already have almost 2 million jobs in the U.S. economy based on the oil and gas industries. Now Obama has proposed spending billions to create 5 million new "green jobs." Which means one of two things—either government will kill the 2 million old jobs related to oil and gas to create a few million new jobs (which makes no economic sense), or we'll create another bloated bureaucracy of 5 million people doing the job once done efficiently by 2 million. Sounds like something only government could produce.

Then the federal government will prop up this bloated, failing bureaucracy with $15 billion to $20 billion per year of taxpayer money (from me and you) paid for with higher taxes and far higher gas and electric rates, and call it a big success. It's amazing how easy it is to create success with someone else's money. If only I could collect taxes, all of my businesses would be remarkable successes.

■ ■ ■

Before we take a chance on crippling the greatest economy in world history and wrecking our future quality of life, let's examine the factual track record of alarmist, extremist environmentalists in the recent past. My guess is that *none* of this has ever been mentioned by the biased liberal mainstream media, or taught by the Kool-Aid-drinking liberal educators in our public schools.

The amazing record of environmentalists:

- At the first Earth Day in 1969, environmentalist Nigel Calder warned: "The threat of a new Ice Age must now stand alongside nuclear war as the likely source of wholesale death and misery for mankind."
- Al Gore is the "King of Global Warming." So it should be valuable to learn that Al Gore's mentor, Professor Paul Ehrlich, predicted there would be a major food shortage in United States in the 1970s and that hundreds of *millions* of people would starve to death. His exact prediction was that by 1999 the U.S. population would have declined to 22.6 million citizens.

    Pretty smart guy that Ehrlich—he was only off by about 277.4 million citizens. Lucky for us he has an advanced graduate degree. Can you imagine how off the prediction would have been in the hands of a *less* educated man?

    But Professor Ehrlich had many interesting predictions. He predicted about the United Kingdom, "If I were a gambler, I would take even money that England will not exist in the year 2000."

    It's lucky that policy wonks don't gamble. But, of course, they'd never risk their *own* money—that's only for entrepreneurs or small businesspeople like you and me. Liberal policy wonks and hare-brained environmentalists only risk *your* money on outrageous, extreme, alarmist predictions.
- In 1975, the Environmental Fund took out full-page ads warning: "The world as we know it will likely be ruined by the year 2000." This statement is reminiscent of what radical environmentalists say today about global warming. Sounds like maybe the children of the executives at the Environmental Fund in 1975 are reading from the same playbook today.
- Harvard biologist George Wald in 1970 warned, "Civilization will end within 15 or 30 years unless immediate action is taken against problems facing mankind." Same storyline. Do these guys with advanced degrees and scientific credentials all drink the same flavor of Kool-Aid?

    Senator Gaylord Nelson in 1970 said in *Look* magazine: "By 1995, somewhere between 75 and 85 percent of all species of living animals will be extinct." The interesting thing to note about

Gaylord's prediction is that the only things extinct in 2009 are Senator Gaylord Nelson . . . and *Look* magazine!

- In 1939, the U.S. Department of Interior predicted that U.S. oil supplies would last only another 13 years. In other words, we'd run out of oil by 1952.

- In 1974, the U.S. Geological Survey predicted that the United States only had a 10-year supply of natural gas left. What is it with this need for "experts" to predict that oil will run out in the near future? Well, at least the idea that we'd run out of oil in 1984 is a better prediction than 1952. The government experts were getting *closer* to the facts by 1974.

The only thing that we can conclude from all these predictions is that the only thing worse than an environmentalist or scientist making predictions, is a government bureaucrat making predictions. You know what another word for predictions is? *Guessing.*

But perhaps my favorite example of the hyperbole of the environmental movement is the headline from *Time* magazine on June 24, 1974, "Another Ice Age?" Read the paragraph below from this *Time* article from 35 years ago. Substitute "global warming" and today's date and you'd swear you were reading an article from *Time* in 2009:

As they review the bizarre and unpredictable weather pattern of the past several years, a growing number of scientists are beginning to suspect that many seemingly contradictory meteorological fluctuations are actually part of a global climatic upheaval. However widely the weather varies from place to place and time to time, when meteorologists take an average of temperatures around the globe they find that the atmosphere has been growing gradually cooler for the past three decades. The trend shows no indication of reversing. Climatological Cassandras are becoming increasingly apprehensive, for the weather aberrations they are studying may be the harbinger of another *ice age*.

The list goes on and on. Scientists, policy wonks, radical environmentalists, government bureaucrats, and their lackeys in the biased liberal media have made alarmist, hysterical, outrageous, and simply dead wrong predictions for decades. Keep in mind that it's their job to alarm you and me. They need to inspire fear and create mass hysteria to sell their radical agenda. You're not going to be willing to double your gas bills, triple your electric bills, or sacrifice your job, unless you can be convinced that your family's lives are in danger. You certainly won't be willing to make these huge sacrifices to prevent one or two extra rainstorms per year. But you might be willing to sacrifice your quality of life today if you are convinced that your entire city will be under 20 feet of water tomorrow. Hysterical headlines get the attention of the public (and taxpayers).

So now let me ask a few important questions:

- When environmentalists and the liberal media were screaming about global cooling and "a new Ice Age" causing hundreds of millions of people to starve to death, what policies should U.S. government have implemented or changed back then to prevent this cataclysmic "end of the world"? Should we have put into place policies that tripled your utility, gas, and grocery bills and made your job extinct? Should we have radically changed government policy? Should we have radically changed the economy of the United States?

- When we hear experts or government bureaucrats make predictions like this, should we assume these predictions are straight from the mouth of God, or should we listen with a healthy dose of skepticism and cynicism?

- Just because a teacher, scientist, professor, media authority, government bureaucrat, or "expert" of some kind says it, does that make it true?

- What makes any of us think that today's global warming scare is any more accurate than the global cooling/Ice Age scare of a few decades ago?

- Even if the threat from greenhouse gases is real, it's a fact that natural wetlands alone produce more greenhouse gas contributions annually than all human contributions combined. So what effect would any of the drastic changes that radical environmentalists demand we enact, actually make on the environment? And would the accompanying loss of jobs and damage to the economy be worth it?

Most importantly, we have taken our eyes off the *real* threat to the futures of our children and grandchildren. It is in fact the deficit and national debt that should be the real "global threat" taught in schools and exposed in the media.

Do not get me wrong—I am not saying that global warming isn't real, or a threat. I am not saying it's a bad thing to be environmentally conscious. I am not saying that creating green jobs is not a worthy goal. But I am saying that further study is needed before we make decisions based on political correctness, or the political agenda of special interest groups interested in creating more jobs, more power and more government contracts for themselves.

The world has warmed up and cooled down for millions of years. We survived in the past without government intervention, but rather based on free markets and personal ingenuity. As an example, the Vikings took advantage of ice-free oceans to colonize Greenland. They were the beneficiaries of a long-ago period of global warming. A *temporary* period.

What I am saying is that we should maintain a healthy dose of skepticism, before we radically and drastically change our economy, or hand over the creation of 90 percent of our future jobs to Obama's friends, supporters, and contributors. And if we do eventually determine that global warming is a fact, I believe our dynamic free market economy will respond to the challenge, much better, far faster, and more efficiently than government ever could. Let the private sector respond to global warming, *not* the government.

■ ■ ■

Although contradictory evidence exists that global warming is a threat to future generations, there is actually 100 percent proof that continuing to run up huge deficits, debt, and unfunded liabilities (for government employee union pensions) is a betrayal of future generations. In an ever more dangerous world, it is quite frankly a national security threat for our federal government to run up mountains of debt—making us dependent on our rivals and enemies. It is also a national security threat to heed environmentalists' demands for a ban on offshore oil drilling, thereby making us more dependent on nations that use our billions of energy dollars to fund a war on terrorism against us.

When you read my ideas for dramatically cutting government, you now understand that I'm not proposing those massive cuts simply because I'm ideologically or philosophically opposed to big government. Opinions don't matter. *Facts do.* The fact is that the future of our children, grandchildren, our national security, and our U.S. standard of living all require these cuts. The very politicians who scream about the still unproven environmental disaster of global warming are not only ignoring this proven looming economic disaster of national debt, but they are *contributing* to it with their calls for more spending and taxes to combat global warming. This is not compassionate, brilliant, or politically correct on their part. ***It is self-destructive.***

And it will lead to the destruction of our great and wealthy country, just as it led to the destruction of the formerly great and wealthy Greek and Roman empires. It will destroy our children and grandchildren's futures.

Global warming hysteria has fed on the fact that people *do* care very much about the health and survival of future generations. That's a good thing. I'm proud of my fellow citizens. Unfortunately they care too much about the wrong issue. Look at all the symbolic things people are willing to do to fight the threat of global warming—like driving hybrids, switching to expensive new "green" light-bulbs, recycling, conserving energy by turning thermostats down, and so on (many actions that my family and I take as well). They make these sacrifices because they believe they can make a difference. They have a deep desire to "save the earth" for future generations.

These are all positive actions and I applaud you for your willingness to sacrifice. But the reality is that these efforts have little or no impact on global warming (which may or may not exist). By all means keep doing them—because they can only help make this planet a better, cleaner, and healthier place. And they are good habits to teach our children, so that future generations will live healthier lives with cleaner air and water.

But these same people, willing to sacrifice, spend, and fight in the name of leaving future generations a better planet, need to grasp the *real* global threat that we all face—an economic tsunami of epic (perhaps Biblical) proportions. These same people, so willing to sacrifice in the name of global warming, now need to decide that they will apply this same level of energy, enthusiasm, and passion to solving our government spending addiction and debt crisis, as to global warming. These same people must start to behave fiscally responsibly in their corner of the world, stop expecting government (and their neighbors) to provide for them what they can and should provide for themselves, and stop supporting politicians who are fiscally reckless and promoting the same government spending addiction (or even higher levels) that has put us in this dangerous position in the first place. They are promoting the same deadly addiction that threatens our children's and grandchildren's future.

We got in this fiscal mess by spending too much, by growing entitlements too much, by asking government to do too much, by hiring too many government employees, and by abdicating our own personal responsibilities. Now we're responding to the present economic crisis by turning to *more* government, *more* government spending, *more* government handouts, *more* government employees, *more* government intervention, and willingly offering to give up *more* of our own freedoms and responsibilities as individuals? This is a recipe for disaster. As workout guru Susan Powter used to say—*stop the insanity!*

Chapter 28

The Commonsense Answer to the Energy Crisis

Less Government, More Entrepreneurship!

If a government were put in charge of the Sahara Desert, within five years they'd have a shortage of sand.

—Dr. Milton Friedman

I t's one thing to complain about global warming and big government intrusion in the economy. What's more important is to propose solutions to the energy and economic crisis. Seldom are there easy answers to such complex problems. But this time the answers are simple. When it comes to energy we must encourage more entrepreneurship, more free market capitalism, and less government interference. That means deregulation and decontrol. That means lower taxes and more incentives for private investment. That means *unleash the free market*. Government doesn't solve problems, government causes them. When it comes to high gas prices, our government is smack dab in the middle of the problem. Only U.S. entrepreneurs and free market capitalism will put the United States on the road to solving our economic problems, but first government has to get out of the way.

■ ■ ■

This energy crisis and the economic crisis go hand in hand (and to some extent, the terrorist crisis as well). Our oil purchases abroad account for almost half the U.S. trade deficit. Every dollar we spend on foreign oil is a dollar that could be better spent growing the U.S. economy. How do we find the massive money required to buy all that oil? We borrow it from those same countries. What do they do with *our* money? They turn around and use it to fund terrorism.

So, how do we stop this vicious, self-destructive cycle? I am sure by now that you know the answer—we get government out of the way. Please, do not get me wrong. There is one area in which I am in consensus with the environmentalists and Democrats. There is no question that the only *long-term* solution for our country's energy independence is to wean ourselves off of fossil fuel (oil) and replace it with clean and renewable energy. The fact is, that process has been underway for years and I am in total agreement that it must be accelerated.

But, the reality is that it may take another 20–30 years to be accomplished. In the meantime, the answer is more of the Libertarian free market variety—drill, drill, and drill some more. President Bush took a first step by lifting the Executive Ban on offshore oil drilling (one of the few good decisions of his presidency). But that was only a small and symbolic start, and it may be overturned soon.

Congress must greatly reduce the draconian bureaucracy that has prevented the creation of any new oil refineries or nuclear power plants in more than 30 years. Get government out of the way and let U.S. ingenuity and entrepreneurship do what it has always done to make our country the leading economic power in the world. Stop listening to liberal environmental extremists who want to drive the United States (by horse and buggy) back to the dark ages. They couldn't care less about the average working person. These radical, big-government environmentalists want to keep us poor and beholden to government for handouts—that is how they buy your vote and keep themselves in power. But I believe it is time to put the interests of U.S. citizens and the U.S. economy *first*.

Consider the ethanol mess as Exhibit A for why government must get out of the way in order to solve the energy crisis. As discussed previously, government tried to solve the energy crisis by picking ethanol as the winner. Big mistake. Ethanol has not only done nothing to solve our energy crisis, it has caused a worldwide food shortage and economic crisis. And, it turns out that ethanol causes more pollution than gas as well. The result is an energy and economic crisis *caused* by government.

As evidenced throughout this book, government bureaucrats and politicians have always played "big shot" and tried to pick winners versus losers. Why? To prove how important they are—to justify their big titles, big salaries, and big egos. It's the "lawyer complex" that I spoke about earlier in this book. And, of course, the politicians also pick winners in order to reward their friends and big business contributors. But, what can you expect? It's happening again as I write this chapter—Senators from states that grow corn (which produces ethanol) are demanding that we pass a bill increasing the percentage of ethanol allowed in a gallon of gas from 10 percent to 15 percent. You would never know that ethanol is a big failure from the speeches these corrupt politicians give on the Senate floor. What they forget to mention is that U.S. automobiles aren't engineered to accept more ethanol. Cars have been ruined by using 20 percent ethanol in experiments. Now we're going to pass laws that mandate more ethanol, without any idea of the long-term consequences, or damage to the cars? Once again, here is insanity and corruption being spread by our politicians.

The government is still asleep at the wheel. All politicians talk nonstop about change. But their version of change is nothing more than allowing government to play hero and pick the winners and losers of the energy business. And that is the root of the problem—government itself is a failure, a monumental screw-up. You can't use a failure to fix a failure, especially when government, if given the choice, always makes the wrong choice.

■ ■ ■

Politicians of both parties think that big government has the answer to solve the energy crisis and it is safe to assume that neither Republicans nor Democrats offer a creative or innovative solution to our energy crisis. President Obama (the man with the most extreme liberal voting record out of 100 U.S. Senators) stands vehemently against offshore drilling. He supports more of the same extreme environmental policies, heavy taxes, and big-government regulation that led to our dependence on foreign oil in the first place. But now he has a new trick in his bag. President Obama will attempt to impose even more rules and regulations, and even heavier taxes on business (called "Cap and Trade")—all in the name of global warming. These draconian new energy taxes will then trickle down to consumers (like you and me). Business will have two choices—go out of business, or raise the prices on everything they produce and sell.

His opponent in the 2008 election, John McCain, was not much better. It is true that McCain experienced a miraculous last-minute conversion (during the election) to support offshore drilling, but he still refuses to support any drilling in ANWR, which potentially offers 10 *billion* (or more) barrels of oil to U.S. consumers. Worse, McCain is also a believer in big-government solutions for global warming. Make no mistake, no matter who won the election of 2008, nothing was going to change to solve our energy crisis or dependence on foreign oil.

McCain's Senate colleague John Warner proposed a "big energy solution" during the election (drum roll please): lowering the national speed limit to 55 MPH. After more than 30 years of inaction, the best the Senate could come up with was more draconian federal government control over our lives and a violation of States' Rights (as well as another stupid law that drivers will ignore). No matter how much gas it saves, drivers will not obey a 55 mph speed limit, simply because it is far too slow for our modern highways and for our technologically advanced automobiles.

What Obama, McCain, and a host of other government officials fail to see is the obvious solution. This solution is so simple and costs taxpayers absolutely nothing: Get government out of the way. Put U.S.

consumers and the U.S. economy *first* by encouraging more domestic exploration, drilling, and production; eliminating red tape, rules, and regulations that hinder U.S. energy explorers and producers; and encouraging entrepreneurship and ingenuity by unleashing the power of the free market capitalist system. How do we accomplish that? Lower tax rates—individual, corporate, and capital gains—to the lowest in the world. Then get out of the way, so that the greatest entrepreneurs and capitalist cowboys (investors) in this country can lead us to energy independence (and the greatest economic boom in world history).

But first let's drill, drill, and drill some more. Build new oil refineries. Build new nuclear plants. Encourage oil shale exploration and gas to liquid production. Build new clean coal plants. Our country has one of the biggest deposits of coal on the planet earth. Find a way to burn coal without emitting hydrocarbons and we become one of the world's biggest energy *exporters*. We can beat the oil-producing nations of the Middle East at their own game. We can become the energy leader of the world with clean coal. We can create millions of energy jobs. In doing so, the U.S. trade deficit becomes a trade *surplus*.

The liberal mantra that removing government restrictions on drilling would not affect oil prices for many years to come was proven to be pure propaganda during the 2008 election. Just as I predicted in a political commentary in early 2008 (with gas prices above $4 per gallon), as soon as politicians started to debate (for the first time in years) ending the ban on offshore drilling, the price of oil started dropping like a rock. Just as I predicted in that same commentary, in response to that national discussion, the energy speculators and traders who were undoubtedly partially to blame for sky-high gas prices, had no choice but to sell their oil contracts with both fists. My exact prediction was that the mere discussion and debate of offshore drilling, would not just pop the "oil bubble," but induce a crash of epic proportions. I'd call a decline from $140 per barrel to less than $40 per barrel a crash of *epic proportions*. Can you imagine what would happen to the price of oil if we actually did more than discuss deregulation and offshore drilling, but actually took action?

The beauty of my plan is that not only would energy prices for U.S. consumers drop dramatically (and stabilize long term) as we produced more of our own oil, but that we'd be able to enjoy at least some partial level of energy independence. That translates to spending less of our national treasure on foreign oil, thereby starving terrorism (by exporting fewer dollars to the countries that fund terrorism). That's one heck of a commonsense one-two punch. Unfortunately common sense and government don't often mix. Certainly not with a big government dominated by radical left-wing environmentalists.

Chapter 29

The End of Prohibition

Why Gamblers Will Empower the Citizen Revolution

> *. . . law is often but the tyrant's will, and always so when it violates the right of an individual.*
>
> —Thomas Jefferson

We are a nation of gamblers. We always have been. We always will be. It was daring Pilgrim gamblers who left Europe to found our country (in the name of freedom). They were taking risks with their lives, traveling on disease-infested boats to a New World. Lotteries helped to fund the original colonies of the United States of America—even George Washington and Benjamin Franklin were known to enjoy wagering on those lotteries! It was daring gamblers like George Washington, Thomas Jefferson, John Adams, and Benjamin Franklin who risked their lives and fortunes to start the

American Revolution against the most powerful army in the world (in the name of freedom). They had the most to lose—yet they were willing to risk their fortunes and lives and even families in order to taste freedom. It was daring frontier riverboat gamblers who tamed the Wild West. It was the daring gamblers of Ireland, Germany, Italy, and Eastern Europe who came to our shores at the turn of the twentieth century, who arrived at Ellis Island to start a new life without money, family, or job prospects waiting on the other side. It was daring entrepreneurial gamblers who created the Internet (and were rewarded for their big risks with billions of dollars during the Internet boom).

Gambling is in our blood—that's the very quality that makes the United States the greatest nation the world has ever known. We are rebels. We are rule-breakers. We are riverboat gamblers. We are cowboys forever roaming and conquering the wild frontier—craps games, and poker will always be part of the Wild West landscape. We are leaders, not followers afraid of our own shadow. The United States is a nation of bold dreamers and risk-takers who don't understand the word "impossible." A nation of people that does whatever others say cannot be done. Those who succeed in this country (entrepreneurs, business owners, commissioned salespeople) are world-class risk-takers. These are people who live on commission or profits—they refuse to accept a safe weekly paycheck. A willingness to gamble is therefore *the* necessary ingredient to achieving financial success.

That willingness to dare fate and roll the dice would explain why we are the most gambling-crazed nation in the world. More money is risked on our stock markets (Wall Street) than any other place in the world. We are also a nation of entrepreneurs—we lead the world (by far) in entrepreneurship, venture capital, and small business creation. What could be a greater gamble than betting your life savings on opening an unproven business with no guaranteed income ever again—instead of keeping a safe job with a guaranteed weekly check, health insurance, and a pension? And the dollars that Americans spend at casinos, racetracks, lotteries, and tribal casinos dwarf that of the rest of the world.

These same people, with gambling in their blood, are also the most willing to pick up and move to another place in order to find new opportunity. Last year, 8 million American citizens relocated to another state. In almost every case, they left a big-spending, big-tax, big-government state to move to a low-tax, limited-government state where economic free-dom is more abundant (meaning taxes are lower and government leaves us alone). It's no coincidence that the state where taxes are zero and gam-bling is legal—Nevada—has been the fastest growing state in our country for the last quarter of a century. They may not know it yet, but all these risk-taking, opportunity-seeking U.S. citizens searching for more eco-nomic freedom and their own piece of the famous American Dream are *Libertarians*. Or certainly they are libertarian (with a small l) leaning. They just want to be left alone by government to achieve their own destinies.

■ ■ ■

Want more proof that we are the most gambling-crazed nation in the world? During the last decade (until the U.S. Congress voted to ban on online gaming), Internet gambling and poker were a global phenom-enon. Billions of dollars changed hands—*daily*. The United States was the only major country that considered making a bet on the Internet, on your own computer, a crime. England, Canada, Australia, and virtu-ally every other industrialized nation either legalized online gaming, or looked the other way. Yet, guess where the majority of the gambling dollars came from? You guessed it—*the United States*. Experts estimated that 70 percent of all the dollars wagered on the Internet came from U.S. gamblers—despite the fact that it was considered illegal. Can you imagine—the rest of the world said it was legal, and all those countries *combined* only added up to 30 percent of the dollars wagered!

How popular is gambling in this country? How much has gambling grown legally in the past 25 years? In 1980, about $1 billion was legally wagered in the United States. Today almost $50 billion is legally wagered in one *state*—New York. In 1980, there were no legal casinos outside of Nevada or New Jersey. Today there are 400 tribal casinos across the United States producing more than $20 billion in revenues. California alone now has 60 tribal casinos that, remarkably, just surpassed the famous Vegas Strip casinos in revenues.

There were 376 million trips made to casinos in 2007 by the U.S. public—that means that one quarter of all adults in our country visit a casino each year. Remarkably, it's now far easier to buy a lottery ticket than a Big Mac—there are 14,000 McDonald's in the United States versus 185,000 lottery retail establishments. But here's the statistic that should open the eyes of Libertarians (and political leaders) everywhere as to how popular, accepted, and mainstream gambling is in this country: In "The States Bet More On Betting" (May 18, 2003), Alex Berenson reports for the *New York Times* that more money is spent on gambling in the United States than books, movies, music, videos, and DVDs *combined*.

Gambling has never been more widespread or accepted by voters. According to the annual poll of U.S. adults, conducted by Luntz, Maslansky Strategic Research, and Peter D. Hart Research Associates, 84 percent of U.S. adults view casino gambling as acceptable for themselves or others. An even larger majority, 86 percent of adults believe that people in individual states and communities should be allowed to decide what is best for them with respect to gambling. When it comes to gambling, people in the United States display a strong Libertarian bent.

But no form of gambling is more woven into the U.S. fabric than sports gambling. According to the U.S. Congress Impact Study on Gambling in 1997, more than $380 billion is wagered on sports annually in the United States, making sports gambling the most widespread form of gaming. That $380 billion figure makes sports gambling bigger than the entire U.S. auto industry.

In "The Man Who Shook Up Vegas," which was published January 5, 2007, by the *Wall Street Journal*, author Sam Walker reported of sports gambling, "If you've never placed a sports bet in America, you are fast becoming a member of the minority. Since its beginnings at Colonial horse tracks in the 17th century, the amount of money Americans wager on sports has grown to rival the gross domestic product of New Zealand . . . through the next calendar year, more than 100 million Americans will wager . . . on sports. The bulk of it . . . flows through office pools, local bookies and offshore online casinos."

The popularity of sports on television in this country can be directly attributed to the popularity of *betting* on sports. The biggest sports gambling event of the year is Super Bowl Sunday—with $6 billion to $8 billion being wagered annually on that one day, on that one game. Not coincidentally, Super Bowl is the highest-rated television event, of any kind, each year.

NFL football is the TV ratings king, with the highest TV ratings by far of any sport. Not coincidentally, NFL football is the king of sports gambling, too—with 50 percent (or more) of all gambling dollars being wagered on football. Can you guess which are the two biggest *betting* games of each week? Of course they are the two highest-rated TV games of the week—NBC Sunday Night Football and ESPN Monday Night Football.

But football is not the only big betting sport. The popularity of March Madness has made college basketball the second most popular betting sport in the United States. More money is now bet on the three weeks of March Madness than the Super Bowl—more than $8 billion. Not coincidentally, March Madness is now the second highest TV sports ratings event.

Then there's poker. One poker site alone—Party Gaming, a public company—reported $45 billion of wagering on their poker site in 2005. Their revenues on that $45 billion in action were just shy of $1 billion—all on one web site. There were approximately 2,400 poker web sites on the Internet at that time. Then the U.S. Congress passed an online gaming ban (called UIGEA), which prevented the transfer of monies for online gaming purposes through banks, credit cards, or other financial instruments. Since then, more than 1 million U.S. poker players have joined the political and lobbying arm of poker, the Poker Players Alliance (PPA). The Chairman of the PPA is former U.S. Senator Al D'Amato.

I believe that those one million (and growing) PPA members can be harnessed by the Libertarian movement to support, contribute, and vote for LP candidates at all levels of office—especially if a high-profile friend of gaming is the nominee. Add to that group the 10 million to 12 million online poker fans in the United States . . . the 50 million people who choose to play poker the old fashioned way (in person) . . . and all the other fans in this country of lotteries, horseracing, and tribal casinos.

■ ■ ■

Now who should enter the picture to try to create a new form of Prohibition? Nanny State politicians—backed by a bunch of straight-laced, out-of-touch busybodies who have never made a bet in their lives (which means they understand nothing about success)—want to tell us what we're allowed to do in the privacy of our own bedroom, on our own computer, with our own money. They want to *police* cyberspace. They want to limit our freedoms and choices. They want to rule our lives—even though your choice to make a bet online does not affect their lives in any way, shape, or form. Or perhaps it does—perhaps these moral busybodies are unhappy that anyone else is having too much fun? Perhaps they are annoyed that you're enjoying your freedoms just a tad too much for their tastes? You know what we call people like this in the Middle East? *The Taliban.*

Well, I happen to enjoy gambling. And I believe in freedom. Freedom is precisely why we fought the American Revolution. Freedom was why we fought the Civil War and two World Wars. We may have chosen the wrong war in Iraq, but we fought it for the same reasons—the freedom of the Iraqi people, and even the freedom of Muslims enslaved and terrified by Islamic radicals trying to control their lives, enslave their minds, and impose their intolerant ideas and laws. The first thing these intolerant Muslim fanatics do to control the people is to ban leisure endeavors in the name of morality—gambling, dancing, drinking, and so on. Sound familiar? U.S. service members die every day in Iraq and Afghanistan to protect the *freedom* of Muslim strangers. To give Muslim girls the freedom to go to school. Yet back home in the United States, our own version of intolerance is alive and well. Our own homegrown version of anti-gambling zealots and moralizers, thought police, and intolerant Nanny State hypocrites tries to impose its definition of right and wrong on U.S. citizens—even if it infringes on your freedom, even if it infringes on your choice of entertainment.

But here's the rub—my neighbor playing online poker in his pajamas doesn't affect me in any way. It certainly doesn't hurt me in any way. It doesn't hurt any Congressperson or U.S. Senator in any way. Many people get in their cars while intoxicated and maim or kill others—yet alcohol is legal. Heck, alcohol companies seem to buy half the ads on U.S. television. Coors *is* the NFL! But in the history of this world, no one has ever been charged with *driving while gambling*. No one has ever been injured or killed by my decision to make a bet online. My decision to gamble does not endanger, or bother, or affect, in any way friends, neighbors, or strangers. The decision to gamble with my hard-earned money (online or otherwise) is my business and *only* my business. There is no difference between using an online gaming site to point and click on a $100 bet on the Dallas Cowboys, versus using my Charles Schwab online account to point and click on a $100,000 bet on Exxon or Microsoft.

Here in my home state of Nevada, gamblers have been playing horses, sports, craps, blackjack, and poker for decades—and Nevada has not fallen off the edge of the earth (not yet anyway). God has not struck us down (no natural disasters of any kind have ever befallen Las Vegas— no fires, floods, earthquakes, tornados, or hurricanes). The earth hasn't opened up and swallowed Nevada whole. As a matter of fact, gambling has been a boon to Nevada. *Reason* magazine in July 2008 rated Las Vegas as the number one major city in the United States for personal freedom. Could that be why Las Vegas is the perennial number one major city in the United States for population growth, economic growth, and job growth for most of the past quarter century? More proof that citizens love limited government, personal freedom, and economic freedom. They go hand in hand. No one forces you to gamble in Nevada. But the choice is yours. That's called freedom. It's a wonderful feeling.

Gambling revenues in Nevada allow our state to feature the ultimate Libertarian style of government: zero state income taxes, zero business tax, zero capital gains tax, zero inheritance tax, and property taxes limited by law. This is the model for the United States. Online gaming, legalized nationally, can become a jackpot for the U.S. government. A 2007 PriceWaterHouseCoopers forecast projected that legalized online sports gambling would produce $30.6 billion in taxes, while legalized online poker would produce $21.4 billion in taxes. Can the United States afford to throw away $52 billion during the worst economic crisis of our lifetimes?

Online gaming is already legalized, regulated, and taxed in England— thereby producing millions of dollars annually in new taxes. Yet the self-deputized Nanny State police here in the United States want to tell untold millions of U.S. gaming enthusiasts whether we have the right (or the *freedom*) to play poker, or to have fun making a friendly wager on a football game.

Most adults in the United States disagree strongly—CNBC and the *Wall Street Journal* surveys both proved that large majorities of respondents opposed a ban on online gaming, while a *USA Today* survey reported that more than one out of two U.S. adults made a bet on sports in the past year. As I write this chapter, I'm watching Florida play Oklahoma for the College Football National Championship on FOX television. I'm only watching because I have a bet on the game. Gambling on sports is my chosen form of entertainment. I've done it for 25 years and I have yet to hurt a single human being with my personal choice of leisure entertainment. *Not one, not once.* Imagine that? I can make a wager on the BCS Championship game and no one in Washington, DC, is hurt. No one in Peoria is affected. No one at the Vatican even knew about it (until now). How can that be possible? The thought police must be notified. Ah, but there's a catch—I made my bet *legally* at a Las Vegas casino.

But what's the difference between a bet made at a Vegas casino . . . or online? Why is one "good" and legal . . . while the other is "bad" or illegal? Who has decided that tribal casinos growing and expanding faster than weeds across the country are good, while online gambling is bad? Who has decided that online horserace gambling is good, but online poker is not? Who has decided that online lotteries are good, but online sports betting is not? Who has decided that sports gambling is bad, but betting on fantasy football is good? Who makes these decisions? Who determines what is legal and what is not? The answer is corrupt politicians and lobbyists pandering to special interests are making those decisions based on who is paying them the most money in lobbying fees and political contributions.

Perhaps people like Jack Abramoff? Remember Jack? He was the morally corrupt lobbyist who pretended to be fighting the spread of tribal casinos—while he was actually *taking* tens of millions of dollars in fees from another tribal casino to cripple the competition. That's "morality" in DC. That's how decisions that affect my freedoms (and yours) are made every day in Washington.

Politicians who represent states with tribal casinos, horserace tracks with slot machines, and state lotteries just happen to think online gaming is a sin (perhaps because it cuts into the profits of the gaming companies that pay huge contributions to those same politicians). Senators who claim to be against online gaming, just happen to accept big donations from billionaires that own horserace tracks in their state. Suddenly online horseracing is *exempted* from the ban. Senators who represent states with lotteries that bring in hundreds of millions in tax revenues just happen to be moral crusaders against online gaming—and suddenly online lotteries are *exempted* from the ban.

States like Louisiana issue arrest warrants against the CEOs of legal publicly traded online gaming companies in England—then we find out that they aren't anti-gaming at all. They just happen to be protecting the interests of a new racetrack with slot machines in guess what state? Louisiana. What a surprise! The governor of Massachusetts tries to push through a law making anyone who plays poker online in his state guilty of a felony—a crime equivalent to molesting a child. Why? It turns out that his state has cut a lucrative deal with land-based casinos and they don't want any competition. Are these politicians, or Mafia hit men? I can't tell the difference. Politicians will do anything, destroy anyone, even destroy our freedom to keep all the money for themselves (and their campaign contributors). Morality has nothing to do with it. That's just the "cover story." *It's all so evil, cynical, and corrupt, it makes gambling itself seem pure and saintly by comparison.*

I'll take Las Vegas any day over the hypocrites who populate Washington, DC. In Las Vegas gamblers wager millions of their own dollars and morality zealots call that evil. In Washington, DC, politicians who call themselves moral and "men of faith" gamble trillions of dollars—and it's not even their own money. *They gamble and waste our money!*

■ ■ ■

The government will fail miserably in their attempt to ban online gaming. The genie is out of the bottle. The train has left the station. You can't stop U.S. citizens from doing what they love to do—gamble or play poker online. You can't control our minds. You can't control our computers. You can't control our wallets. You cannot control what we choose to do in our own homes. There is only one solution—*freedom*. Legalize online gaming, regulate it, and tax it. Then watch the billions of dollars of new tax revenues flow in—money to pay for homeland security, education, deficit reduction, and gambling addiction programs. If you ban it—the tax dollars disappear, the gambling addiction problem moves underground and worsens, the profits go to organized crime, and just like during Prohibition—normally law-abiding people lose respect for the law. The longer this ignorant, misguided, and hypocritical attempt to ban online gambling goes on, the more I think that organized crime is behind it all (after all, they are the biggest beneficiaries of a ban). Perhaps we should name this ban "The Sopranos Support Bill."

To those who say, "Wayne, with issues on the table like war, illegal immigration, the health care crisis, foreign energy dependence, Social

Security facing bankruptcy, soaring budget deficits, and government bailouts, how can you possibly think playing online poker is an important political issue?" My answer is simple: If our federal government thinks they have a right to tell you and me what we can do on our own computer, in our own bedroom, with our own money, can you even *imagine* what else they have in store for us? Can you even *imagine* how badly they want to control our lives? At its core, the ban on online poker perfectly represents the extremes our government will reach, in order to take away our freedoms. It is a battle the freedom movement was born to fight. It is a battle that must be won to overturn the Nanny State.

Now you understand why I added gambling to the subtitle of this book. First, because the great state of Nevada offers the perfect model for our nation—limited government, lower taxes, more economic and personal freedom, and sin tax to reduce the tax burden on our citizens.

Second, because the freedom to gamble is *that* important to the citizen revolution. It is that important because of the civil liberties it involves. It is that important because of the issue's massive power to harness the support of gaming and poker enthusiasts. The freedom to gamble must be the centerpiece of any movement to overturn the Nanny State. Because gambling is such a big part of the crucial issue of this technology age: *Internet Freedom*. Because in a time of declining tax revenues and burgeoning budget deficits on the state and national level, the legalization of online gaming and poker has the potential to provide $50 billion (or more) in tax revenues to the U.S. government.

And finally, because the younger generation plays online poker virtually nonstop, the politician or political movement that supports personal freedom and the rights of consenting adults to do what they want in their own homes, on their own computers, with their own hard-earned money will win elections for years to come. Gaining the support of poker and gaming enthusiasts holds the potential to fuel the citizen revolution.

Chapter 30

The Inalienable Right to Pursue Happiness

"If It Is to Be, It Is Up to Me"

The human race divides itself politically into those who want to be controlled, and those who have no such desire.

—ROBERT A. HEINLEIN, NOVELIST

You've now read multiple chapters about my support of the libertarian ideals of dramatically cutting spending, entitlements, and taxes; radically cutting the size, scope, and power of government; and increasing economic and personal freedom for the individual citizen and taxpayer. Having done so, it is important to note that this philosophy is not just good for your wallet, it's good for your spirit, too. In this chapter, you read of long-term studies that prove that simply

333

believing in the power of the individual versus that of government makes all the difference in whether you are successful and satisfied in life. What a bonus! You thought you were picking up a financial and political book. *But here in this book, I've handed you the key to a happier and more fulfilling life in the bargain.*

Back in October 2008, newspapers across the country trumpeted the news that being a Republican automatically makes you happier than being a Democrat. But headlines rarely tell the full story. Happiness is certainly not about political party affiliation. It is about a mind-set. When you read beneath the surface of these long-term studies, to the real nitty-gritty details, you find that the mindset that leads to satisfaction and happiness in life is quite simply the philosophy of this book. What leads to happiness is *freedom*—free will, free markets, free speech, and freedom from government interference in your decisions, choices, and life. None of us is guaranteed happiness on the day of our birth. As great as the United States is, no government can guarantee happiness. But what our Founding Fathers guaranteed is the *freedom* to pursue happiness.

The studies you will read about in this chapter prove that happiness comes from the belief that you as a free individual, citizen, and taxpayer are in control of your own life. That "if it is to be, it is up to me." That you—and only you—have the free will to determine your destiny. That is the mind-set that leads to success, wealth, health, and happiness. Whether it's true or not is immaterial. It is the *belief* that produces higher levels of success and happiness.

■ ■ ■

The actual study, released by the Pew Research Center, is called the "Pew Social & Demographic Trends Project." This poll is built around "detailed and long-term research." The dramatic partisan "happiness gap" that Pew found in favor of Republicans has held steady for nearly four decades—since 1972 when surveys funded by the National Science Foundation first began to ask the happiness question. Remarkably, it has held steady during both Republican and Democratic presidential administrations. Republicans weren't just happier under Reagan or Bush, but they were also happier under Carter and Clinton. Republicans were happier than Democrats while Democrats dominated Congress. Republicans were happier than Democrats even during the darkest days of Watergate. The happiness gap actually widened in the fall of 2008—Republicans were far happier even as the economy tanked, the stock market collapsed, the credit markets froze, and it became obvious that Democrats would win the White House and control all levels of government. Is happiness in the DNA of Republicans?

Republicans in the study actually rated as happier at both ends of the spectrum—pure joy and pure depression. Republicans lead at the top of the study, where almost half of Republicans consistently report being "very happy," compared to only 25 percent to 30 percent of Democrats and 29 percent of independents (in the latest version of the study). And Republicans lead at the bottom of the latest study, too, where only 9 percent of Republicans are "not too happy" versus a whopping 20 percent of Democrats.

I understand exactly why Republicans are happier. But it has nothing to do with party identification. It is about a belief system—a positive conscious mind-set that helps to create health, wealth, success, and happiness. The proof is that the same results hold true in places across the globe where the words "Republican" and "Democrat" don't exist. In countries all over the world, those who identify themselves as "conservatives" are far happier than those who identify themselves as "liberals." Again, it is a long-term pattern.

None of this actually has anything to do with political party identification. Being a card-carrying Republican is certainly not what makes a person happy. It is the libertarian, fiscally conservative belief system—the idea that *you*, not government, are in control of your own destiny. It is the belief that government should be smaller, the individual stronger, government spending lower, and taxes cut dramatically—so that the individual can choose what to do with his or her own money. It is the belief that government isn't the solution, but rather the problem. That's what conservatives and free market libertarians share the world over.

The Pew study found that a key factor for happiness is whether you believe that success is determined by outside forces, or if it is personal initiative that determines your level of success. It is that core belief that changes lives. As the *Washington Post* put it, "The hypothesis: Those who think they can control their destinies are happier." My heroes Barry Goldwater, Ronald Reagan, and Thomas Jefferson, would be proud. That was their philosophy. That is my philosophy. I hope it is now yours.

Arthur Brooks, the author of one of my favorite books, *Gross National Happiness: Why Happiness Matters for America—and How We Can Get More of It* (Basic Books, 2008) was quoted in the *Washington Post* about the Pew happiness survey. He told the *Post* reporter that the results of this study revolve around the answer to a simple question: "Do you believe that hard work and perseverance can overcome disadvantages?" He reports that conservatives are more likely to say *yes*! And I'll bet that those who identify themselves as libertarians are even more likely to share this sentiment.

To me, it is simple and straightforward. If you believe that government can make your life better, and because of that, you are waiting around for government to save you—you are destined to fail. If you believe in handouts, entitlements, bailouts, and stimulus checks, you are destined to fail. And perhaps most importantly, if you are waiting for government to make your life better, you are destined to be disappointed, thereby creating unhappiness and depression. Anytime you hand your power, the power that God gave you, to someone else, you are destined to be disappointed, dissatisfied, and unhappy. If you believe the world is a terrible place and success is not in your control, you are destined for failure and disappointment. If you believe you are powerless, and only government has the power to change your life, you are destined to be depressed and miserable. If you spend your time complaining and protesting about how unfair and unjust the world is, you are destined to fail.

There is no reason to protest against external forces, when it is *internal* forces that determine your level of success in life. I've seen it again and again—even in the gambling world. Yes, fate often hands poker players lousy cards. But it's amazing how often a great poker player, with superior talents and skills, and supreme confidence, overcomes those lousy hands and impossible odds. It's amazing how often poker players with inferior skills, a lousy attitude, and a lack of confidence, seize defeat from the jaws of certain victory (even while being blessed with the best cards).

As an entrepreneur in the business world, I've seen luck play a huge factor in achieving success. I've experienced luck my whole life—*and all of it has been bad!* Yet I've remained an incredibly positive and happy person. Why? Because I believe that a talented, confident entrepreneur can overcome long odds and surmount challenges that others see as insurmountable. I've never waited for opportunity to knock. In my opinion, opportunity *never* knocks. I believe you have to create your own opportunity. I've always seized opportunity like a caveman—beating it over the head with a club, knocking it unconscious, and dragging it home. I don't wait for life, society, the universe, or government to save me. I know that my best chance for success is if I save myself.

It is you who creates your own destiny. You, the individual, are responsible for your own life. If it isn't working out, you have no one to blame but yourself. Yes, you might have been given a lousy set of cards. But it's your job to figure out how to use what you've been given to the best of your abilities. Individuals with talent, confidence, and chutzpah are experts at turning lemons into lemonade. This kind of individual is self-reliant and believes in personal responsibility. This kind of individual understands that government can't help you, only *you* can help you. It is the mind-set of waiting for government to help that wastes so many precious lives. You can wait an awful long time for government to help—pretty soon your whole life has passed by. Successful and happy people the world over wait for nothing and no one—they take action, they take control, they take charge. *If it is to be, it is up to me.*

■■■

This all leads to one conclusion: The key to success isn't in the hands of Obama or Bush or McCain or Pelosi. It's not in the hands of any politician or government official. It's only in your hands . . . in your control. The only way to guarantee happiness is to depend on yourself. No one else can or will take better care of you, than you. No one else believes in you, more than you believe in yourself. No one else can or will fight harder for you, than you can for yourself. And if you happen to be an especially ambitious and success-driven person (as I am), no one will ever buy you a Ferrari or Aston Martin . . . but you. *If it is to be, it is up to me.* Those who sit around waiting for government to make things better, to right the wrongs, to improve their lives, to create equality and fairness, will be sitting around waiting for a lifetime. And it will be a long, depressing, miserable life.

Those who desperately depend on safety nets rarely achieve success. Safety nets damage the attributes that lead to success: ambition, drive, commitment, courage, and tenacity. As John F. Kennedy said, "Only those who dare to fail greatly, can ever achieve greatly." The individuals that are happier, healthier and more successful on this planet tend to run toward risk, not run away from it. They don't expect the government to guarantee safety, any more than the government can guarantee happiness.

Benjamin Franklin understood the relationship between risk and reward, safety and security. He once said, "They who can give up essential liberty to obtain a little temporary safety, deserve neither liberty nor safety." Safety nets and the mentality that goes with them (asking government to protect you) actually limit your thinking, limit your creativity, limit your potential, limit your freedom, and limit your success. You can't protect everyone from everything negative in life. And even if you could, why would you want to? Good things come from adversity. Facing life's obstacles, challenges, and failures is what makes you stronger and tougher. Being shielded from adversity makes you weaker. Ask any entrepreneur— they will tell you that most successful businesses are built from the lessons learned from the ashes of failure. Why would we want government to shield our citizens from failure? How would you pick the leaders of society, if not by watching how they overcame challenge and adversity?

The reason that conservative/libertarian thinkers in every country are happier than liberals is because people with this mind-set believe in the power of the individual, not the government—just like our Founding Fathers. They are happier because they believe their destiny is in *their* hands. It's much harder to feel happiness when you believe that luck, fate, strangers, or government holds your future in their hands. It's easy to feel frightened, depressed, or stressed when you believe you are powerless to control your own future. Those who ask for no help from government; those who feel free to dream, to achieve, to succeed—with their own wits, ideas, creativity, commitment, tenacity, perseverance, relentless spirit—*those individuals are more likely to succeed.* And remarkably, this long-term Pew study proves that they are destined to be *happier* while doing it.

Capitalism works because individualism works. The group isn't the answer. Success isn't found in "group think." The government isn't the answer. The Nanny State isn't the answer. New laws to limit our abilities to make our own decisions and choices are not the answer. Government handouts, bailouts, entitlements, and stimulus packages are certainly not the answer.

The answer is to empower the *individual*. The solution is to get government out of the way, so that we are all free to fulfill our great destinies. The answer is to inspire, empower, and motivate U.S. citizens, taxpayers, and individuals by allowing us to keep more of our own money. Allow the individual to choose what to do with it, how to spend it, how to enjoy it, how to multiply it. Then get out of the way—and watch the greatest economic recovery and expansion in world history.

Freedom and individualism is what made the United States the greatest nation in world history. Courage in the face of great risk is what made us great. There were no safety nets in 1776 when we fought the British. There were no safety nets in 1860 when we fought the Civil War. There were no safety nets in 1800 when we fought the Indians and settled the American West. There were no safety nets when we fought Hitler during WWII. It was courageous risk-takers and pioneers that made us the greatest nation in world history. It was personal responsibility, self-reliance, and rugged individualism. That same combination will solve this economic mess that we find ourselves in today. That same combination will fuel the resurgence of this great country. The individual is the key to the greatest success story known to mankind—the American Dream. It isn't our country that is great, it is the individuals who make up our country.

Greatness comes from the freedoms our Founding Fathers gave to our citizens, in the form of a Constitution, which *limited* the power of government. It is this remarkable Constitution that has unleashed such incredible creativity, productivity, and achievement in our economy. It is this remarkable Constitution that gives us our freedoms. It is this freedom that makes us (at least some of us—the fiscal conservatives) happy.

Only our Founding Fathers, among all the other nations of the world, had the wisdom and foresight to include "the inalienable right to pursue happiness" in our founding document. Jefferson, Madison, Franklin, Washington, Adams—perhaps the most brilliant thinkers ever assembled—all recognized that free individuals had the inalienable right to pursue happiness, not the inalienable right to achieve it. No government can guarantee you happiness. Nor can government provide it. Government can only guarantee you the freedom to pursue it.

Our Founding Fathers were remarkable men. They understood that happiness is an automatic by-product of freedom and individualism.

It is time to get back to the principles that founded this country and made it great. Only turning the individual loose from the shackles of dependency on government will return us to happiness, greatness, and beyond. God Bless the citizens and taxpayers of this great nation. God Bless our inalienable right to pursue happiness. And most importantly, may God Bless the *freedom* that makes it all possible.

Parting Words: Relentless!

Relentless is what separates the men from the boys. Relentless is that special ingredient that allows nobodies to become somebodies. Relentless empowers anyone with a big enough heart to overcome insurmountable odds; to smash though barriers; to break glass ceilings; to surmount adversity, challenge and fear; to make the impossible, possible.

—WAYNE ALLYN ROOT

As I say good-bye, I want to first thank you for reading my book and showing your interest in my thoughts and opinions. The United States is under siege. We are a family, all of us in this together. We will have to work together, fight together, and most of all, be *relentless* together to change the direction of this economy and this great country. I also want to address a crucial question. I can hear you asking it right now: "I agree with what you have to say Wayne. I want to change the status quo. I want to throw the bums out. I've had enough of big and bigger, dumb and dumber. I want to get you elected President of the United States. But the Libertarian Party has never elected anyone to a major national office. How are we going to do something that has never been done before?"

The answer is simple: *Get Involved. Get Passionate. And, Follow Me!* I'm a huge sports fan. One of the great things about sports is that every year people achieve things that no one ever expected, or believed possible. Examples abound in sports of players and coaches who struggle and lose year after year. Fans may give up on them, but they never give up on themselves. Then, they are signed, or hired in the right place at the right time, in the perfect situation for their talents. Suddenly coaches that have been losers their entire careers win Super Bowls or World Series. Suddenly quarterbacks who have been losers their entire careers wind up in the Hall of Fame. Running backs who couldn't find a hole move to another team, and wind up in the Pro Bowl. Career backups become stars with a change of scenery or game plan. Teams with a history of losing pathetically win the championship—and then create a long-term tradition of excellence.

The Boston Red Sox are a perfect example. For almost a century they were cursed and considered losers—until they won a World Series . . . and then another. Now they are a dynasty. The curse is forgotten. Few experts believed the hapless Red Sox were capable of this kind of success—until it happened.

Joe Torre was a subpar baseball manager who was fired from three jobs—until he joined the Yankees and became the best manager of his generation. Joe was a miserable 286–420 as manager of the New York Mets. Then he was a mediocre 351–354 as manager of the St. Louis Cardinals. Both stints led to firings. When he was later hired as manager of the New York Yankees, the media and fans rebelled. The New York media called him Clueless Joe. That was before he led the Yankees to six World Series and four world championships in 12 glorious seasons as manager. Now Joe is a surefire Hall of Famer. Few experts believed Joe Torre was capable of this kind of success—until it happened.

The New England Patriots were perennial losers until they found the right owner (Robert Kraft), who hired the right head coach (Bill Belichick), who found the right quarterback (Tom Brady). That was four Super Bowl victories ago. Now it's hard to remember a time when the Patriots weren't an NFL dynasty. But no one believed it was possible a few years ago—until it happened.

Ironically, Pete Carroll was the New England Patriots' head coach before Bill Belichick arrived on the scene to build a winning tradition. Carroll failed miserably, fired after only three seasons at the helm of the Patriots. That was better, however, than his record as head coach of the New York Jets where he was fired after only one short season. Carroll's NFL head coaching career was over. Soon after he was hired as head coach of the USC Trojans. The media and fans reacted in outright shock and dismay. The choice appeared so flawed that thousands of USC alumni threatened to withhold donations to the school until Carroll was fired. That was before he won two national championships, seven consecutive PAC 10 championships, and coached the USC Trojans to seven consecutive 11 win seasons (an all-time college football record). As I wrote this chapter, Pete Carroll became the first coach in history to win three consecutive Rose Bowls (and four of the last six). Carroll is today the winningest active coach in college football. His USC Trojans were voted the "Team of the Decade" by ESPN. He is considered to be one of the greatest coaches in college football history. No one is complaining now. Few experts believed Pete Carroll was capable of this kind of success—until it happened.

But the best coaching turnaround in history has got to be the magic act performed by Turner Gill as head coach of the Buffalo Bulls. Never heard of this small college team? Join the club. Most fans didn't even know that Buffalo had a college football team until Turner Gill came along. When Gill arrived in 2005, Buffalo was one of the worst teams in college football. They had won only 10 games over the past seven seasons. But Turner Gill believed. He told the players and press that "UB (University of Buffalo) now stands for *you believe!*" By 2008, Gill's third year as head coach, Buffalo won the MAC championship game, propelling the Bulls to their first bowl game in the football program's 92-year history. No one ever believes—until it happens.

A fact of life is that timing is not important . . . *it's everything!* Things change in a hurry when the right man (or woman) meets his destiny. Mountains can be moved when the pieces of the puzzle fall together, in the right situation, at the right time, in the right place. Suddenly the impossible becomes *possible*. It happens virtually every year in sports. That's why our country loves sports—because of the magical moments. But before you can move mountains or pull off miracles, first you've got to believe in yourself . . . and then you've got to be *relentless*.

The impossible and magical happens in politics, too. I'm living proof. I was there at the very beginning of the New York State Conservative Party. I was just a kid, but I clearly remember how futile it all seemed. We were like rebels with pitchforks fighting the powerful British Empire. I remember Republican leaders literally snickering at my father and mother. The big shots that ran the New York State GOP were all politically connected—lawyers and political power brokers with Ivy League degrees. My dad was just . . . gasp . . . a *butcher*. My mom was the cashier at the butcher store. To the New York crowd we were just a bunch of poor, powerless, amateur nobodies. We must have seemed like Jed Clampett and his family of hillbillies arriving in Beverly Hills (except without the money).

The odds were insurmountable that this ragtag third party would ever elect anyone—until 1971 when we elected James Buckley as U.S. Senator in perhaps the biggest political upset *ever*. From that point on the Conservative Party was known as the kingmaker of New York state politics. From that point on Republicans literally begged for our endorsement. Since 1974, no Republican has won a statewide race in the state of New York without Conservative Party endorsement. That means it's been over 30 years since the big, bad, powerful Republicans won a statewide race without the help of the Conservative Party. Score a big victory for the peasants with the pitchforks. Who would have ever believed that? No one ever believes—until it happens.

It's remarkable how it can all change overnight. But first you've got to believe in yourself . . . and then you've got to be *relentless*.

■ ■ ■

Let's fast-forward a few years to 2008. I'm sure no one thought a Las Vegas odds maker, a complete unknown in political circles, was going to win the Libertarian Party vice presidential nomination either. My odds looked insurmountable. Then things got *worse*—a former four-term U.S. Congressman (Bob Barr) and former U.S. Senator (Mike Gravel) entered the race. At that point my odds looked downright infinitesimal. At that point my odds were so bad that the *Washington Post* erased me from a photo of the Libertarian presidential debate. Now that's pretty pathetic. But I never lost faith. I never stopped believing that I would make the impossible, *possible*. But then I am *relentless*.

Relentless is in my genes. Let me tell you a remarkable, magical, extraordinary story that literally defines relentless—the story of the last hours of my mother's, Stella Root's, life. My mother and father died of cancer 28 days apart in 1992, the hardest year of my life. I spoke at my father's funeral in New York and returned to my home in California only to get a call a few days later from my sister telling me that our mom had gone into a tailspin after the funeral. Twenty-eight days later she was gone. But it was the remarkable last hours of Stella Root's life that I will remember and cherish forever.

"Wayne, I'm sorry to tell you this, but your mom is gone. Her brain no longer has activity, so we're disconnecting life support. Please don't rush home. She's gone. You've had enough tragedy in your family for one month. You have a new baby on the way that depends on you. So be careful, take care of yourself, breathe deep, and don't rush. Doctor's orders. Got it?"

That was the phone message I received from my mother's doctor on the last day of her life. Then he handed the phone to my sister, who whispered because she was afraid the doctor would hear what she had to say and she'd sound foolish, "Wayne . . . rush home. Because you and I both know that mom won't die until you get here. *Rush home!*"

I caught the red eye flight that night out of Los Angeles to New York. The flight left late. It taxied on the runway forever. I ordered a car to pick me up at JFK airport to rush me to the hospital in Westchester County. But the car was caught in traffic and arrived late. Everything that could go wrong, did. By the time I walked into my mother's hospital room it had been 12 hours since I got that terrible phone call; 12 hours since life support had been disconnected; 12 hours since that doctor said, "Don't rush home, your mom is gone."

Yet when I raced through the door to her room, I heard the most beautiful sound I'd ever heard. Beep . . . beep . . . beep. It was her heart monitor beeping. Despite being disconnected from life support, her heart was still beating. My sister had sat by her bedside all night saying, "Mom, hang on, Wayne is on the way. Don't die, Wayne is on the way." Medical science may have determined that her brain was dead, but that beeping heart monitor told another story. She'd lived through the night on sheer willpower. Some might call it a miracle. I simply called it *relentless*.

I hugged my mom and grabbed her hand. I kissed her cheek. I couldn't stop crying. I said, "Mom, I love you. Thank you for waiting for me. I know how hard that was. But I made it . . . and you made it. I'll always remember what you did for me. You showed those doctors. I love you . . . but now it's time to go. You deserve a rest. Heaven is waiting. You can go. I give you permission to *let go*."

And within 10 seconds, her heart monitor went beep . . . beep (fainter) . . . beeeeeep . . . flatline. She was gone.

Medical science may have considered her brain dead, but somehow, someway, my mother had understood what was being said. She heard my sister's pleas to hang on all night long. If her brain was dead, how did she know to hang on all night long . . . and into the next morning? How did she know that her son Wayne was on the way? If her brain was dead, how did she hear me say that it was time to let go? Why did her heart monitor stop within seconds of my giving her permission to let go?

My mother may not have had any brainpower left, but she had willpower. She certainly had *heart*. And that's the most important thing in the world—no matter what your goal. All success, all progress, all the miracles in this world are based on heart, on spirit, on will, on being *relentless*. My mother was relentless. She beat cancer for six long years, coming back from dead a dozen times. She beat the odds because she had a huge heart. She had spirit and relentless willpower. In those last hours of her life, she refused to lose faith, to give up, to give in—even though medical science had written her off. To the medical experts, she was brain dead.

Stella Root defined relentless her whole life. She wasn't going to die without saying good-bye to her only son, her baby boy Wayne. Stella Root proved that heart is what matters in life. Heart is more important than the diagnosis of experts, or doctors, or scientists, or science itself. Hard facts don't matter when heart is involved. Heart is what makes miracles happen. Heart makes the impossible, *possible*.

My mom's story proves that if your heart is big enough, it doesn't even matter if your brain is *dead*.

When I'm asked why the Libertarian Party (LP) hasn't elected anyone to major national office in the past, my answer is "I don't care. That was then. This is now." The Libertarian Party has had fine candidates, smart candidates, even brilliant candidates in the past. The LP certainly has a great message . . . the right message. But the missing ingredient up until now has been *heart*. I am Stella Root's son. I am *relentless*. I have a bigger heart than a thousand candidates. More heart than all the others that came before me—*combined*. Heart is the missing link . . . the missing ingredient that has the power to turn the right message into a *winning* message. Heart is the straw that stirs the drink.

Being smart is a good thing. Being educated is a good thing. Brainpower in a political leader is a good thing. But they are not the most important things. Willpower trumps brainpower. Heart is the intangible that's impossible to replace. Heart is the game-changer. Heart is that special ingredient that brings it all together to win Super Bowls, and World Series, and championship boxing matches . . . and, yes, national political elections. Heart is what determines champions. Heart is the thing that separates life's winners from losers. Heart, as the younger generation might say, is the *bomb*.

I inherited heart, spirit, will, and a tenacious, passionate, never-say-die attitude from my mother. I am relentless. If I have to, I will drag this party . . . like Jack LaLanne celebrating his 70th birthday by dragging 70 rowboats with 70 people through Long Beach Harbor . . . with his *teeth*. That's relentless. That's heart. That's what this party, this freedom movement, has been missing. We have had plenty of intellect, plenty of brainpower, plenty of good ideas, but up until now, not enough heart. Without that one ingredient, all the rest is rendered meaningless.

From this day forward, the buck stops here. The Libertarian Party has a fighter to lead the way—a passionate, committed, tenacious, relentless fighter with the biggest heart in all of politics. It may take 8 years . . . or 12 . . . or 16 . . . or even 20 years. But I'll see you at the White House. And the day I put my hand on that bible, I know one thing for certain—David and Stella Root will be looking down from heaven with the biggest smiles ever, with their hearts bursting with joy. They'll look at their son, shake their heads, and say, "*Relentless.*"

I hope you enjoyed *The Conscience of a Libertarian.*

God Bless,
Wayne Allyn Root

The day will come when we entrust the conduct of our affairs to men who understand that their first duty as public officials is to divest themselves of the power they have been given.

> Barry Goldwater's words. My promise. On the day
> I am sworn in, I pledge to put my hand on the Bible
> and vow to give the power back to the people.

The Root Revolution

Nothing great was ever achieved without enthusiasm.
—RALPH WALDO EMERSON

This isn't an ending. It's only a beginning. If you're excited, enthusiastic and committed to changing the direction of this country—Please join the ROOT REVOLUTION. To join my mailing list, e-mail list, or to volunteer for future ROOT campaigns, please go to:
www.ROOTforAmerica.com

I'd enjoy hearing from you. Please e-mail me with your comments, requests or questions. You can e-mail me directly at:
Wayne@ROOTforAmerica.com

For information on my other books, videos, DVD's, CDs, or audiotapes on politics, success, sales, risk, or being RELENTLESS; or my availability for speeches and seminars anywhere in the world; please visit my web sites at www.ROOTforAmerica.com or www.WayneROOT.com or www.ROOTofSuccess.com

About the Author

Wayne Allyn Root is one of the most charismatic, telegenic, passionate, fiery, outspoken, and controversial political personalities in the United States today. Wayne was the 2008 Libertarian Party vice presidential nominee. A college classmate of Barack Obama at Columbia University, Wayne is now the leading contender for the Libertarian Presidential nomination in 2012. Wayne is the quintessential "Citizen Politician" envisioned by our Founding Fathers. He is an S.O.B. (son of a butcher) from humble beginnings, second-generation American, small businessman, and home-school father of four young children. Wayne is proud of his Nevada roots, a Western frontier state known for smaller government, rugged individualism, personal responsibility, and zero state income tax.

A nationally recognized sports celebrity, Wayne has been dubbed by the media as "The King of Vegas." He has been honored as the youngest recipient of his own star on the Las Vegas Walk of Stars. A former anchorman and host on Financial News Network (now known as CNBC), Wayne now serves as national spokesman and chief economic and political strategist for Rare Coin Wholesalers (www.RCWroot .com), one of America's premier rare coin and gold bullion companies.

He is spokesman, board member, and senior economic advisor for Wealth Masters International (www.wmitoday.com), a global financial education company. He is also the founder of the popular sports handicapping web site www.WinningEDGE.com. His political and business web sites include www.ROOTforAmerica.com and www.ROOTofSuccess.com.

Wayne's business and political careers have been profiled by CNBC, the *Wall Street Journal*, *Time*, *Fortune*, *CNN/Money*, *Equities*, *Millionaire*, *Robb Report*, *Reason*, *American Spectator*, and the *New York Times*. He is a frequent guest on FOX News, FOX Business, and many national radio shows including *Savage Nation*, *The Jerry Doyle Show* and *The Mancow Show*. Wayne is the leader of a new American revolution for smaller government and more power and freedom for the people.

Index